*perspectives on*

# CASE

# MANAGEMENT

# PRACTICE

*Edited by Carol D. Austin
and Robert W. McClelland*

Families International, Inc.
Milwaukee, Wisconsin

Copyright 1996
Families International, Inc.
Publishing in association with Family Service America
11700 West Lake Park Drive
Milwaukee, WI 53224

**Library of Congress Cataloging-in-Publication Data**

Perspectives on case management practice / edited by Carol D. Austin
    and Robert W. McClelland.
          p.    cm.
      Includes bibliographical references.
      ISBN  0-87304-285-9
      1. Social case work.    2. Psychiatric social work.    3. Medical
    social work.    I. Austin, Carol D.    II. McClelland, Robert W.
    HV43.P473    1996
    361.3'2—dc20                                                                96-619

Printed in the United States of America

*For Mary and Moe*
*Auretta and Ray*

# Contents

# Contributors

**Carol D. Austin,** Professor, Faculty of Social Work,
University of Calgary

**Candyce S. Berger,** Director, Department of Social Work,
University of Michigan Medical Center

**James Brennan,** Senior Staff Associate for Health,
National Association of Social Workers

**David Este,** Assistant Professor, Faculty of Social Work,
University of Calgary

**Rae Johnson,** Research Assistant, School of Social Welfare,
University of Kansas

**Walter Kisthardt,** Research Assistant, School of Social Welfare,
University of Kansas

**Robert W. McClelland,** Assistant Professor, Faculty of Social Work,
University of Calgary

**Sue Pearlmutter,** Research Assistant, School of Social Welfare,
University of Kansas

**John Poertner,** Professor, School of Social Welfare,
University of Kansas

**Charles A. Rapp,** Professor and Associate Dean,
School of Social Welfare, University of Kansas

**Dean Schneck,** Director of Field Program, School of Social Work,
University of Wisconsin–Madison

**W. Patrick Sullivan,** Assistant Professor, School of Social Work,
University of Indiana, and Director, Indiana Department of
Mental Health

**Joan Levy Zlotnik,** Project Coordinator, Social Work Education
and Public Human Services: Developing Partnerships Project at the
Council on Social Work Education, and graduate research assistant
and doctoral student, School of Social Work, University of Maryland
at Baltimore.

# *Foreword*

## *Joan Quinn*

C ase management has come of age. From its early development in the mid-1960s in aging and mental health programs, it has evolved and become important to many population groups in our society. As the chapter authors of this book aptly state, the ever-increasing complexity of the service and financial reimbursement systems for care have made access to care very difficult to obtain for certain groups. The diversity and complexity of caregiving and caregivers make the case manager role essential.

Even though the case management function can be described with common terms—screening, assessment, care planning, monitoring, periodic reassessment, and discharge—how case management services are delivered varies according to the diverse populations benefiting from case management and the diverse practice settings in which they are served.

*Perspectives on Case Management Practice* will prove useful to case managers, regardless of their client base and practice setting. Case managers may become myopic in their work with their particular clients. Information on the work of case managers serving other kinds of clients can be very useful. Case managers in managed care have a focus different from that of case managers working with older adults or substance-abuse victims. Although managed-care case managers focus on cost containment and substance-abuse case managers on appropriate treatment and follow-up, each can learn from the other.

Case managers need to master a great deal of information to fulfill their role. They need to know what their clients' needs are, how the service system works, and how the financing system operates. Key components that allow case managers to function in service and reimbursement systems that are dysfunctional include flexibility, tenacity, creative problem solving, and core competencies. The authors in this well-edited collection provide excellent suggestions for comprehensive curriculum development in the training of case managers.

Although case managers play a small role with respect to system change and policy direction, they are at the front line of care. From this vantage point, the case manager can provide an enlightened agency administration with important information to effect system change and care reimbursement. Improvement in these areas is occurring, in some systems more quickly than in others. Regardless of the speed of change, the case manager must work persistently within the care and reimbursement system on behalf of clients who need help. This book affirms the case management function while presenting conceptual and theoretical questions that need to be addressed.

The contributing authors clearly understand case management in their practice environment. And they do not present "cookie cutter" descriptions of case management practice. Fiscal, structural, environmental, professional, and political constraints are considered for each population group discussed in the book.

With the advent of managed care for diverse population groups, gathering client and family information and acquiring knowledge about care options are important case management functions. The client/family needs to know when care is inferior, how much care costs, and who is delivering the care. Adequate fiscal resources and services must be found to meet client/family needs.

Case management service is often interdisciplinary and must minimally include provision of health and social support services. One must avoid the trap of labeling various population groups as "patients" rather than persons. The majority of people, even those with chronic disability, spend only a small portion of their life as patients. In chapter two, on mental health case management, proactive planning and consumer empowerment, ideas that have spread to work with other population groups, are emphasized. The need to avoid being crisis reactive and paternalistic toward clients must be taught to case managers regardless of their professional background.

Role changes are occurring in many professions, including medicine, nursing, and social work, and it is a good time to teach and learn comprehensive case management practice. The authors in this volume discuss case management roles across disciplines and population groups. They raise provocative system and policy questions that must be addressed as case managers continue to help individuals obtain the necessary services to enhance their independence and self-determination. In addition to being an excellent tool for case managers, educators, and students, this book can help policymakers understand the complex issues that surround case management practice today.

*Joan Quinn is President, Connecticut Community Care, Inc., and the National Case Management Partnership. Ms. Quinn is founder and editor of the* Journal of Case Management; *her most recent book is titled* Successful Case Management in Long-Term Care.

*Chapter* 1

# Introduction: Case Management—
# Everybody's Doing It

*Carol D. Austin and Robert W. McClelland*

C ase management is alive and well, which is testimony to its capacity to adapt to diverse program settings. It has become, and apparently will continue to be, a critical component in the delivery of health and social services to a wide range of populations. This is not a new observation: "Different forces contributed to a similar need within different client populations" (Rothman, 1992, p. 1). Across North America case management has been included in child welfare, mental health, programs for severely emotionally disturbed children, substance abuse, developmental disabilities, corrections, teen pregnancy, youth employment, health care, managed care, long-term care, AIDS programs, programs for children with special health care needs, and employment programs for welfare recipients, to name a few. If case management did not exist, someone would surely invent it.

Case management is the common ground upon which diverse actors in the human services fields can come together. Its popularity is quite understandable. Despite its limitations, case management may be the most pragmatic approach to addressing the daunting realities of service delivery. Fragmentation of services is a real issue. Clients need assistance from savvy, "system-smart" case managers who are also skillful practitioners. Something or someone is needed to deal with the complex barriers, rules, paperwork, and inevitable frustrations in the system. Although it may be preferable to restructure the delivery system, clients need services today. The genius of case management is its extraordinary flexibility. Each professional group has about as firm a claim on case management as has any other. The component tasks of case management practice are highly flexible; each can be adapted to a wide range of programs. Case management is a pragmatic response to the realities of today's delivery systems.

What is case management? Considerable time and energy have been spent trying to answer this question. Discussion has taken place on

*1*

two levels. At one level, focus has been on comparisons among and between case management services at the direct-service level. On another level, discussion has focused on identifying a generic model, a common framework that is shared across programs and providers.

Various activities have been called case management. Services provided as case management will vary considerably from one agency to another. Frequently, it is safe to assume that "if you have seen one case management program, you have seen one case management program." Today it is difficult find a provider agency that does not deliver case management services of some kind as part of various programs targeted to a range of populations. In some quarters case management has been seen as a fad, while elsewhere it has been hailed as a panacea. Although case management continues to be the source of controversy, it has become and remains a key cornerstone in contemporary human service programs, including those discussed in the chapters that follow.

Intaglia (1982) observes that "case management is a process or method for ensuring that consumers are provided with whatever services they need in a coordinated, effective and efficient manner" (p. 657). Geron and Chassler (1994) define case management as "a service that links and coordinates assistance from both paid service providers and unpaid help from family and friends to enable consumers . . . to obtain the highest level of independence consistent with their capacity and their preferences for care" (p. v). In a slightly different vein, Libassi (1988) states that "case management, over and above its specific functions, is integrative, rational, proactive and individualized" (p. 93). Another definition describes case management as "the process of planning, organizing, and monitoring the services and resources needed to respond to an individual's . . . care needs" (American Hospital Association, 1987, p. 2). Another perspective holds that "case management is widely viewed as a mechanism for linking and coordinating segments of a service delivery system . . . to ensure . . . the most comprehensive program for meeting an individual client's needs for care" (Austin, 1983, p. 16).

The National Association of Social Workers (1992) promulgated Standards for Social Work Case Management, defining social work case management as

> a method of providing services whereby a professional social worker assesses the needs of the client and the client's family, when appropriate, and arranges, coordinates, monitors, evaluates and advocates for a package of multiple services to meet the specific client's complex needs. . . . Social work case management is both micro and macro in nature; intervention occurs at both the client and system level (p. 5).

The focus on service coordination and the description of case management as a process at both client and system levels are consistent themes in these definitions.

Nevertheless, considerable ambiguity remains, partly because case management's role and function are usually designed to pursue multiple and conflicting goals. Berger (chapter 7) highlights these issues in her examination of case management in health care settings. She distinguishes between case management and benefits management, case management and utilization management, system and client-centered case management, and quality and cost-effectiveness considerations. The fact is that case management services can address each of these familiar and frequently overlapping goals.

## Origins of Case Management

The recent growth in case management services can be traced to the mid-1970s, although its origins go much farther back. Its roots can be traced to the early history of social work. The early settlement houses and charity organization societies were concerned about and involved in service coordination. In the settlement houses, this represented little more than a box of index cards containing information about families, group activities, the neighborhood, and the environment. In the settlement house movement, coordination often emphasized advocacy and organizing on behalf of immigrant populations. The charity organization societies emphasized the coordination of information. Here the goal was to enhance the rational distribution of charitable relief. Each family was registered at a central bureau, which permitted agencies to determine whether a family was already receiving services from another source when they applied for additional assistance. Carter (1978) states that the purpose of registration was clear: "to prevent cheating and duplication of assistance to the needy poor" (p. 2). Although it may appear that case management is a relatively new development, early concern for carefully coordinated and fiscally accountable service delivery has its origins in the record-keeping methods created by these historic movements.

Mary Richmond is credited with the further development of the concept of social investigation, which stressed the importance of client-centered approaches to interagency coordination and cooperation. In 1901 she identified problems associated with service expansion, most notably the absence of adequate coordination and communication among agencies. Her approach was multifaceted and occurred on multiple levels, including the identification of forces at various levels: family, personal, neighborhood, civic, private charitable, and public relief. Her model foreshadows contemporary concepts such as the person-in-environment and the dual focus (client and system) of case management. With these historical roots, it is ironic that "case management is [now] one of the most popular current 'new' approaches to organizing care" (Baker & Vichi, 1989, p. 204).

## Contemporary Case Management

The emergence of case management as an important mechanism for coordinating service delivery can be traced to the Allied Services Act in 1971. This proposal recognized the need to improve programs at state and local levels for the Department of Health, Education and Welfare (HEW). To this end, HEW initiated a series of demonstration projects—the Services Integration Targets of Opportunity (SITO)—to demonstrate various coordinating mechanisms, primarily at the local level. Integration techniques included newly developed information and referral systems, client tracking systems, comprehensive service centers, and case management procedures. The SITO sites developed several significant integrative features: case management, client's pathway, data units, and service-provider contracts. Experience at the SITO sites suggests that unless the structure of funding is modified, the progress toward integrated delivery systems will be thwarted. Funding patterns contribute greatly to the fragmentation evident in the current system.

Since the early 1970s case management has been mandated in federal legislation affecting child welfare reform, long-term care for frail elders, mental health, health care, welfare reform, services for children with special health needs, children who are severely disturbed, and specially targeted populations (populations affected by AIDS, substance abuse, developmental disabilities, homelessness, family circumstances that pose risks). No human service program is immune to the problems produced by program and fiscal fragmentation. Case management has become a permanent part of the service-delivery landscape. It has become acceptable to key stakeholders. Although it does not significantly alter the *status quo*, it is a flexible vehicle for promoting service coordination.

Radol Raiff and Shore (1993) described characteristics of what they call the "new" case management. Their description of this new form captures case management's common features across program areas and client populations. The new case management is a core service. It does not play a secondary role. Case managers drive service delivery in programs targeted to selected populations. The new case management is not a repackaged version of traditional social casework; it is made up of a mixture of specialized skills and concentrated knowledge within diverse practice settings. The new case management has gained currency partly because it is seen as a way to contain costs. Contemporary case management is a critical part of program development and a familiar tool of public policy.

The new case management is a core component in the deinstitutionalization movement, whether in programs designed to divert people from institutional placement or in programs that discharge residents to the community. The major goal of such programs was normalization. Persons returning to or remaining in the community required services, monitoring, and supervision. Someone had to coordinate services for clients needing assistance in dealing with the complex community-services-delivery system. That person was called case manager. The new role arose in the context of

> the rise of community psychiatry and community mental health centers, the growing awareness of a burgeoning aging cohort with its service needs and hopes that moneys would be saved (and individuals better served) if services were offered in the community rather than in hospitals and nursing homes (Wood & Middleman, 1989, p. 165).

## *Variations on the Theme*

Models of case management abound. In the following chapters, the authors identify, describe, and discuss various case management models. Some models were developed for a specific program or client group, whereas others have been adapted from one setting to another. The number and range of models are testimony to case management's adaptability. The program-specific implementation of case management services is extremely flexible.

Various constraints and parameters (fiscal, programmatic, and organizational) significantly affect program operations and service delivery—another key reason for the proliferation of case management services today. For example, Sullivan (chapter 6) identifies nine key variables: duration of services, intensity of contact, focus of service, availability of service, site of the intervention, consumer direction, professional training, authority, and team structure. Each of these significantly affect how key case management functions are performed. In a similar vein, Rapp and Kisthardt (chapter 2) state that various models emphasize differing goals and may adhere to specific treatment ideologies. Austin (chapter 4) specifies four programmatic variables (targeting, gatekeeping, reimbursement, and financing) as significantly influencing the character of the case management function in any given setting.

The professional group designated to perform case management also affects how services are provided. The core case management tasks represent, in the most generalized and abstract case, good professional practice with attention to comprehensive assessment, continuity of care, monitoring, and reassessment. Obviously, most human service professional groups strive to perform these tasks.

Another source of variation in case management arises at the task level. Each case management task can be implemented in myriad ways. Furthermore, each task can be operationalized within very wide parameters. Comprehensive assessments, screening potential clients, and developing care plans can be conducted in many ways. This flexibility and adaptability of the basic case management model is extremely attractive. Fiorentine and Grusky (1990) noted that "because the case management role is necessarily diffuse and influenced by structural constraints, client contingencies and case manager preferences, there is likely to be a great deal of variation in role performance" (pp. 80–81).

## *The Generic Model: A Common Framework*

Despite diverse implementation of case management services, professionals generally agree about the core functions of case management. These functions appear in one form or another in case management programs, regardless of the specific program area. The totality and sequence of these tasks constitute case management.

- Outreach
- Screening and intake
- Comprehensive assessment
- Care planning
- Service arrangement
- Monitoring
- Reassessment

The authors in this volume describe and examine how these tasks are operationalized in their settings.

*Outreach activities* are designed to identify and enroll the most appropriate clients. These efforts require a definition of the target population that can be accurately implemented (Steinberg & Carter, 1983; Weil, Karls, & Associates, 1985). The reality of scarce service resources means that it is necessary to take steps to ensure accurate case finding and to prevent the inappropriate use of resources.

*Screening,* which is performed at intake, is a preliminary assessment of the client's circumstances in order to determine presumptive eligibility. Screening criteria are applied to determine whether the client's needs and circumstances match the target population definition of the program. The screening process is designed so that only those clients whose needs and circumstances appear to meet the program's eligibility criteria receive more lengthy and costly comprehensive assessment. Screening activities are normally used to accomplish the program's targeted goals.

*Comprehensive assessment* has received considerable attention as a key task in the case management process (Burack-Weiss, 1988; Kane & Kane, 1981). Comprehensive assessment is "a method of collecting in-depth information about a person's social situation and physical, mental and psychological functioning which allows identification of the person's problems and care needs in the major functional areas" (Schneider & Weiss, 1982, p. 12). Formal assessment normally includes the use of a systematically developed assessment instrument. Assessment functions as both a targeting mechanism and as a first step in the service-allocation process.

*Care planning* is the process by which information gathered during assessment is translated into a recommended service package (Rose, 1992; Schneider, 1988; Vourlekis & Greene, 1992). It serves as a resource-allocation process whereby a service prescription is written for a client. Program financing fundamentally shapes the nature of the care-planning process. Care planning is particularly important because the cost of the care plans developed by case managers directly affects program expenditures.

The *service arrangement* function is a process of contacting both formal and informal providers to arrange for services outlined in the care plan. Service arrangement and plan implementation involve negotiations with provider agencies and with family caregivers. The care plan cannot be successfully implemented if the community does not have a sufficient supply of services. In many cases, the care plan is highly dependent on the presence of a willing and able caregiver. The presence of sufficient and appropriate supports, in both formal and informal categories, cannot be assumed.

*Monitoring* is a critical case management task that enables the case manager to respond quickly to changes in the client's status and increase, decrease, terminate, or maintain services as deemed necessary. The frequency of monitoring varies, depending on the intensity of client needs and the type of services being delivered. Responsiveness to changes in clients' needs can have a dramatic impact on service costs.

*Reassessment* can be routinely scheduled and/or initiated by events. During the reassessment process, the case manager examines the client's situation and functioning in order to identify changes that have occurred since the most recent assessment. Routinely scheduled reassessments provide a method of determining how and to what extent clients are progressing toward goals specified in the care plan.

As indicated by these tasks, effective case managers must be skilled and knowledgeable. The job requires comprehensive knowledge of the local delivery system, providers, services, programs, eligibility requirements, and financial arrangements. Well-developed assessment skills and informed care planning are important elements in case management practice. The capacity to engage in creative problem solving and the ability to function as a system-level change agent are core competencies that demonstrate the range of knowledge and skills needed for effective practice. The role of case management is challenging and demanding.

## *Persistent Themes*

The case management literature consistently presents several themes and issues common to various program and practice settings. Case management practice is constrained by fiscal, structural, environmental, professional, and political realities. System dysfunction, role conflict, and resource allocation are fundamental problems.

### ❏ System Dysfunction

Rose (1992) charges that "the need for case management constitutes an indictment of existing organizational and interorganizational patterns of service design and delivery" (p. vii). Case management developed as a response to dysfunctional delivery systems, delivery systems that were structured, for the most part, to accommodate providers, funders, and professionals, rather than to strengthen their autonomy in order to ensure a steady and predictable flow of resources. Curiously, coordination is generally seen as neutral. In reality, coordination is a mixed blessing. It entails substantial costs to the agency in areas such as funding, time, and consultation. Moreover, enhanced coordination among agencies increases their interdependence, thus creating uncertainty and unpredictability in agency operations. The desire to protect and maximize agency autonomy and the pressure to coordinate service delivery can create considerable tension. Effective provision of case management services requires that agencies confront the fragmentation of service delivery and create ways to balance autonomy and service-coordination goals.

Service coordination is at the core of case management. It is such a familiar concept that its underlying complexity can be obscured. On closer examination, however, it is clear that as case managers attempt to coordinate services for their clients, they encounter numerous system level obstacles. Rothman (1992) provides an illuminating example.

*Case management emerged during the movement toward deinstitution-alization [of] client groups that had been served in large and costly self-contained settings. At the time . . . it was understood that ample funds would follow clients back into the community in order to provide for continuing care in that environment. . . . Such funding did not materi-alize. . . . Clients needing basic support services from community orga-nizations were left to fend for themselves without a funding policy or mechanism to assure service provision. Into this breach was thrown a cadre of service professionals, designated case managers, whose role was to extract a range of services from community agencies that were coming under extreme fiscal constraint. Structural problems are rarely amenable to solution through actions of individuals. Yet this is the task that has been imposed on case managers (p. 7).*

Are there other ways to address service-delivery fragmentation? And if there are, why is case management so consistently chosen to fix such unrelenting problems in the delivery system? A basic observation is that fragmented funding creates discontinuous and costly delivery sys-tems. Another strategy is to consider options for achieving structural change that will create greater integration.

Greater system integration can be created by co-location of ser-vices, coordination of information, joint funding of programs involving several providers, preadmission screening, and the development of con-solidated delivery systems. Consolidated delivery systems are based on single-source funding of comprehensive services. Each of these integra-tive approaches could also involve case management, but case manage-ment is not the primary method for coordinating services and integrat-ing programs. System change leading to fiscal and structural modifica-tion is the ultimate goal. Clearly, however, the favored strategy for man-aging service fragmentation has been case management. "Perhaps case management has enjoyed such widespread acceptance because it has not been viewed as a systemic reform, but as a function that can be incor-porated into ongoing service delivery systems without changing struc-tural relationships among the providers" (Austin, 1983, p. 17). Case management usually focuses on coordinating services to individual clients rather than on reducing fragmentation in the delivery system. Case managers rarely produce system change, perhaps because they are not supposed to. Case managers responsible for large case loads are undoubtedly overwhelmed by the demands of direct service as well as by responding to clients' unmet needs.

Is fragmented service delivery inevitable? It is important to pose this fundamental question. The presence of professional specialization, splin-tered funding, and pressures for organizational autonomy suggest that the future of fragmented service delivery is unfortunately secure. Without attention to structural and fiscal realities, case management alone will not accomplish ambitious program goals.

## ❏ Role Conflict

Case managers perform a common set of client- and system-level interventions. The National Association of Social Work Standards for Social Work Case Management speak to these responsibilities. Standard 5 states, "The social work case manager shall intervene at the client level to provide and/or coordinate the delivery of direct services to clients and their families (National Association of Social Workers, 1992, p. 12). Client interventions are the various tasks included in the generic model of case management (screening, assessment, care planning, plan implementation, monitoring, and reassessment). Standard 6 states that "the social work case manager shall intervene at the service system's level to support existing case management services and to expand the supply of and improve access to needed services" (National Association of Social Workers, 1992, p. 15). System interventions include agency policy review and change, resource development, data collection, information management, and social action.

Can case managers function as client advocates and system agents simultaneously? Are client goals and system goals consistent? Can case managers actually intervene in a comprehensive fashion when their effectiveness is limited by multiple and partially conflicting goals, differing frameworks of practice, and insufficient authority? In some settings, case management is an inherently conservative activity, which reinforces dysfunctional systems and does not sufficiently stress client advocacy. For example, why do consumers have a hard time gaining access to the delivery system and receiving services? One answer is that clients lack information. That is, if clients had accurate information about how services are organized, they would be more successful with system entry and obtaining services. This view suggests that clients need to improve their knowledge. If case managers primarily attend to client-level interventions, they run a substantial risk of blaming the victim. "Such dilemmas make many case management systems highly fluid and politicized arenas in which to work" (Vourlekis & Greene, 1992, p. 16). Rothman (1991) argues,

> Without adequate funding and supportive services, case management can be used to project an illusion of being responsible caregivers and can take pressure off politicians and government leaders to respond to needs. Human service professionals ought to avoid becoming a part of such an illusion and should keep a clear perspective (p. 521).

The intrinsic stress between the client-oriented and system-focused responsibilities will not disappear. For example, Baker and Vichy (1989) state,

> For mental health case managers, a conflict may soon intensify as they face the dilemma of seeking to provide a full continuum of quality care while their sponsoring agencies are forced to control the cost of services. This conflict has barely emerged largely because so few settings in which the financing and management of community services for severely mentally ill persons have been organized into coherent, integrated, managed care systems (pp. 207, 209).

Increasingly, case managers are becoming responsible for cost containment. This is particularly true in managed-care systems. Managed care received considerable attention during the health care reform debate in the United States. Despite the failure to produce comprehensive reform, managed-care systems are proliferating. The managed-care model is becoming an attractive method and may very well become a method for financing and organizing health care services for specific population groups. Managed-care systems are supposed to produce changes in utilization and expenditure patterns. This model, at its best, stresses quality of service as well as controls costs.

Case management in managed health care has been defined as "a systematic approach to identifying high-cost patients, assessing potential opportunities to coordinate their care, developing treatment plans that improve quality and control costs, managing patients' total care to ensure optimum outcomes" (Fisher, 1987, p. 287). McClelland (chapter 9) notes that the case manager in managed care may assume a gatekeeping function to control utilization of expensive services. Managed-care case management is designed for prospectively financed systems, in which funding is provided on a capitated basis and providers are at risk for their fiscal performance. In health care, perhaps more clearly than in other settings, questions arise about whether quality services and cost containment can be successfully integrated.

## ❑ Resource Allocation

Case management requires the allocation or distribution of resources. Case managers make important decisions about the type, duration, and intensity of service that consumers will receive; the time and agency resources that will be allocated to each consumer; and which providers will deliver services. Thus case management can be a powerful strategy for shaping delivery systems. If case managers can purchase services directly on behalf of their clients, they assume a significant position within the local delivery system. In many case management programs, care planning is carried out within clearly defined financial limits. The funding source is the basis for the case manager's power to authorize services, and the case manager is the fiscally accountable person (Applebaum & Austin, 1990; Austin 1983; Rose, 1992).

Cost containment is consistently identified as a major goal of case management. Many case management programs have adopted methods to control care-plan costs. On the other hand, Rose (1992) observes that

> *articles discussing case management . . . begin with its central tasks unquestioned: containing costs and rationalizing care. . . . Thus case management becomes a service rationalizing function, orchestrating the most effective and efficient coordination of services (p. 131).*

An expert advisory committee in long-term care reported that "case management's ability to control costs is enhanced when case managers consider the full range of providers . . . and make referrals to lower cost and nontraditional service providers" (Geron & Chassler, 1994, p. 83). Shapiro (1994) disagrees, contending that cost containment has been overemphasized. First the cost-containment goal

> *implies that case managers have been profligate with the available resources heretofore. This is doubly unfortunate because the resources allocated [have] generally been so minimal that stinginess has too often been the benchmark of case management. . . . The other unfortunate aspect of setting cost containment as a goal of case management is that it raises serious issues about the real and potential conflict between the achievement of other goals and this one (p. 5).*

Nevertheless, cost containment and quality services are usually twin goals in case management systems. These goals are clearly observable in managed care, in which various carefully designed and tested methods are routinely present in the service-delivery context. These methods are designed to ensure quality care while containing costs. Thus, the core conflict surfaces again. Can case managers function as system agents and client advocates at the same time? How do case managers resolve these dilemmas when the goal of cost containment is so pervasive and frequently dominant? An unfortunate consequence is that with the

> *denigration of the advocacy function of case management or in its expression in co-opted or provider driven form . . . advocacy [is reduced to] case specific measures to gain access to traditional service offerings. . . . While the client may benefit from the outcome [the] central concern remains the provider system (Rose, 1992, pp. 271–272).*

## *This Volume*

The authors in this volume describe and analyze case management practice in various program settings. These settings represent a mix of programs, some with extensive experience with case management and others in which case management is a relatively recent development.

The book is organized chronologically, moving from the earliest to the most recent development of case management practice in particular settings. Program settings are divided into three groups. Programs with extensive case management experience constitute the first group. These innovative projects were initiated in the early 1970s. This group includes programs targeted at individuals suffering from severe and persistent mental illness, child welfare programs, and community-based long-term-care projects designed to serve the elderly and disabled adults.

Rapp and Kisthardt (chapter 2) trace the earliest development of case management from programs for the chronically mentally ill to research in the late 1960s. Extensive provision of case management services did not occur until the Community Support Program was launched in 1978. Rapp and Kisthardt systematically compare various case management models and provide information about their relative effectiveness. Case management in programs for the chronically mentally ill has received considerable empirical attention. This chapter combines findings from various evaluation studies with a discussion of hands-on case management practice.

The most recent impetus for case management in child welfare programs is the Family Preservation Act of 1993. Zlotnick (chapter 3), however, identifies the beginning of child welfare programs in the Social Security Act of 1935 and its amendments of 1961 and 1967. Child welfare programs have an extensive legislative history that has stimulated various program models. Zlotnick analyzes the family-focused, comprehensive, and intensive models and discusses creative approaches that blend funding from various sources.

In the early 1970s the Health Care Financing Administration funded a number of innovative demonstration projects that tested different approaches to assisting chronically ill elders in avoiding or delaying nursing-home placement. Since that time, 17 demonstrations of various magnitudes have been tested and evaluated. Austin (chapter 4) focuses on this demonstration experience in the chapter on aging and long-term care. Contextual variables consistently influenced the effectiveness of the demonstrations, although evaluations emphasized client satisfaction and cost. Analysis of demonstration experience indicates the limits imposed by funding and delivery-system structure.

Case management emerged in the second group of programs during the 1980s. This group includes programs serving severely emotionally disturbed children and adolescents, substance-abuse services, and health care. Programs for severely emotionally disturbed children and adolescents and substance-abuse programs were developed from the early experience in programs for the chronically mentally ill. In this sense, these programs represent dissemination of earlier experience to a second generation of case-managed programs. The 1980s saw the beginning of what has become a revolution in health care delivery and financing. These changes are reflected in the nature of case management in health care settings.

The Child and Adolescent Service System Act of 1984 had a major influence in the development of children's mental health case management. Poertner (chapter 5) links these programs to the community support programs that served adults with chronic mental illness. Poertner provides a thoughtful and thorough analysis of the range of case management models used to serve this target population and discusses caregivers' expectations of case management as another perspective on case management service and practice.

Contemporary substance-abuse programs developed out of employee assistance programs of the early 1980s. Sullivan (chapter 6) reports on findings of recent evaluation studies, with particular attention to the length of the treatment program and the variability of the case management role. Sullivan notes the development of the behavioral health care industry and examines challenging ethical dilemmas confronting case managers in this setting.

Berger's discussion (chapter 7) of case management in health care settings illustrates the complexity of health care delivery and the importance of quality in a funding-driven system. Case management in this setting has numerous dimensions. She differentiates between case management and case coordination, between case management and utilization management, and between system- versus client-centered case management. The emergence of case management in health care is partially a result of legislative mandates in the Medicaid program. Berger stresses that a significant difference between case management in health care and in other settings is health care's emphasis on gatekeeping.

The last group includes case management programs that have developed recently; case management in public welfare, in managed care, and in programs serving HIV/AIDS populations.

Perlmutter (chapter 8) discusses the emergence of case management in public welfare programs. The Family Support Act of 1988 created the Job Opportunities and Basic Skills Training program, whereby public-assistance recipients receive education and training to improve their employability. A key part of this program is case management. Although the focus is training and employment, the case managers' scope of responsibility is broader. Perlmutter reviews findings from several evaluations and examines various case models that have emerged in various locations.

Managed care was a hotly debated type in recent health care reform efforts. As McClelland (chapter 9) points out, however, managed care is not a new idea, although interest in it has exploded in the 1990s. Here, case management has developed within the context of private health insurance. Gatekeeping is emphasized in managed care case management. Case managers control access to services. Health maintenance organizations can take various forms; however, each includes some form of case management. McClelland also examines the nature of case management in managed mental health programs.

Case management for HIV/AIDS populations is a recent development. Brennan's (chapter 10) discussion addresses the complex issues involved in serving these populations. This complexity is reflected in the depth and breadth of case managers' responsibilities. In addition to medical care, case managers may need to work with a range of programs, from financial services to housing and counseling. Brennan explores a developmental model of case management in which services are contingent upon the course of the disease.

The provision of case management services creates substantial challenges for both practice and policy. In the final chapter, McClelland, Austin, and Schneck (chapter 12) discuss implications for practice and policy, with attention to the relationship between these two levels of analysis.

## References

American Hospital Association. (1987). *Long-term care case management.* Report of the American Hospital Association Section for Aging and Long Term Care Services. Chicago: Author.

Applebaum, R., & Austin, C. (1990). *Long-term-care case management: Design and evaluation.* New York: Springer.

Austin, C. (1983). Case management in long-term care: Options and opportunities. *Health and Social Work, 8*(1), 16–30.

Austin, C. (1992). Have we oversold case management as a "quick fix" for our long-term care system? *Journal of Case Management, 1*(2), 61–65.

Baker, F., & Vichi, T. (1989). Continuity of care and the control of costs: Can case management assure both? *Journal of Public Health Policy, 10,* 204–213.

Burack-Weiss, A. (1988). Clinical aspects of case management. *Generations, 12*(5), 23–25.

Callahan, J. (1989). Case management for the elderly: A panacea? *Administration in*

*Social Work, 1,* 122–130.

Carter, G. (1978). Service coordination: Recycling tested concepts. In *Case coordination and service integration projects: Client impact, program survival and research priorities.* Los Angeles: Social Policy Laboratory, Andrus Gerontology Center, University of Southern California.

Fiorentine, R., & Grusky, O. (1990). When case managers manage the seriously mentally ill: A role contingent approach. *Social Service Review, 64,* 79–93.

Fisher, M., (1987). Defining the practice content of care management. *Social Work and Social Services Review, 2,* 204–230.

Geron, S., & Chassler, D. (1994). *Guidelines for case management practice across the long-term continuum.* Report of the Robert Wood Johnson grant to Connecticut Community Care, Bristol, CT.

Intagliata, J. (1982). Improving quality of community care for the chronically mentally disabled: The role of case management. *Schizophrenia Bulletin, 8,* 655–674.

Kane, R., & Kane, R., (1981). *Assessing the elderly.* Lexington, MA: Lexington Books.

Libassi, M. (1988). The chronically mentally ill: A practice approach. *Social Casework, 69,* 88–96.

National Association of Social Workers. (1992). *NASW standards for social work case management.* Washington, DC: Author.

Netting, F. (1992), Case management: Service or symptom? *Social Work, 37,* 160–164.

Radol Raiff, N., & Shore, B. (1993). *Advanced case management.* Newbury Park, CA: Sage Publications.

Rose, S. (1992). *Case management and social work practice.* New York: Longman.

Rothman, J. (1991). A model of case management: Toward an empirically based practice. *Social Work, 36,* 518–529.

Rothman, J. (1992). *Guidelines for case management: Putting research to professional use.* Itasca, IL: F. E. Peacock.

Schneider, B. (1988). Care planning: The core of case management. *Generations, 12,* 16–19.

Schneider, B., & Weiss, L. (1982). *The channeling case management manual.* Prepared for the National Long-Term-Care Channeling Demonstration Program. Philadelphia: Temple University Institute on Aging.

Shapiro, E. (1994, September 17). *Case management: Status, trends and issues.* Opening plenary session, 2nd International Conference on Long-Term-Care Case Management, Toronto.

Steinberg, R., & Carter, G. (1983). *Case management and the elderly.* Toronto: Lexington Books.

Vourlekis, B., & Greene, R. (1992). *Social work case management.* New York. Aldine de Gruyter.

Weil, M., Karls, J., & Associates. (1985). *Case management in human service practice.* San Francisco: Jossey-Bass.

Wood, G., & Middleman, R. (1989). *The structural approach to direct practice in social work.* New York: Columbia University Press.

# Chapter 2

# Case Management with People with Severe and Persistent Mental Illness

*Charles A. Rapp and Walter Kisthardt*

For nearly 20 years, case management services have been used with people who have severe and persistent mental illness. Case management in mental health has been driven by concern about effectiveness of services rather than cost containment. The consequences of early deinstitutionalization and research suggesting the effectiveness of community interventions has flavored and directed the practice, research, and policy-related developments of case management in the mental health field.

## History

Case management as a concept first appeared with the establishment of the Community Support Program (CSP) in 1978. The CSP was developed in response to the massive deinstitutionalization movement that commenced in the mid- to late 1950s. From 1955 to 1980, the population in state hospitals was reduced from 558,992 to 175,000 (Division of Biometry, 1979). Unfortunately, many patients were discharged to urban ghettos without access to adequate housing and services, resulting in a large homeless population. Families lacking personal and financial resources carried the burden of caring for mentally ill members. Unemployment rates for deinstitutionalized adults exceeded 80% and few were involved in vocational training. In many respects, quality of life outside the institutions was lower than it was inside. The stresses of daily life exacerbated symptomatology for many mentally ill persons. Concern about protracted stays in psychiatric hospitals was replaced with concern about the "revolving door," whereby people with severe and persistent mental illness were frequently admitted, released, and readmitted to institutions for short periods (General Accounting Office, 1977; President's Commission on Mental Health, 1979).

The theoretical rationale for designating case management an essential service within CSP was also influenced by studies conducted in the 1960s, 1970s, and 1980s. These studies increased our under-standing of the types of helping activities that contributed to positive outcomes for people with persistent mental illness. Although the stud-ies did not describe case management as an independent variable, they did describe activities that resembled many of the functions of case management as we know it today. For example, these studies discussed the need for resources and supports in naturally occurring contexts in the community as well as for consistency and a spirit of closeness and collaboration with individuals and families.

Pasamanick, Scarpitti, and Dinitz (1967) showed that intensive sup-portive services in the homes of persons with persistent mental illness significantly reduced the likelihood of hospital treatment. In support of this finding, Langsley and Kaplan (1978) provided in-home crisis inter-vention for families with members with persistent mental illness and found that 77% of the mentally ill persons who received this type of home-based care were able to remain in the community.

Hogarty, Schooler, Ulrich, Mussore, Ferro, and Herron (1979) focused on biochemical and social factors as they relate to people with persistent mental illness. They found that people with persistent mental illness were able to remain in the community longer when their med-ication regimen was combined with "sociotherapy." Four randomly assigned groups of consumers were exposed to different treatment con-ditions. One group received medication and sociotherapy; one group received just medication; another group received sociotherapy without medication; and a fourth group served as a no-treatment control group. The medication and sociotherapy group was the only group that demonstrated a statistically significant difference in rate of relapse. Hog-arty and colleagues' work suggested that successful intervention with people with persistent mental illness addresses social needs as well as medical needs.

Ewalt and Honeyfield (1981) surveyed several hundred people with persistent mental illness who were receiving care in the VA system in an effort to learn what consumers felt they needed to live and func-tion well in the community. Overwhelmingly, consumers reported that they needed assistance with basic resources such as money, housing, friends, medical care, and transportation. Interestingly, the treatment needs frequently noted by professionals, such as "improve personal hygiene," "become more medication compliant," or "interact appropri-ately with peers," were not identified by consumers as being important. This study supported the notion that case management should focus more on helping people to secure needed resources or "supplies" (Caplan, 1964) than on providing traditional treatment.

The emerging consensus that many people with persistent mental illness could be treated in the community was validated by the work of Marx, Test, and Stein (1973). These researchers identified 60 people who were currently being treated at a hospital and determined to be in need of continuing care. These individuals were then randomly assigned to one of three groups. The experimental group was discharged to receive total treatment in the community. A second group was treated in the usual way on the hospital ward. A third group was transferred to a special research unit of the hospital. This group was given equal time and attention, but the focus was on preparation for release by means of group therapy, ward work details, medication, and instruction in problem solving and daily activity skills. It was emphasized in the study that all treatment with this group was provided in the hospital.

The experimental group focused on five elements. First, treatment emphasized teaching skills in the community. Second, the team refused to use the hospital as a backup but rather responded to crises with community alternatives. Third, treatment emphasized work with family and significant others. Fourth, the mentally ill person was responsible for his or her decisions, and natural consequences of decisions were supported by the treatment team. Finally, staff emphasized establishing a close relationship with other community providers and stressed the advocacy function (Rappaport, 1977). The results of this study suggested that people with persistent mental illness can cope in the community if they have needed supports. At the end of the study, those in the experimental group spent an average of 6.33 days in the psychiatric hospital compared with 103.05 days for the hospital research unit and 98.55 for the regular hospital unit. This study had a significant impact on the direction of community mental health policy and practice.

By the mid-1970s, it was clear that more needed to be done for people with persistent mental illness if they were to live in the community. The CSP was initiated through the National Institute of Mental Health (NIMH). The program had two main goals. The first goal was to identify a range of services to support people with severe mental illness in the community. The 10 functions of CSP were:

- Location of clients/outreach
- Assistance in meeting basic human needs
- Mental health care
- Twenty-four-hour crisis assistance
- Psychosocial and vocational services
- Rehabilitative and supportive housing

- Assistance/consultation and education
- Natural support systems
- Protection of client rights
- Case management

Services at that time were generally limited to day treatment or partial hospitalization, outpatient psychotherapy and counseling, vocational rehabilitation for the few clients who were deemed eligible, and an occasional group-living arrangement. The effectiveness of these services was and continues to be poor (Bond & Boyer, 1988; Stuart, 1977).

The second goal was to improve access and coordination of services through case management. Although efforts to understand mental illness through biological and neurological research continued, the consequences of mental illness in terms of social functioning were brought into sharper focus. As Turner and Shifren (1979) noted,

> One person, or team of people, would now be responsible for remaining in touch with each client regardless of how many agencies get involved. This can provide the glue that binds otherwise fragmented services into arrangements that respond to the unique and changing needs of clients (p. 9).

## What Is Case Management?

Case management has been subjected to numerous definitions. Moxley (1989) defines case management as "a client-level strategy for promoting the coordination of human services, opportunities, or benefits" (p. 11). Johnson and Rubin (1983) describe case management as being concerned with achieving continuity of care for persons with multiple needs at different times. In a similar vein, Chambers (1986) identifies case management as a strategy that seeks to integrate a highly complex and fragmented social welfare system so that clients' needs may be met in the most efficient and cost-effective manner possible. Each of these definitions emphasizes mental health workers who work with the social welfare system to ensure access to resources and services on behalf of a person rather than who treat a particular patient, group, or family at a mental health center. In other words, case managers do not provide treatment; they coordinate the efforts of others who provide services.

Others highlight the interpersonal nature of case management. Rapp and Chamberlain (1985) discussed the importance of establishing a collaborative relationship with people with persistent mental illness. Lamb (1980), suggesting that a trusting relationship is critical, argued that therapists are best suited for the case management function. He further suggested that case management, when done well, should be part of any therapeutic endeavor.

These interpretations of the role and function of case managers vary. A common thread runs through these descriptions, however. Case managers are expected to assess personal needs of clients as well as monitor the responsiveness of the service system, an approach that incorporates the person-in-environment philosophy of social work (Gordon, 1965). Johnson and Rubin (1983) also encourage social workers to view case management as part of their domain, and Wintersteen (1986) challenges social workers to assume leadership roles in the development and implementation of this approach. Roberts-DeGennaro (1987) suggests that case management integrates the various aspects of traditional social work practice: casework, group work, and community organization.

Moxley (1989) summarizes six core functions of case management:

- **Assessment:** The process of gathering information about the person's circumstances and needs. The helping plan should flow naturally and logically from the data recorded on the assessment.

- **Planning:** The process of identifying the activities that will promote the attainment of consumer goals. Identifying what consumers, the manager, other providers, and significant others will do becomes an essential part of effective planning in case management services.

- **Implementation:** Putting the plan into action. This function involves linkage and advocacy efforts on the part of the case manager. Consumers may be expected to perform short-term goals or tasks such as taking their medication as prescribed, attending particular skill-training groups, or attending support groups.

- **Monitoring:** Remaining involved with consumers through regular meetings to determine progress toward completion of stated goals. This function often leads to reassessment and modification of the plan.

- **Evaluation:** Determining the effectiveness of the helping effort. Were goals achieved? What was the outcome of the case management process?

- **Involvement:** Remaining involved with people in a helping capacity as determined by their desire and need as well as the policy of the agency/organization.

These general similarities in conceptualizing the functions of case management camouflage many differences. Some have suggested that the primary function of case management is to link or refer consumers to services or programs. This linkage may occur within their own agencies or with other agencies in the community (Turner & TenHoor, 1978). Others argue that case managers establish a trusting therapeutic relationship with people and, in fact, do provide a direct helping service (Deitchman, 1980; Harris & Bergman, 1987; Rapp & Chamberlain, 1985). Others suggest that case management functions should be handled by a team of professionals within the context of a comprehensive program (Test & Stein, 1980). As noted earlier, some suggest that case management is not needed, that the community functions inherent in this approach should be provided within the context of the client–therapist relationship (Lamb, 1980).

## *Case Management Models*

In the early 1980s, specific models of case management were developed and evaluated. The four dominant models were the broker model, the strengths model, the Program for Assertive Community Training (PACT), and the rehabilitation model. Robinson and Bergman (1989) described their key features as follows:

*Broker model.* This model focuses on assessing the need of an individual for particular services and identifying and ensuring availability of those services. However, it stops short of coaching the client or taking responsibility for making sure the client gets the service. The broker places much of the responsibility for obtaining services on the client or identified family members.

*Strengths model.* This model addresses the social desires and needs of people with severe and persistent mental illness and rests on two underlying assumptions about human behavior. The first is that people who are successful at living have the ability to use and develop their own potential and have access to resources that allow them to do this. The model identifies a person's strengths and actively creates situations (environmental or personal) in which success can be achieved and personal strength enhanced. The second assumption is that human behavior is primarily a function of the resources available to individuals and that a pluralistic society must value equal access to resources. People who are mentally ill may need help securing resources in important life domains essential for human growth and development. These domains include employment, housing, education, social support, and medical services. A primary focus of this model is securing environmental resources. The community (people, groups, and organizations) is broadly conceived as a network of resources available to enrich the client's life.

Given the assumptions, case management in the strengths model focuses on building clients' personal strengths and self-identity through existing and newly created environmental transactions. It is a form of personalized helping directed at connecting individuals to resources that will improve the quality of their community life. Rather than focusing on intervention and treatment for an "illness," this model aims to provide the environmental support needed to develop and move closer toward goals identified by the individual.

**PACT model.** This model combines clinical and case management services by providing direct assistance with symptom management as well as by meeting basic needs and improving social, family, and instrumental functioning. A primary function of PACT is developing a primary clinical relationship with the client and family, teaching individuals about their symptoms, and helping them manage symptoms so they function optimally in the community. This model is characterized by interdisciplinary service teams responsible for a fixed group of patients, assertive outreach and *in vivo* treatment in the community, individualized treatment using client-tailored interventions, and ongoing treatment and support.

**Rehabilitation model.** This model views case management as representing more than a response to a dysfunctional system (Anthony, Cohen, Farkas, & Cohen, 1988). The client's goals and needs, rather than preestablished system goals, dictate the response and form of case management services. Therefore, the case management system must be flexible enough to accommodate individual needs (Marlowe & Weinberg, 1982). Rehabilitation-oriented case management helps clients find success and satisfaction in the social environment of their choice with the least amount of professional intrusion. Although the rehabilitation model focuses on identifying and supporting the unique strengths of clients, it also attempts to identify and evaluate skill deficits that act as barriers to achievement of personal goals.

Key differences among the models include the following:

- Although all are client centered, only the strengths approach is client directed; the others incorporate the person's "perceived needs" into the service plan.

- The four models differ in their underlying focus: the broker model stresses the linkage function, the strengths model a mentor approach and systems advocacy, the rehabilitation model improving living skills, and the PACT model reduction and management of symptoms.

- Client assessment focuses on functional elements (strengths or deficits in life domains and skills) in all the models except the PACT model, which stresses clinical assessment.
- Staffing can consist of a case manager working alone with a specified case load (broker, rehabilitation), an individual case manager working with a team (strengths), or an interdisciplinary team performing case management as one of its functions (PACT).
- Responsibilities added to the core functions of the model differ in each model: systems advocacy (broker, strengths, rehabilitation), crisis intervention (strengths, PACT), symptom management (PACT), and skills training (rehabilitation).
- The underlying focus is different for each model: The broker model links individuals with community services, the strengths model improves quality of life and individual achievement, the rehabilitation model attempts to remedy deficits in order to overcome barriers, and the PACT model attempts to reduce symptomatology and improve functionality.

These models also share important features:

- Focus is on individual clients.
- Case management services are provided *in vivo* (where the client is located) rather than in the clinic setting.
- Staff–client ratios are kept as low as possible, ranging from a low of 1–10 to a high of 1–25, with the exception of the broker model, which has ratios as high as 1–40.
- Case managers without graduate training generally are supervised by a staff person with a master's degree or higher.
- Case management services range from daily to weekly.
- The core functions covered by case managers include client identification and outreach, individual assessment, service planning, linkage with requisite services, monitoring of service delivery, and client advocacy.
- No time limit is placed on the duration of case management services.
- Case managers often have authority over a discretionary fund to

assist clients in emergency situations.

• These four models are the only models that have been subjected to empirical testing.

## *Research*

### ❏ Brokerage Model

Franklin, Solovitz, Mason, Clemons, and Miller (1987) tested the efficacy and cost of the brokerage model. The study was designed to determine whether a "generalist" model of case management yielded specific outcomes for consumers. Specifically, "as compared with the services that are already provided in the community, does case management reduce admissions, increase the utilization of community-based services, affect the cost, and improve the quality of life of [consumers] who live in the community?" (p. 674).

The study used random sampling to create two groups of consumers. The E group ($n = 213$) received the generalist model, and the C group ($n = 204$) received all other services except case management. At the conclusion of the 12-month project, 138 members of the E group and 126 members of the C group were reinterviewed.

The findings served as a counterpoint for those who had concluded that the primary focus of case management should be to link consumers with mental health and community social services. Those who received the generalist model were hospitalized more frequently than were the control (3,173 vs. 1,671 bed days). Moreover, the consumers in the E group cost more to maintain ($304,924 vs. $145,000). Finally, no significant difference in quality of life was noted for those who received case management, despite the fact that case managers in the study successfully implemented the linking function. In fact, 95% of the services received were received by people in the experimental group, which suggests that the case managers did fulfill their role as linkers and brokers of services and programs.

Fisher, Landis, and Clark (1988) conducted a regression study to determine whether case management in a linkage/brokerage model correlated to client change. Specifically, they viewed case management as "not being designed to provide direct services, but to link clients with other services" (p. 136). Five case management functions were analyzed: advocacy, linkage/referral, intake/assessment, monitoring, and transportation. The results suggested that the case management functions, as defined within a brokerage approach, are not correlated with client change. Data suggested that "less than three percent of the variance in overall client change was explained by all five services combined" (p. 134).

These studies suggest the following: First, the findings indicate that merely linking consumers to existing mental health and social services does not necessarily result in positive outcomes for people. Second, consumers who are influenced to avail themselves of mental health and social services may realize iatrogenic consequences in the form of increased need for in-patient care.

## ❏ PACT Model: Case Management in the Context of Comprehensive Programming

The PACT model, which was originally called the Training in Community Living (TCL) program served as a prototype for the development of many community case management systems. Most of the research on this team approach to case management has been carried out in Illinois, Indiana, and Washington.

Witheridge and Dincin (1985) conducted outcome research on consumers engaged in the Bridge Program in Chicago. They reported that involvement in the program resulted in longer tenure within the community. Consumers used the hospital less frequently and for fewer days if they were hospitalized, resulting in a savings of $5,700 per member per year.

Bond and Boyer (1988) conducted experimental outcome research on an adaptation of the "full support" case management approach labeled assertive case management (ACM). One-hundred and sixty-seven consumers at three mental health centers in Indiana were randomly assigned to receive the full-support team approach or assigned to receive all other aftercare services at the center. The findings provided further evidence of the efficacy of case management. At two of the three centers, statistically significant differences were noted in rehospitalization: Overall, consumers in the ACM group were rehospitalized an average of 9.2 days, significantly less than the 30.8 days recorded for controls. The most cost-effective center reported a savings of approximately $5,500 per ACM consumer. This study did not find statistically significant differences between ACM and control-group consumers in quality of life, medication compliance, involvement in community mental health center programming, or contacts with the legal system in any of the three centers. The researchers concluded that "assertive case management appears to have the greatest impact on the clients in greatest need, particularly those who are frequently hospitalized and who refuse other aftercare services" (Bond, Miller, Krumweid, & Ward, 1988, p. 417).

Borland, McRae, and Lycan (1989) replicated the PACT model and tracked outcomes for 72 consumers during a five-year period. A time-series design was used whereby the consumers in the project served as their own controls, with baseline determined from retrospective data (two years prior to the project). The researchers were interested in discovering (1) if reduction in hospital use could be maintained for five years, (2) if improvements in patients' functional levels noted in prior studies continued for longer periods, (3) whether net cost savings generated by the provision of case management would be demonstrated for five years, and (4) to what extent the use of case management services affected hospitalization, patients' functioning, and cost of patient care.

The results of this longitudinal study were mixed. In terms of reduction of in-patient care, the consumers in the project used 75% fewer bed days during the five years when data were compared with baseline. Results indicated a 193% increase, however, in the use of structured residential bed days in the community. Consumers' level of functioning in the community as measured by the Global Assessment Scale (GAS) remained essentially the same during the project. The data indicated a decrease in consumers' use of crisis and emergency services during the five years. Finally, a comprehensive cost analysis suggested that the savings realized through reduction in in-patient bed days were offset by increased costs for intensive structured support in the community.

McRae, Higgins, Lycan, and Sherman (1990) carried out a follow-up to the Borland et al. (1989) study. This group of researchers was interested in whether the consumers who were involved in the Borland study would "withdraw or refuse to participate in CMHC services, clinically deteriorate, and again require frequent hospitalization" after the intensive supports of the five-year study were withdrawn (p. 176). The researchers were also interested whether a significant increase in cost associated with these hypothesized changes in consumer functioning would occur.

The results of this study suggested that consumers fared better than expected after the intensive support program was discontinued. Of the 69 consumers who were living two years after the study, 91% remained involved in community treatment of some kind; 70% of this treatment was provided at the CMHC. The authors reported a statistically non-significant increase in annual hospital admissions and bed days, concluding that "overall patient care costs were 12% less during each of the two years of the follow-up period, representing a savings of approximately $1,500 per patient annually" (p. 178).

McRae and associates' study provided a more optimistic outlook regarding consumers' ability to grow and change as a consequence of intensive involvement with a comprehensive program. Prior to this study, many believed that consumers would regress as a consequence of discontinuing specialized CSP programming (Stein & Test, 1980).

The PACT model was evaluated recently. Bush, Langford, Rosen, and Gott (1990) studied consumers who received case management within the context of a comprehensive program to determine whether they fared better than did "some of these same services, but at a less intensive level and only at the offices of the case managers" (p. 647). The number of psychiatric days and medication compliance were used as dependent variables.

Consumers who received the TCL model had an average of 10 fewer days of hospitalization than did those in the control group. Additionally, consumers in the TCL group adhered more consistently to their prescribed medication regimen and followed through more regularly with the agreed-upon service plan than did those in the control group. The most consistent outcome in this and other studies of TCL has been the reduction in hospitalization. Results in other areas, such as employment and other quality-of-life measures, have been uneven at best.

❏ **Rehabilitation Model: Case Management in the Context of Skill Training in the Community**

Anthony (1979) extensively developed the principles and skills employed in psychiatric rehabilitation. The philosophy and methodology of the approach has been incorporated into a model of case management that has been delivered and evaluated in Toronto, Canada.

Goering, Wasylenki, Farkas, Lancee, and Ballantyne (1988) tracked outcomes for 82 consumers in a rehabilitation-oriented case management program six months and two years after they were discharged from an inpatient setting. These outcomes were compared with the same outcomes for 82 matched controls who were discharged from the same inpatient settings before the project began. The model emphasized

> serving the patient's functional needs through the techniques of resource linking and patient-centered interviewing [not defined]. Each case manager ensured that the patient received support with crises, coping with bureaucratic confusion, and acquiring personal and social skills (p. 273).

This research suggested that the rehabilitation approach could promote positive outcomes in several areas of consumers' lives. For example, two years after discharge those who received case management realized higher levels of occupational functioning than did those in the control group. This difference, however, was not statistically significant (20% of those in the program vs. 13% of those not in the program). The researchers also reported that consumers who received case management were more likely to have independent housing arrangements than were the controls (32% vs. 13%), a finding that was statistically significant. After two years in the program, consumers who received case management realized statistically significant improvements on all three indicators of social isolation.

This study found no statistically significant differences between the case management and control group in hospital recidivism or length of stay. Goering et al. (1988) noted that this finding should not be given more importance than it deserves. They also alluded to the fact that preventing hospitalization is not the primary goal of the rehabilitation model. The success of rehabilitation programs cannot be measured simply or exclusively by whether they reduce reliance on in-patient care. Improvement in the patient's quality of life is an important benefit that must remain a primary goal of our treatment efforts.

## ❏ Personal Strengths Approach:
## People, Not Patients; Possibilities, Not Problems

The strengths model, developed by Rapp and associates at the University of Kansas, was originally referred to as the Developmental-Resource Acquisition Model (Modrcin, Rapp, & Chamberlain, 1985). The initial evaluation of the strengths model examined the outcomes for 19 consumers (Rapp & Chamberlain, 1985). The researchers were interested in determining whether case management that focused on the unique strengths of each individual as well as the naturally occurring resources in the community would result in positive outcomes. Specifically, would consumers set and achieve personal goals? How would consumers rate the case management process? How would therapists evaluate the case management process? To what extent would consumers require inpatient psychiatric care during the six-month intervention period?

Findings suggested that consumers who received intensive case management under this model did have positive outcomes. For example, 13 of the 19 consumers achieved at least 51% of their goals. Seven consumers met all of their goals; only three consumers met none. Moreover, 91% of the consumers reported that they were satisfied with case management, and 74% said that the case manager helped them do things they found difficult. During the course of the project, no consumer was hospitalized in a state psychiatric hospital.

Building on Rapp and Chamberlain's work, Modrcin, Rapp, and Poertner (1988) developed an experimental design to test the comparative efficacy of the personal-strengths approach. Consumers were randomly assigned to receive this model or to receive other case management services provided by the agency. With the experimental model, case management contacts were more frequent, usually out of office, and focused more on consumer interests, strengths, and personal goals than on problems, behavioral deficits, and diagnostic factors.

Results indicated significant differences between the two groups on five of the six discriminating variables used in the study. Consumers who received the strengths model were more likely to be involved in vocational training. Moreover, they were rated by significant others as being better adjusted in terms of community-living skills and acceptable community behavior. Also, consumers in the experimental condition showed more tolerance of stress than did consumers in the control condition. Finally, consumers who received the strengths-based model perceived their use of leisure time as more meaningful from pre- to posttest than did controls. No significant difference was noted between the groups in terms of hospitalizations or medication compliance.

In the most recent research on the strengths model, Rapp and Wintersteen (1989) reported on the impact of the strengths model as documented in 12 different projects. In this evaluation design, care was taken to monitor the process closely to ensure fidelity of the model. Data were gathered for 235 consumers served in 12 different units; 72% of the consumers involved in the projects had experienced multiple psychiatric hospitalizations. The results of this six-year project suggested that people with persistent mental illness respond positively to a case management approach that focuses on their unique interests, knowledge, and abilities. Across all 12 projects, a total of 5,635 goals were set, with 4,456 (79%) being achieved. In addition, consumers who received the strengths model tended to have a lower hospitalization rate than did CSP consumers statewide (15.5% vs. 30%).

This study has several implications. First, consumers who are difficult to engage (the projects tended to include consumers who did not engage readily with program-based CSP) may respond enthusiastically to this type of approach. Second, working with consumers in a way that conveys realistic short-term expectations regarding personal goal attainment did not exacerbate symptomatology in work with the majority of people engaged in the project. Third, the case management model was provided by BSW and first-year MSW students, many of whom had no prior experience working with people with persistent mental illness. As the authors noted, however, the experienced MSWs provided diligent supervision.

## A Decade of Case Management: What Have We Learned?

Three of the four models of case management reviewed in this chapter appear to contribute to positive outcomes for consumers. Moreover, these three models (strengths, PACT, and rehabilitation) appear to focus on three areas of helping: working out of the office, involving consumers in development and implementation of their plans, and helping people access community resources.

The research suggests that the broker model is not effective for people with persistent mental illness in terms of community outcomes. Case management is more than merely linking people to existing social services or mental health programs. The most effective approaches are characterized by lighter case loads, proactive planning rather than reactive crisis intervention, and a relationship characterized by consumers assuming a more active role as director of the helping process.

Some have argued that the PACT model is not a case management model, but rather is an organizational arrangement of which case management is a part. Consumers in this program tend to receive a wide range of services. In fact, Len Stein, one of the originators of the PACT approach, called for the abolition of case management as a strategy in his 1993 keynote address at the National Association of Case Management Annual Conference.

The strengths model has generated positive outcomes both in terms of quality-of-life measures and decreased use of psychiatric hospitalization. Consumers have consistently displayed high levels of personal goal attainment in every replication site. Consumers as well as providers and therapists have reported positive experiences with this approach (Kisthardt, 1993).

That which was identified as a desired outcome of the work appeared to be positively affected. For example, the studies that focused on reducing the use of hospitalization showed promising results. However, in studies in which hospitalization was not a designated outcome variable, case management services appeared to have no effect.

## A View of Practice

With the history and research results as a backdrop, we now turn to a finer focus on actual case management practice. Although the material presented here is based on the strengths model, many of the methods and techniques are common to other case management models. The following practice guidelines have been drawn from more than a decade of delivering and evaluating case management services, consulting and training in more than 40 states, and, most important, from research that sought to amplify the consumer's perspective on effective case management (Kisthardt, 1992). This section presents practice guidelines that seek to amplify the consumer voice in the following areas of practice: engagement, assessment, and case (personal) planning.

## ❏ Engagement

The case manager's first meeting with consumers sets the tone for the emerging relationship. At this meeting, consumers conduct their own assessment of the case manager. Consumers shared many insights regarding their first meeting with a case manager. The following comments illustrate common themes (Kisthardt, 1993).

- We just talked like friends.
- They bought me a coffee and we talked and laughed.
- They told me I was the boss and they worked for me.
- They asked me where I wanted to meet, when was it convenient for me.
- They didn't ask a lot of personal questions, didn't impress me as "snoopervisor."
- They asked me what I wanted in my life, not what they think I needed.
- They told me they had a lot to learn from me, that I was the expert on how mental illness has affected me, not them.
- We shared a lot about what we had in common, like how we get angry at our mothers.
- They told me it was not their job to change me, that they could only help me make the kind of changes I wanted to.
- They really seemed to be listening to what I was saying, showed a lot of respect. I could see in their eyes that they really cared about what I was saying.
- They did not assume that I was their patient or client, said they would respect my decision to choose not to work with them.
- They were really nice to my cat. When I saw her go on his lap, I knew he was O.K.
- They commented on the things that were important to me, especially my plants.

- She didn't judge things I said. She said we all make mistakes and hopefully we learn from them.
- She let me work the radio when we were in her car.

These statements suggest principles and strategies to guide case managers' efforts early in the case management process.

*The primary agenda of the first meeting should be to engage another human being in a purposive conversation.* The case manager should not attempt to complete a needs assessment or other one-sided interview protocol. The task is to get to know the individual as a person and to share information about oneself that will help establish a trusting relationship.

*The case manager's primary consideration should be the comfort and convenience of the consumer.* Where the meeting will be held, when, and for how long will vary. If the case manager is concerned about personal safety, a public location within the community may serve as an effective compromise.

*As much, if not more, information may be gathered through good observation compared with asking a series of predetermined questions on the intake or assessment form.* Useful information can be gathered from noticing posters on the walls, pets, plants, displayed crafts, tapes or CDs, television show being watched, brand of cigarettes, whether things are well-ordered or chaotic, family pictures, and the like. Noticing the details helps remind the case manager to focus discussion on the elements of consumers' life that hold meaning and value for them.

*As case management expands the boundaries of the mental health relationship, it becomes necessary to share in words and symbols the purpose of the work.* The following excerpt illustrates how one case manager uses this principle in her work.

> *If you choose to allow me to work with you, I will try to help you to get what you want and need to live the kind of life that holds meaning and value for you as a citizen. It's my job to help you get things you want and need and also to help you to sustain and maintain what you already have without having to go to the state hospital to get them. I also will try to be honest with you and I will not support things that are not legal. A big part of my job is to help you to get people in your life to help you or do things with you, people who are not being paid but are are friends whom you can count on. I hope you feel comfortable with me like a friend, but it's important for you to know that this is different from a friendship.*

Symbols include sharing the strengths assessment form with clients and documenting pertinent information together. Also, documenting helping activities serves as a visual cue indicating that the relationship is purposive.

Although the primary focus of the first meeting is to engage the consumer, information is clearly being gathered. The strengths assessment tool may in many cases not be used during the first meeting. However, case managers may have an opportunity to explain the tool and leave it with consumers to begin recording information about their life. During the next several meetings, case managers and consumers work together to identify pertinent information to guide and direct the helping efforts.

## *Assessment*

In being given the opportunity to talk about their strengths and abilities, consumers are energized and in general feel comfortable with the assessment process (Kisthardt, 1993).

- We worked on it together; it wasn't them doing it on me.

- They didn't ask me questions about things that happened 20 years ago. That's over, I can't change that and I want to focus on the here and now.

- They asked me about what I wanted and they wrote that down. They didn't tell me I'd never be able to do it. They validated my visions.

- They were interested in what I wanted to talk about, what I liked, the things that are important to me. Like spirituality, they seemed real comfortable with that.

- They didn't keep telling me about things I should do. I hate it when people *should* on other people.

- They made me feel good about things I'd done in the past, told me that living in my car really took a lot of strength and resourcefulness. And, you know, I never thought of it that way, but it did.

- They said that I did not have to say I had a goal just to make them happy, that if things were O.K. in my life now that they would try to help me keep it that way.

- They asked me what my priorities were, where I wanted to start—that felt good.

- We spent about 20 minutes just talking about shark week on the Discovery Channel. It was great.

- It felt really good to talk about the things I liked and things I did well. It made me feel really good. I guess I can do things. Sometimes I don't give myself enough credit 'cause I think a lot about being mentally ill and all the problems I have.

On the basis of consumer feedback and evaluations of the multiple sites where the strengths model was implemented (Rapp & Wintersteen, 1989), the following principles appear to help guide the case management assessment process.

*The assessment process should focus on gathering information about what people want in their lives, not on what they need.* When people make a cognitive connection between what they need and what they desire, they are more likely to follow through with constructive behaviors. For example, most people would rather not *need* to take medication. In fact, the medication noncompliance rate for people in general (not just people with mental illness) is 75% (Sands, 1991). A well-developed strengths assessment will indicate why taking medication is important—to stay out of the hospital, to live free of troublesome voices, and so forth. The informed consumer will ask questions: How will taking this medication help me? How will coming to this group contribute to my parenting abilities? Conceptually, the strengths assessment begins to document areas of the consumer's life that will eventually serve as outcomes of community treatment. What must be done in order to get there becomes the focus of the personal planning process.

*The assessment provides a detailed description of what people are able to do, what they enjoy, and the things that hold meaning for them; it does not focus on problems, deficits, or pathology.* The challenges of mental illness are quite real. However, mentally ill people do survive, cope, and live their life with a measure of quality. The idiosyncratic ways in which each person responds to daily events are the keys to unlocking new opportunities and options. For example,

A young man receiving case management had difficulty with personal hygiene. During the assessment process, it was listed as a primary need. The man refused all efforts to get him to bathe. The case manager attempted to persuade him by saying things such as "People at the day program are beginning to complain," "You won't be able to get a job if you don't attend to your hygiene." For this young man, these "motivators" were not relevant because he didn't want to be at the day program and he didn't want to get a job. The case manager decided to take a different tack. She explained the strengths-assessment tool, and at a fast-food restaurant over coffee, he agreed to work on it with her. He talked about how he loved to listen to the radio. She asked him what his *favorite station was and who his favorite D.J. was. Armed with this information, she asked him if he would like to go to the station and actually watch the D.J. do his show. He said this would be something that he would love to do. She pointed out that he would need a shower and some new clothes, because the station manager would be sensitive about having other people at the studio. Together, they planned how they could achieve this goal. The young man showed up on the day of the show showered, clean shaven, and wearing a suit. Currently, they are working together on his goal to be a D.J.; he is planning a two-hour show at the day program during which he will take requests from other consumers and staff.*

**Motivation.** A tenet of the strengths approach is that all people are motivated and that they make decisions in their daily life. The purpose of the assessment is to identify and validate, not to judge, the motivations and decisions that are expressed through behavior. This process may in turn stimulate ideas and other options for the individual.

This perspective creates dissonance for some case managers. Consider the dually diagnosed alcoholic. Do we enable the person to drink when we do not focus on abstinence as a goal? Certainly it would be wonderful if people agreed with our assessment that they should stop drinking. Unfortunately, many people do not want to stop. They have not made a cognitive connection between stopping and the benefits they might accrue. By helping consumers with other wants and needs, such as housing, entitlements, advocacy with utility companies, and the like, case managers gradually build a "capacity to influence." Consumers are more likely to be open to suggestions and advice from someone who has helped them in other ways.

*A case manager worked with a 27-year-old man who suffered from schizophrenia and alcohol abuse. This young man had had multiple hospitalizations, which were usually precipitated by drinking while taking medications. The case manager expressed his concerns about mixing medications and alcohol but also stated that he realized this was the young man's choice and that he would probably maintain this pattern until he decided that it was creating problems for him. The case manager helped the man move out of a group home (despite objections from staff) into his own small apartment. He also helped him feel more comfortable in the community by accompanying him to the mall and to the grocery store. One day the consumer told his case manager that he was going to be more cautious about his drinking. He really liked his apartment and wanted to keep it. He didn't want to go back to the state hospital. The young man stated that he would take his medications Mon-*

*day through Thursday. He would then stop taking the medication and not drink until Saturday. He also said that he had decided to drink a six-pack rather than a whole case of beer. This young man continues to live in his apartment and has remained out of the hospital.*

This example illustrates an action plan and coping strategy that is consumer driven. This man took personal ownership of the plan, and it worked. The personal planning process (or treatment plan) in strengths-focused case management may sometimes take a "risky" course. However, if consumers' perspectives and desires are to be incorporated into the plan, some risk is inevitable. Case managers discuss a wide range of options with consumers and negotiate rather than prescribe and/or dictate to people.

## ❏ Case Planning

A well-developed assessment leads clearly and logically to documentation of consumers' goals and action steps. Consumers indicated possible reasons for the high level of achievement in the projects we have evaluated (Kisthardt, 1992).

- I was working on things that were important to me, not what somebody else said was important to me.

- Before all my goals were in my head. When [the case manager] put them on paper for me they became real–I could see them.

- It felt great to actually accomplish things; I could see that I was making progress in my life.

- I didn't want to do the plans at first, but she said she would write down what we were doing anyway and I could see what she was writing anytime I wanted. When I decided to see them, it was neat to see how far I had come.

- She asked me if I wanted to write my own. That blew me away. I was afraid at first, but I did it, and it felt really great, like I was in charge.

- I get really overwhelmed real easy, and my case manager [using the personal planning tool] helped me to break them up into real small, comfortable steps that I could manage no sweat.

- She told me I was in charge. Like this was my own to-do list, and I was not locked in and could change my mind whenever I wanted.

- I get copies of my plan, and I keep them and look back on all the things I've done when I'm feeling depressed, and it lifts me up.

- When I told her I wanted to go back to school, she did not try to talk me out of it as some other people did, saying I was not ready and needed to do a whole bunch of other things before I could try this big step. She wrote it down, and then we talked about all of the things that needed to get done for this to happen.

- We get together and we review the sheets. I check off all of the things that I've done, and my case manager puts a sticker on the page—I love that. One time she forgot to put my sticker on and I let her have it!

- I'm gonna try now to not have case management for a while. I think I can do it. I told my case manager I'm going to keep using the personal plan as my stress-management strategy.

Several principles or guidelines for the goal-attainment process may be gleaned from these comments.

- People will follow through with the action steps/needs determined through negotiation with case managers if the steps are clearly and logically related to something that they desire.

- Personal plans should incorporate consumers' resources, talents, interests, documented on the strengths assessment.

- Personal plans should reflect creativity and innovation in the helping process

- Personal plans should individualize each consumer.

- Personal plans should build in opportunities for success.

- Personal planning becomes a symbol of the professional nature and purpose of the work. This is especially important in case management situations in which people are being helped in ways that traditionally have been viewed as transcending the boundaries of the helping relationship.

- The personal plan should reflect what consumers want and believe they need, not what the providers want for them and think they need.

In our evaluation of case management programs throughout the country (and in Great Britain), these three core functions—engagement, strengths assessment, and personal planning—are essential components of effective community-care programs. Conceptually, a case may be made that other functions of case management (e.g., brokering, advocacy, counseling, graduated disengagement) are subsumed within these three helping activities (Kisthardt, 1992).

## *Organization and Funding*

The 1963 Community Mental Health Centers Act (P.L. 88-164) succeeded in establishing mental health centers across the country. These centers are the logical and predominant organizations for community support services and case management services. Case management can occasionally be found as part of psychosocial clubhouses, which typically are not affiliated with mental health centers. Psychosocial clubhouses emphasize member involvement and control of program activities.

Medicaid and Medicare are the principal sources of funding for case management. With Medicaid, expenses are paid through both federal and state funds. A major funding issue is the discrepancy between regulations describing services eligible for reimbursement by Medicare and Medicaid and research on the most effective case management models. Both Medicaid and Medicare standards describe a brokerage model of case management and prohibit some of the services provided by other models. Ironically, the brokerage model is the least effective case management model.

Other sources of funding for case management include state grants and local mill levies. State support for case management has increased as funds have been reallocated from state psychiatric hospitals to community-based agencies. Mental health reform in Ohio, Vermont, New York, and Kansas has led to significant increases in case management funding. The State Comprehensive Mental Health Planning Act (P.L. 99-660) required states to develop community-based (as opposed to hospital-based) systems of care for adults suffering from severe and persistent mental illness and for youth suffering from emotional disturbance. Failure to do so could lead to reductions in block-grant funding. Thus case management is singled out as an important service in such legislation.

## *Costs*

With the exception of the Franklin et al. (1987) study of the broker model, all studies that included cost analysis indicated that case management is more cost effective than are traditional service-delivery mechanisms. Whereas the Franklin study reported that the case management group cost more than twice as much to serve as did the control group ($304,924 vs. $145,000), other studies have reported no difference in average cost per patient (Weisbrod, Test, & Stein, 1980) or have found case management intervention to be less expensive. Witheridge and Dincin (1985) reported per-client savings at $5,700 per year,

Bond et al. (1988) at $5,500 per year, and McRae et al. (1990) at $1,500 per year.

The results of the studies described above seem to be primarily a function of high hospital or nursing home costs and the use of community resources. Institutional costs dramatically increase per-client costs (Goffman, 1961). Research suggests that case management reduces bed-day utilization in institutions, resulting in considerable savings. For example, persons who are able to cook for themselves in the community will have meals prepared for them in an institution. In an institution, a patient gets everything regardless of individual capacities or available support. Case management, on the other hand, tailors services and resources to the circumstances and needs of the individual.

Another issue concerns case managers' use of community resources. Costs escalate with the use of formal services. For example, day-treatment programs that teach skills in daily living (cooking, hygiene, shopping) are commonly used. However, if the case manager solicits the help of neighbors, friends, family, and so forth, costs are negligible.

## Issues in Case Management

### ❏ Attrition

Many programs experience a high turnover rate for case managers—in some places as high as 50% annually. This is cause for concern in that hiring and training new case managers is expensive and lack of continuity in the relationship between consumers and case managers is unfair to the consumer. As one consumer put it, "I should get paid for breaking in all these new case managers."

Why are turnover rates so high? Many case managers are young and have minimal experience working with adults with persistent mental illness. Often, they do not receive ongoing training and close supervision. Moreover, many supervisors of case managers are required to carry a case load of their own in addition to their supervisory duties. Case managers are often the least paid professionals on staff, despite the fact that they frequently spend more time with consumers and are expected to provide services in creative ways. These work conditions often lead to frustration, anger, low morale, and job dissatisfaction.

### ❏ Consumerism

A marked shift has occurred in recent years toward viewing clients as consumers of mental health services. Changes in the nature of the physician–patient, therapist–client roles have given rise to assertive, informed consumers of services who often do not comply passively with recommended treatment regimens. In some programs, this shift has been welcomed and supported by community mental health professionals. Other programs, often with a long history of clinic-based medical services, are less sanguine about the change.

Many successful case management programs have embraced an approach that emphasizes consumer wants and choices in housing, education, vocational pursuits, and social involvements. Case managers report feeling frustrated in their efforts to convince psychiatrists, therapists, and other staff with "higher credentials" to support consumers. The philosophical differences regarding who is in charge can lead to conflict between consumers and staff; case managers are caught in the middle. In these situations, the guiding concern is frequently "liability" rather than "do-ability."

Many innovative case management and community support programs that have embraced a person-centered approach are addressing this important issue head-on. It is important to include psychiatrists in case management training. Providers must understand that their expertise *is* needed but that the goal of case management is to work *with* not *on* people. The stance of helping professionals should be that of discussion rather than lecture, negotiation and compromise rather than compliance and prescription.

## ❏ Ethical/Professional Dilemmas in Case Management

The expanded boundaries of community mental health intervention in case management has generated concern. Case managers often wonder whether they are doing too much, getting too close to the consumer, or making the consumer too dependent. These are important questions that defy simplistic answers.

Case management is not a profession; it is a methodology. People who are hired to deliver this methodology have diverse educational training. Social work, psychology, counseling, education, theology, nursing, and a range of other professional disciplines are frequently represented. Each discipline has its own set of standards for professional conduct. Although we do not believe that a separate ethical code for case managers is needed at this time, case managers should review the ethical guidelines of their respective disciplines. Many programs have adopted the National Association of Social Workers (1980) Code of Ethics and have asked case managers to become familiar with it. We offer the following guidelines for case managers to consider:

- Sexual involvement with consumers is never justified.

- Any intervention that appears to overstep the limits of the help-ing relationship should be discussed in depth with the supervi-sor and team members.

- From the beginning of the relationship, case managers should explain to consumers the concept of graduated disengagement (Kisthardt & Rapp, 1992). In this regard, the ultimate aim of case management is to help consumers develop relationships with people (non–mental health professionals) with whom they can do things in the community.

- Each activity that case managers engage in with consumers should be documented on the personal plan, with the consumer signing and thus indicating informed consent. Each activity should be logically and clearly related to a consumer-stated long-term goal.

Working with consumers as partners, collaborators, and fellow stakeholders in the community has led to shifts in thinking about the efficacy of traditional helping protocols and conditions. Professionals are now being asked to recognize the power, wisdom, desires, cultural beliefs, gifts, and talents of consumers, regardless of diagnosis, history, and functional limitations. They are being asked to attempt to share their agendas with consumers and not impose their agenda upon them. Case management is driven more by notions of individuality and citizenship than by patienthood and clienthood. It is driven by an appreciation for culture and for the challenges and consequences of mental illness. Its goal is not to discover a cause or cure for mental ill-ness but rather to attempt to help people discover options and make choices. Accordingly, we must be willing to engage and work with peo-ple in ways that validate and affirm their value while sharing our power and decision-making responsibilities with them.

## References

Anthony, W. A. (1979). *Principles of psychiatric rehabilitation*. Baltimore, MD: Univer-sity Park Press.

Anthony, W. A., Cohen, M., Farcas, M., & Cohen, B. F. (1988). *Case management: More than a response to a dysfunctional system*. Boston: Center for Psychiatric Rehabilitation.

Bond, G. R., & Boyer, S. L. (1988). The evaluation of vocational programs for the mentally ill: A review. In J. A. Ciardello & M. D. Bell (Eds.), *Vocational reha-bilitation of persons with prolonged mental illness*. Baltimore, MD: Johns Hopkins University Press.

Bond, G. R., Miller, L., Krumweid, R., & Ward, R. (1988). Assertive case management in three CMHCs: A controlled study. *Hospital and Community Psychiatry, 39,* 411–418.

Borland, A., McRae, J., & Lycan, C. (1989). Outcomes of five years of continuous intensive case management. *Hospital and Community Psychiatry, 40,* 369–376.

Bush, C., Langford, M. W., Rosen, P., & Gott, W. (1990). Operation Outreach: Intensive case management for severely psychiatrically disabled adults. *Hospital and Community Psychiatry, 41,* 647–649.

Caplan, G. (1964). Current issues relating to education of psychiatric residents in community psychiatry. *Proceedings of the Third Annual Conference of Mental Health Career Development Program.* Public Health Service Publication No. 1245. Bethesda, MD: National Institute of Mental Health.

Chambers, D. E. (1986). *Social policies and social programs.* New York: Macmillan.

Deitchman, W. S. (1980). How many case managers does it take to screw in a lightbulb? *Hospital and Community Psychiatry, 31,* 788–789.

Division of Biometry and Epidemiology. (1979). *Data sheet on state and county mental hospitals.* Rockville, MD: National Institutes of Mental Health.

Ewalt, P. L., & Honeyfield, R. M. (1981). Needs of persons in long-term care. *Social Work, 26,* 223–231.

Fisher, G., Landis, D., & Clark, K. (1988). Case management service and client change. *Community Mental Health Journal, 77,* 134–142.

Franklin, J., Solovitz, B., Mason, M., Clemons, J., & Miller, G. (1987). An evaluation of case management. *American Journal of Public Health, 77,* 674–678.

General Accounting Office. (1977). *Returning the mentally disabled to the community: Government needs to do more.* Washington, DC: U.S. Government Printing Office.

Goering, P., Wasylenki, D., Farkas, M., Lancee, W., & Ballantyne, R. (1988). What difference does case management make? *Hospital and Community Psychiatry, 39,* 272–276.

Goffman, E. (1961). *Asylums: Essays on the social situation of mental patients and other inmates.* Garden City, NY: Doubleday/Anchor.

Gordon, M. E. (1965). Toward a social work frame of reference. *Journal of Education for Social Work, 1,* 19–46.

Harris, M., & Bergman, H. (1987). Case management with the chronically mentally ill. *American Journal of Orthopsychiatry, 57,* 296–302.

Hogarty, G. E., Schooler, N. R., Ulrich, R., Mussare, F., Ferro, P., & Herron, E. (1979). Fluphenazine and social therapy in the aftercare of schizophrenic patients. *Archives of General Psychiatry, 36,* 1283–1294.

Johnson, P., & Rubin, A. (1983). Case management in mental health: A social work domain? *Social Work, 28,* 49–56.

Kisthardt, W. E. (1992). A strengths model of case management: The principles and functions of a helping partnership. In D. Saleebey (Ed.), *The strengths perspective in social work practice.* New York: Longman.

Kisthardt, W. E. (1993). An empowerment agenda for case management research: Evaluating the strengths model from the consumers' perspective. In M. Harris & H. Bergman (Eds.), *Case management with mentally ill patients: Theory and prac-*

*tice*. Langhorne, PA: Harwood Academic Publishers.

Kisthardt, W. E., & Rapp, C. A. (1992). Bridging the gap between principles and practice: Implementing a strengths perspective in case management. In S. Rose (Ed.), *Case management and social work practice*. New York: Longman.

Lamb, H. R. (1980). Therapist case managers: More than brokers of services. *Hospital and Community Psychiatry, 31,* 762–764.

Langsley, D. G., & Kaplan, D. (1978). *The treatment of families in crisis*. New York: Grune and Stratton.

Marlowe, H. A., & Weinberg, R. B. (Eds.). (1982). *The management of deinstitutionalization*. Proceedings of the 1982 Florida Conference on Deinstitutionalization, University of South Florida, Tampa, FL.

Marx, A. J., Test, M. A., & Stein, L. I. (1973). Extrahospital management of severe mental illness. *Archives of General Psychiatry, 12,* 505–511.

McRae, J., Higgins, M., Lycan, C., & Sherman, W. (1990). What happens to patients after five years of intensive case management stops? *Hospital and Community Psychiatry, 41,* 175–183.

Modrcin, M., Rapp, C. A., & Chamberlain, R. (1985). *Case management with psychiatrically disabled individuals: Curriculum and training program*. Lawrence, KS: School of Social Welfare, University of Kansas.

Modrcin, M., Rapp, C. A., & Poertner, J. (1988). The evaluation of case management services with the chronically mentally ill. *Journal of Evaluation and Program Planning, 11,* 307–314.

Moxley, D. P. (1989). *The practice of case management*. Newbury Park, CA: Sage Publications.

National Association of Social Workers. (1980). NASW Code of ethics. *NASW News, 25,* 24–25.

Pasamanick, B., Scarpitti, F. P., & Dinitz, S. (1967). *Schizophrenia in the community: An experimental study in the prevention of hospitalization*. New York: Appelton-Century-Crofts.

President's Commission on Mental Health. (1979). *Report to the President* (Vol. 1). Washington, DC: U.S. Government Printing Office.

Rapp, C. A., & Chamberlain, R. (1985). Case management services for the chronically mentally ill. *Social Work, 30,* 417–422.

Rapp, C. A., & Wintersteen, R. W. (1989, July). The strengths model of case management: Results from twelve demonstrations. *Psychosocial Rehabilitation Journal, 13,* 23–31.

Rappaport, J. (1977). *Community psychology: Values, research, and action*. New York: Holt, Rinehart, and Winston.

Roberts-DeGennaro, M. (1987). Developing case management as a practice model. *Social Casework, 68,* 466–470.

Robinson, G. K., & Bergman, G. T. (1989). *Choices in case management*. Washington, DC: Policy Resources, Inc.

Sands, R. (1991). *Clinical social work practice in community mental health*. New York: Merrill/Macmillan.

Stein, L. I., & Test, M. A. (1980). Alternatives to mental hospital treatment: Conceptual model, treatment program, and clinical evaluation. *Archives of General Psychiatry, 37,* 392–397.

Stuart, R. B. (1977). *Trick or treatment: How and when psychotherapy fails*. Champaign, IL: Research Press.

Test, M. A., & Stein, L. I. (1980). Alternatives to mental hospital treatment, III. Social cost. *Archives of General Psychiatry, 37,* 409–412.

Turner, J., & Shifren, I. (1979). Community support systems: How comprehensive? *New Directions for Mental Health Services, 2,* 1–13.

Turner, J., & TenHoor, W. (1978). The NIMH Community Support Program: Pilot approach to a needed social reform. *Schizophrenia Bulletin, 4,* 319–348.

Weisbrod, B., Test, M. A., & Stein, L. (1980). Alternatives to mental hospital treatment, II: Economic benefit cost analysis. *Archives of General Psychiatry, 37,* 400–405.

Wintersteen, R. T. (1986). Rehabilitating the chronically mentally ill: Social work's claim to leadership. *Social Work, 31,* 332–337.

Witheridge, T., & Dincin, J. (1985). The Bridge: An assertive outreach program in an urban setting. *New Directions in Mental Health Services, 26,* 65–76.

# Chapter 3

# Case Management in Child Welfare

*Joan Levy Zlotnik*

> *We have learned that immediate response to families, low case loads, flexible work hours, and a family empowerment approach to case planning and solution work well. What then is being done inside agencies now to revamp intake and child protective services to conform with the characteristics of the successful program? What is being done to make foster care case management more intensive? I sometimes see case management being used by cynical policymakers or legislators as a ruse to increase the case load of the worker. They believe that it takes less time and effort to provide case management services than it did to provide traditional services (Cole, 1993, p. 10).*

State and local child-welfare services are undergoing changes as they struggle to improve service delivery through implementation of the Family Preservation and Support Services (FPSS) provisions enacted as part of the Omnibus Budget Reconciliation Act of 1993 (P.L. 103-66) while coping with increasing case loads, negative media attention, diminished community resources, and difficulties recruiting staff. Intensive, family-focused case management is an important component of efforts to improve service delivery now under way (Kahn & Kamerman, 1992).

Case management is closely associated with both the delivery of traditional child-welfare services and the new vision fostered by the FPSS initiative. How case management is defined and implemented has changed, however. This chapter explores the history and definition of child-welfare services and addresses variations in case management practice in a range of child-welfare settings since the mid-1970s. Innovative models of case management practice, as well as implications for staffing, training, and research, are described and discussed.

## Defining Child Welfare

Just as child-welfare services are evolving, so too are definitions of child welfare. The developmental view defines child welfare as services directed to meeting the needs of all children, recognizing that no family is entirely self-sufficient to meet all of their children's needs (Kadushin & Martin, 1988). The predominant definition of child welfare throughout the past half century focused on family breakdown: "social services to children and youth whose parents are unable or need help to carry out their child-rearing responsibilities" (Child Welfare League of America, 1982, p. 8). A more recent definition incorporates both the developmental and residual perspective, defining child welfare as "those areas of social service designed to protect children from abuse and neglect, improve opportunities for optimal child development, help establish and fortify family structures, and improve the level of family functioning" (Child Welfare League of America, 1993, p. 7). This contemporary perspective views the child within the context of the family, and provision of services focuses on both the child and the family. The development of community-based family support and family-preservation services envisioned in the FPSS legislation incorporates the developmental and residual perspective.

Child welfare encompasses a broad range of prevention and intervention services, including foster care, adoption, child protection, family preservation, family support (e.g., drop-in centers, child and family counseling, home visiting, parenting education, respite care), and child day care. Preventive programs such as Head Start and the Maternal and Child Health Bureau's Healthy Start can be considered child-welfare programs under this enhanced definition (Kamerman & Kahn, 1989; Wells, 1985).

## Historical Overview

Child-welfare services are provided through agencies serving children and families in both the public and private sectors. Early child-welfare services were provided by charitable organizations that created services, including orphanages and institutions, for delinquent, homeless, and handicapped children. Today, services include foster care, adoption, residential and group care, and child protective services.

Until the passage of the Social Security Act in the 1930s, child-welfare services were provided by voluntary agencies. Federal funding began at that point and established public child-welfare agencies as major providers of child-welfare services. Federal funds are the major funding source for child-welfare services in both public and private agencies (Costin, Bell, & Downs, 1991; Rapp & Poertner, 1980). In a recent survey by the American Public Welfare Association (1990), the only child-welfare services available on a state-wide basis in all 50 states were child protective services, foster care, and special-needs adoption, that is, those programs mandated specifically through federal funds.

Historically, among the helping professions, social work has been predominant in the delivery of direct services, administrative support, research, advocacy, program planning, and worker preparation for child welfare (Child Welfare League of America, 1982). Social work values, theory, and knowledge support child-welfare practice, including the application of systems theory, ecological theory, and family systems theory to service delivery (Family Impact Seminar, 1994; Family Partnership Project, 1994; Kadushin, 1987). Since social agencies joined together to establish schools of social work in the early twentieth century, child-welfare research and practice have been major aspects of social work education (Zlotnik, 1993).

The Social Security Act of 1935 and amendments in 1962 and 1967 created the federal foster-care program. More recently the Child Welfare and Adoption Assistance Act of 1980 (P.L. 96-272) represents the most sweeping legislation affecting the delivery of foster care and adoption services in states (Allen & Knitzer, 1983). The intention of the Title IV-B and Title IV-E programs was to provide strong accountability measures to ensure that states made reasonable efforts to move children through the child-welfare system and to find them permanent homes. Child-welfare advocates and service providers hoped for a new era in the delivery of services to children and families.

The legislation was based on model permanency-planning programs implemented in the 1970s that demonstrated significant achievements in preventing children from lingering in foster care. Permanency planning is a goal-directed, time-limited process to help reunite children with their biological families or to find permanent homes with other relatives or through adoption (Pecora, Whittaker, & Maluccio 1992). States were required to make reasonable efforts to prevent children from being placed in foster care. For each child in placement, a permanent plan was required. The status of children in placement was to be regularly reviewed, and every effort made to reunite children with their birth families, to place children with relatives, to make adoptive placements, or if no other appropriate alternative was available, to make foster care a permanent placement. The goal was to make families partners in the placement process and participants in the review process. New funds were made available for the provision of subsidies to encourage the adoption of special-needs children and to eliminate incentives for keeping children in foster care.

The Child Abuse Prevention and Treatment Act (CAPTA) of 1974 (P.L. 93-247) provided some funding to state agencies, supported child-abuse research, and created requirements regarding child-abuse reporting and child-abuse and -neglect definitions. The 1991 amendments to

CAPTA (P.L. 102-295) provided incentives to states to make improvement in their child-protection system, including enhancing "case management and delivery of ongoing family services" (U.S. Advisory Board on Child Abuse and Neglect, 1993a, p. 203). Unfortunately, funding for CAPTA has not reached the levels needed for making these system improvements (T. Birch, personal communication, January 12, 1995). Since passage of CAPTA in 1974, child protective services have become the core public child-welfare service in many states. Kamerman and Kahn (1989) assert that

> the social service system has become so constricted that children gain access to help only if they have been abused or severely neglected, are found delinquent or runaway. Doorways for "less serious" or differently defined problems are closed (p. 13).

Title XX of the Social Security Act was created in 1974 and became the Social Services Block Grant in 1981. It supports many child- and family-focused social services, including child protective services, child care, and homemaker services (Harris, 1987). These provisions stimulated the extensive use of purchase of service from private agencies (Rapp & Poertner, 1980).

The Indian Child Welfare Act of 1978 (P.L. 95-508) encouraged tribal governments to assume responsibility for American Indian children who needed child-welfare services (Mannes, 1993). This legislation was intended to help American Indian children who needed to be separated from their biological family to remain connected to their tribe, community, and heritage.

After enactment of the Child Welfare and Adoption Assistance Act of 1980 (P.L. 96-272), the number of children in foster care fell from an estimated 502,000 in 1977 to 302,000 in 1980 (U.S. House of Representatives, 1989) to 262,000 in 1982 (Tatara, 1993). Increased attention on family reunification and specialized adoption efforts stimulated this dramatic reduction of children in foster care. The passage of P.L. 96-272 encouraged permanency-planning efforts throughout the country. Many successful programs were developed to prevent out-of-home placement or to reunify foster children with their families. Generally, comprehensive case management was a major element of these programs (Maluccio, Fein, & Olmstead, 1986). Characteristics of these programs are described in the section headed Intensive and Family-Focused Case Management in Child Welfare.

Unfortunately, the goals for P.L. 96-272 were never realized. The federal government did not commit resources for implementation. Consequently, the training needed to help front-line workers, supervisors, and administrators understand and implement the vision and service-delivery components was not provided. As case loads increased, agencies focused more on crisis intervention, and fewer resources were available to provide the broad multidimensional response required of effective child-welfare services (American Public Welfare Association, 1991; Kamerman & Kahn, 1989).

The number of children in foster care remained relatively steady between 1982 and 1986. However, the number of children in care began to increase dramatically in 1987. By 1992, approximately 442,000 children were in substitute care (Tatara, 1993), with projections that 550,000 children would be in foster care by 1995 (U.S. House of Representatives, 1989). This growth in case load was related both to the increasing number of children entering care and to declining rates of children leaving care (Stagner, 1993). The number of reports of child abuse and neglect increased from 1.1 million in 1980 to 2.9 million in 1992 (American Humane Association, 1993). These increases in child abuse and neglect were accompanied by increasing rates of substance abuse, especially crack cocaine. Research indicates a link between drug abuse and foster-care placement (Stagner, 1993). In addition, financial and programmatic initiatives have supported kinship care (care of children by relatives); such care is considered foster care and thus has added new children and maintained other children on the foster-care roles.

Increases in child abuse and neglect and in the number of children in foster care have created a situation whereby families usually are served only at the point of crisis, because increasing needs have not been counterbalanced by additional resources for child-welfare agencies. Little or nothing is available to provide preventive services. Case loads are high—sometimes in excess of 100 cases per worker. In addition, liability concerns, violence in the workplace, and the increasingly complex problems of children and families as a result of substance abuse, violence, homelessness, and poverty have contributed to problems in the service-delivery system (Pecora, Briar, & Zlotnik, 1989). The intent of the Child Welfare and Adoption Assistance Act of 1980—to decrease the number of children in foster care and to find permanent homes for children—has not been realized to the extent expected.

## New Child-Welfare Reform Initiatives

Prompted by the rising rates of child abuse and foster care, the scarcity of prevention services, and increasing service-delivery problems, several reports (American Public Welfare Association, 1991; National Commission on Children, 1991; U.S. Advisory Board on Child Abuse and Neglect, 1990) examined problems regarding the delivery of child-welfare services and recommended implementation of preventive, family-focused services to help decrease out-of-home placements. These reports highlighted successful models of family-focused prevention, early intervention, and crisis-intervention programs as well as community-based systems reform efforts supported by federal, state, and foundation dollars (Family Impact Seminar, 1994; Kahn & Kamerman, 1992; Kamerman & Kahn, 1989; Ooms & Owen, 1992).

Their recommendations called for providing services in a "new" way through a continuum of family-focused prevention, early intervention, and intensive-intervention services; improving operations of the child-welfare system; and collaboration with other human services. These recommendations stimulated efforts to create new federal legislation that would build on the intent of P.L. 96-272 to prevent child abuse and neglect and to keep children from moving into foster care.

In August 1993, after several years of advocacy efforts, the Family Preservation and Support Services provision of the Omnibus Budget Reconciliation Act of 1993 (P.L. 103-66) passed Congress and was signed by President Clinton. This legislation created a capped entitlement funded at $1 billion over five years to stimulate the development of family-support and family-preservation programs in order to enhance the availability of family-centered, community-based prevention, and early intervention services to families to prevent crises and to reduce the need for out-of-home care (Administration on Children, Youth, and Families, 1994). Family support services as defined by the Department of Health and Human Services are:

> Community-based services to promote the well-being of children and families designed to increase the strength and stability of families (including adoptive, foster, and extended families), to increase parents' confidence and competence in their parenting abilities, to afford children a stable and supportive family environment, and otherwise to enhance child development.
>
> [Family support services may include the following.] (1) Services, including in-home visits, parent support groups, and other programs, designed to improve parenting skills (by reinforcing parents' confidence in their strengths and helping them to identify where improvement is needed and to obtain assistance in improving those skills) with respect to matters such as child development, family budgeting, coping with stress, health, and nutrition; (2) respite care of children to provide temporary relief for parents and other caregivers; (3) structured activities involving parents and children to strengthen the parent–child relationship; (4) drop-in centers to afford families opportunities for informal interaction with other families and with program staff; (5) information

*and referral services to afford families access to other community ser-*
*vices, including child care, health care, nutrition programs, adult edu-*
*cation and literacy programs, and counseling and mentoring services;*
*and (6) early developmental screening of children to assess the needs of*
*such children, and assistance to families in securing specific services to*
*meet these needs.*

*[Family preservation services are] services for children and fami-*
*lies designed to help families (including adoptive and extended fami-*
*lies) at risk or in crisis, including (1) services programs designed to help*
*children, where appropriate, return to families from which they have*
*been removed, or be placed for adoption, with a legal guardian, or, if*
*adoption or legal guardianship is determined not to be appropriate for*
*a child, in some other planned, permanent living arrangement; (2) pre-*
*placement preventive services programs, such as intensive family*
*preservation programs, designed to help children at risk of foster care*
*placement remain with their families; (3) service programs designed to*
*provide follow-up care to families to whom a child has been returned*
*after a foster care placement; (4) respite care of children to provide tem-*
*porary relief for parents and other caregivers (including foster parent[s]);*
*and (5) services designed to improve parenting skills (by reinforcing par-*
*ents' confidence in their strengths, and helping them to identify where*
*improvement is needed and to obtain assistance in improving those*
*skills) with respect to matters such as child development, family bud-*
*geting, coping with stress, health and nutrition (Family Preservation and*
*Support Services, 1994, p. 50647).*

Activities such as respite care, home visiting, and assistance in
obtaining services may be considered either a family-support or a family-
preservation service. Intensive family-preservation programs to prevent
out-of-home placement and intensive family-reunification services to
reunite children with their biological families are included in the definition of family-preservation services.

In order to access these new funds, state child-welfare agencies are
required to work together with other human service providers in the public and private sectors, advocacy organizations, and families to create the
services that are needed (Family Preservation and Support Services, 1994).

The following principles for services to children and families undergird many system-reform and service-integration efforts (Kahn & Kamerman, 1992) and guide FPSS implementation efforts:

- *The welfare and safety of children and all family members must be*
  *maintained while strengthening and preserving the family whenever*
  *possible. Supporting families is seen as the best way of promoting chil-*
  *dren's healthy development.*

- *Services are focused on the family as a whole; family strengths are iden-*
  *tified, enhanced, and respected, as opposed to a focus on family deficits*

or dysfunctions; and service providers work with families as partners in
identifying and meeting individual and family needs.

- Services are easily accessible (often delivered in the home or in community-based settings, convenient to parents' schedules), and are delivered in a manner that respects cultural and community differences.

- Services are flexible and responsive to real family needs. Linkage to a
wide variety of supports and services outside the child welfare system
(e.g., housing, substance abuse treatment, mental health, health, job
training, child care) are generally crucial to meeting families' and children's needs.

- Services are community-based and involve community organizations
and residents (including parents) in their design and delivery.

- Services are intensive enough to meet family needs and keep children
safe. The level of intensity needed to achieve these goals may vary
greatly between preventive (family support) and crisis services (Administration on Children, Youth and Families, 1994).

The goal is to create a more integrated system of care for vulnerable children and families. Each state has flexibility in how they priori-
tize use of these new funds; moreover, the new funds cannot be used to
supplant existing funds. States are encouraged to examine all potential
federal funding streams that support services for children and families.
States must collaborate with state mental health, education, and health
agencies, as well as others, to develop a comprehensive array of services
for vulnerable children and their families. They can incorporate school-
linked services funded through education resources as well as comprehensive services for children and adolescents with severe emotional disorders funded through the Center for Mental Health Services (CMHS)
and Maternal and Child Health (MCH) programs as part of their service-delivery strategy. Because funds are scarce, states are encouraged
to target new dollars toward communities or specific populations (Center for the Study of Social Policy, 1994; Family Preservation and Support Services, 1994). Implementation of these programs has brought
renewed attention to the importance of coordinated service delivery
and systems integration. Kahn and Kamerman (1992) define integration
of services as

> a systematic effort to solve problems of service fragmentation and of the
> lack of an exact match between an individual or family with problems
> and needs and an interventive program or professional specialty. The
> effort may take the form of (a) high-level or local-level administrative
> restructuring or collaboration, or (b) case-oriented strategies at the ser-
> vice delivery level (p. 5).

The critical role of case management in the implementation of these new service-reform strategies is described later.

## *Case Management and Casework*

Traditionally, children and families received child-welfare services through direct casework services. Casework tasks include outreach and intake, assessment, planning, intervention or service provision, monitoring, evaluation, and planned termination (American Humane Association, 1991; Child Welfare League of America, 1982). The focus is on the relationship between the client and the caseworker. The caseworker assesses the situation and engages with the client in a problem-solving process through "counseling casework" (Kadushin, 1987). Access to concrete services, such as day care, financial assistance, or employment services, available through the child-welfare agency or other community agencies are obtained through the client's relationship with the child-welfare caseworker. The most common services in traditional child welfare are counseling and placement (Rapp & Poertner, 1980), and the relationship between the client and the caseworker is the most frequently cited factor leading to positive or negative outcomes in child-welfare work (Kadushin, 1987). The caseworker's ability to make timely decisions is a significant factor in children lingering in foster care (Emlen, 1975). Casework services have been described as "goalless" if they do not focus on permanency-planning strategies (Wiltse, 1982). As the array of child-welfare services provided by agencies has expanded beyond casework to include homemaker services, child care, parent aides, and programs for special populations such as teen mothers and children with developmental disabilities, the caseworker's role has become more complex.

There is little agreement in the literature regarding the fit between casework and case management in child-welfare services. Are they distinctly separate services? Do professionals who are called case managers actually provide a set of services different from those performed by people who are called caseworkers? Weil (1985) defines the functions of case management as

> *(1) client identification and outreach, (2) individual assessment and diagnosis, (3) service planning and resource identification, (4) linking client to needed services, (5) service implementation and coordination, (6) monitoring service delivery, (7) advocacy, and (8) evaluation (p. 29)*

These functions are similar to the functions of casework, except that advocacy is noted explicitly in the case manager role. In casework, case-level advocacy is a responsibility of the caseworker, but advocacy for expanded services is perceived as a social-action responsibility of the agency or other child-welfare advocates (Child Welfare League of America, 1982). The case management functions may be subsumed under casework (Weil, 1985) or may be viewed as being distinct from casework because of the focus on service coordination and management of an array of services (Rapp & Poertner, 1980).

Casework focuses on the direct provision of services to children and families, whereas case management emphasizes arranging for the provision of services. Young (1994) defines the case management function as "doing-for" and the child-welfare clinical social worker's task as "doing with."

## Case Management after PL 96-272

In the late 1970s and early 1980s, the term case manager was commonly used to describe the role of workers involved in the delivery of child-welfare services. This occurred as a result of the complex array of child-welfare service options, the use of purchase-of-service contract stimulated by the passage of Title XX, and the new accountability requirements for moving children through the foster-care system (Hegar, 1992; Rapp & Poertner, 1980; Wiltse, 1982). Case management helps reduce confusion, enhance accountability, and provide quality services to children and their families (Wells, 1985).

The increasing complexity of child-welfare services can be seen by comparing typical participants in child-protection court cases in 1975 and 1992. In 1975, the participants typically were the custodial parent(s) and the caseworker. In 1992 typical participants included the caseworker, the custodial parent(s), the attorney for the agency, the attorney for the custodial parent(s), the child's attorney and/or attorney serving as guardian *ad litem* or a court-appointed special advocate, volunteer, foster parents, and noncustodial or putative parent(s), and the attorneys for them (Hardin, 1992).

In the early 1980s, leading social work practitioners and educators examined the critical importance of ensuring that social workers have the skills necessary to provide case management services in child welfare (Saalberg, 1982). Case management was emphasized for several reasons. Interagency coordination is critical in that children and families are often served by several agencies and the worker needs skills to engage several systems, including the family and various service systems, in orchestrating a plan to meet the child's and family's needs and goals (Wiltse, 1982). Caseworkers are increasingly placed in a decision-making position and thus need the tools, resources, and administrative skills to fulfill this function (Rapp & Poertner, 1980). Larger case loads preclude many child-welfare agencies from providing clinical services or gathering detailed social histories. These services may be purchased from other providers; the public agency caseworker is responsible for assessment, service coordination, monitoring, and evaluation (Rapp & Poertner, 1980; Saalberg, 1982). Accurate assessment is important to ensure that the client is directed toward the appropriate set of services. Case management is a way to link vulnerable clients with other services so that clients are not lost in the system (Kamerman & Kahn, 1989).

Many social service administrators believe that in public agencies without resources to provide treatment or sustain ongoing services, case management by public child-welfare agency staff helps ensure that these clients are linked to other services. This perception has tended to limit the services that public agencies offer (Kamerman & Kahn, 1989). In New York City, the Human Resources Administration limits case management to a linkage function only. When referral to a preventive service is made and the case has been accepted, the case is transferred to a case management unit, which assumes responsibility for paying the voluntary agency for services. No one from the case management unit is actually involved with the client (Kamerman & Kahn, 1989).

Little (1982) promotes three functions of case management in child welfare—orchestration of services, monitoring and recording, and financial and service accountability for the plan. Compher (1983) describes general case management as a typical staff role in a public child-welfare agency. The skills needed to perform general case management include listening well in order to clarify complex problems, supporting and encouraging families' strengths, and the ability to develop a feasible service plan. These skills are different from those of comprehensive social workers or clinical case managers who have skills in family counseling and take on both the counselor and case manager roles (Compher, 1983; Kamerman & Kahn, 1989; Young, 1994). Clinical case managers are more likely to be found in private agencies that contract with public agencies for specific services or in a demonstration project (Kamerman & Kahn, 1989).

The move from casework to case management in the 1970s and 1980s resulted in declassification of professional positions and titles in public child welfare agencies. In some agencies, titles were changed from social worker to case manager, although the title change did not necessarily reflect changes in responsibilities. In some instances, job requirements were lowered and case loads increased (Cole, 1993). The lowering of job requirements is in direct contrast to assertions that case management requires a high level of professional skill (Ooms, Hara, & Owen, 1992; Weil, 1985). Moreover, declassification led many professionally trained social workers to leave the child-welfare field, which diminished the high status of child welfare as a setting for social work services (Kadushin, 1987; Rome, 1994).

As public child-welfare agencies assumed the narrow case management functions related to brokering, coordinating, and monitoring services, private agencies under contract with public agencies had opportunities to provide more intensive, holistic case management services (Cole, 1993; Kamerman & Kahn, 1989). For example, an agency providing special foster care to children with developmental disabilities also might coordinate the broad array of medical, educational, therapeutic, and social activities in which a child was involved as well as facilitate work with the biological family, foster family, and public agency caseworker to prepare for the return home or adoption of the child. The case manager needs a high level of skills in the clinical and service-coordination areas as well as knowledge of community resources.

## Intensive and Family-Focused Case Management in Child Welfare

Today "comprehensive" (Weil, 1985) or "intensive" case management is often a key component of service delivery for vulnerable children and families (Kahn & Kamerman, 1992; Melaville & Blank, 1991; Ooms et al., 1992). Comprehensive case management is different from minimal case management, which emphasized the brokerage and monitoring functions (Kamerman & Kahn, 1989; Nelson, 1984; Stein, 1982; Weil, 1985) and was characteristic of child-welfare services in the 1980s.

The current movement toward system reform, system improvement, and integration of services, including the implementation of FPSS provisions, give new emphasis and consensus to case management principles and functions (Ahart, Bruer, Rutsch, Schmidt, & Zaro, 1992; Allen, 1990; Kahn & Kamerman, 1992; Melaville & Blank, 1991).

Guiding principles regarding programs state that programs should be "family-focused, holistic, community-based, consumer-oriented, culturally sensitive, comprehensive, and integrated or coordinated to create a system of care" (Kahn & Kamerman, 1992, p. 8). These principles encompass previously stated principles articulated by the Department of Health and Human Services for the FPSS program. Case management based upon these principles should include the following key elements. Case management practice should reflect family-focused policies and should incorporate the following principles.

- Case management services are family focused (Allen, 1990). Family concerns, problems, and solutions should be approached from an ecological perspective. Rather than focusing on an individual client within a family, family-centered case management requires a holistic, family-systems approach that recognizes families as the "focal point of child welfare services because the conditions of children's lives and their future prospects largely depend on the well-being of their families" (Ahart et al., 1992, p. 14). Family may include parents, siblings, grandparents, and other significant persons.

- Case management is comprehensive. Weil's (1985) definition is modified to include (1) family identification and outreach, (2) comprehensive family assessment, (3) service planning and resource identification, (4) linking family members with needed services, (5) service implementation and coordination, (6) monitoring service delivery, (7) advocacy, and (8) evaluation of service delivery and case management, including planned termination and follow-up.

- Case management should involve working with the family as partners in setting goals and finding solutions (Melaville & Blank, 1991). Families have the potential to change and thus should be active participants in implementing the service plan (Lloyd & Sallee, 1994).

- Family strengths should be assessed and used in the development and implementation of the service plan (Commission on Families, 1991; Family Partnership Project, 1994; Lloyd & Sallee, 1994).

- Effective family-centered case management requires interagency collaboration to meet the needs of the family. Cross-systems collaboration and communication is critical, because many families have multiple needs and receive services from various systems, including child welfare, health, mental health, economic security, housing, juvenile justice, and education (Briar, 1994).

- Case managers have the authority, skills, knowledge, and ability to make decisions and to access necessary services and resources (Ahart et al., 1992; Melaville & Blank, 1991). A pool of money is available to assist families to meet their specific needs, from repairing the stove to purchasing respite care to psychological-assessment services that may not be covered by another funding source.

- Case managers' case loads should be small enough to allow them to provide intensive services to families. Such services are often provided in the family's home or other community-based settings and at convenient times for the client.

- Case managers should work together with the family to tailor a service plan to meet the family's individual needs. Families should not be forced into services that do not fit their needs (Family Partnership Project, 1994).

- Case managers should deliver services in a manner that is culturally relevant to the family and community.

Intensive, family-focused case management may vary in structure from program to program. Variations include:

- *Case management as a primary staff role.* One individual may serve as the case manager. He or she may carry a small case load and have the discretion to call upon specialists to provide resources or expertise (Kamerman & Kahn, 1989; Ooms et al., 1992; U.S. Department of Health and Human Services, 1994).

- *Clinical case manager.* One individual may provide therapeutic intervention as well as link children and families with other services (Kamerman & Kahn, 1989; Weil, 1985; Young, 1994).

- *Case management team approach.* Professionals from several disciplines may work together with the family. Ongoing communication among team members and the family is necessary.

## *Program Models*

In discussing contemporary case management in child welfare, it is important to consider a broad range of case management approaches. Many children and families are served by multiple systems and agencies. Many children in the child-welfare system have special mental health and educational needs. Agencies need to design strategies to facilitate their work together at the administrative level, including the development of work agreements, and case managers need interactional skills (Weil, 1985; Wiltse, 1982) to work with colleagues in other systems and professional disciplines. In family-focused service delivery, case managers are required "to coordinate and facilitate the fit between family system needs and helping system services" (Friedman, 1991, p. 36). In families with multiple needs, multiple case managers may be involved. The plan must coordinate services among case managers and ensure accountability and communication for resources and services available from different systems (Melaville & Blank, 1991).

During the past decades, a range of program models using intensive, family-focused case management has been developed. These models in various human service systems have served as catalysts for one another. In child welfare, intensive, family-focused case management is prominent in family-preservation programs, in family-support programs for at-risk families, and in intensive programs that work to reunify foster children with their families (Ahart et al., 1992; Kamerman & Kahn, 1989; Melaville & Blank, 1991). Intensive, family-focused case management also forms part of the vision of an effective child-protective-services system (U.S. Advisory Board on Child Abuse and Neglect, 1993b) that would provide more preventive and community-based family-support services.

A related program in another system is the Child and Adolescent Services System Program (CASSP). This program was developed at the Center for Mental Health Services, which provides incentive funds for states to establish focal points for interagency collaboration for seriously emotionally disturbed children (Kahn & Kamerman, 1992). Other related programs include the Comprehensive Child Development Program, a family-support program that provides intensive, family-focused case management to high-risk families to help promote self-sufficiency and provide educational services to parents and young children (U.S. Department of Health and Human Services, 1994); a range of public health programs supported by the Bureau of Maternal and Child Health (MCH) that promote early identification, family-centered care, outreach, assessment, coordination, and follow-up (Kahn & Kamerman, 1992); a range of education-related programs established under the Individuals with Disabilities Education Act and school-linked services (Behrmann, 1992; Melaville & Blank, 1993); and family-focused case management efforts implemented after passage of the Family Support Act of 1988 that evaluate the complex set of services needed to assess and establish employment plans (American Public Welfare Association, 1992; Kahn & Kamerman, 1992).

Several states are attempting to maximize federal funding for services to vulnerable children and families, including making efforts to consolidate funding sources such as Title IV-B, Title IV-E, CASSP, MCH, and Part H. Medicaid funds cover a range of nonmedical services for high-risk children, including case management (Bruner, 1990). In addition, some states are using Title IV-A Emergency Assistance funds to meet family needs and develop an intensive strategy to keep children and families together (Joe & Farrow, 1992).

These efforts represent an attempt to institutionalize comprehensive, family-focused services across a continuum of services–from preventive services to intensive interventions. Such initiatives go beyond earlier programs that were funded with discretionary grants and foundation dollars and were often terminated when the special funding ended. Several foundations, including the Annie E. Casey and Edna McConnell Clark foundation, are working in partnership with public and private agencies at the state and local level to develop comprehensive, family-focused services across human service systems. Case management is integral to implementation of such programs.

The Services Reform Initiative in Maryland is a good example of coordinated, cross-system reform to serve children and families in the child-welfare system. The reform was initiated in 1988 as a result of various factors and concerns, including the need to "fix" the foster-care system and provide mental health services to children; practitioners' belief that social services needed to be more family-focused and integrated; a grant from the Annie E. Casey Foundation to implement a child-welfare reform initiative; and the development of a government subcabinet post for children, youth, and families. Reform goals included (1) preventing unnecessary out-of-home placement, (2) reducing the number of out-of-state placement, and (3) redirecting funds into preventive services. Intensive case management services are provided for families at risk of child placement and that fall into other high-risk categories. The case manager may be drawn from any of several different systems, including mental health, education, juvenile justice, and child welfare. Local planning entities have been established, and funds are used flexibly to serve the needs of the children and families (Family Impact Seminar, 1994).

To track cases and to enhance communication across the agencies involved with the families, a comprehensive case management information management system, HomeBase, was developed. The system is especially designed for intensive, family-focused case management and is intended to produce management and evaluation data as well as to aid the front-line worker in service delivery. It provides family profiles, goals, outcomes, strategies, and information about service providers and financing. It can be accessed from several agencies that are networked together because they serve the same clients. The development of the system was supported by the Casey Foundation and based on CareTrack, which was developed under a grant from the Robert Wood Johnson Foundation (Services Reform Initiative, 1994).

The FPSS encourages state child-welfare agencies to work together with health, education, and mental health agencies from the public and private sector to develop plans for the use of FPSS funds (U.S. Department of Health and Human Services, 1994). Cooperative relationships also exist among CASSP, MCH, and Part H programs (Kahn & Kamerman, 1992). The National Association of Public Child Welfare Administrators (NAPCWA) (1991), an affiliate of the American Public Welfare Association (APWA), and the State Mental Health Representatives for Children and

Youth, a division of the National Association of State Mental Health Program Directors (NASMHPD), developed *The Child Welfare/Children's Mental Health Partnership: A Collaborative Agenda for Strengthening Families* and have launched a multiyear effort to improve the delivery of services to children who are served by both systems. This initiative is taking place at the national, state, and local levels.

## *Key Skills*

### ❏ Assessment Skills

The ability to carry out a family-focused biopsychosocial assessment is key to developing an appropriate case management action plan. The assessment should be face-to-face and include more people than the mother–child dyad. All significant individuals in the child's life should be included in the assessment in order to ensure that all potential resources and strategies are explored. The National Association of Social Workers (1992) recommends that case managers be skilled in identifying "strengths as well as weaknesses through a systematic evaluation of the client's current level of functioning" (p. 13). The interplay among physical, environmental, behavioral, psychological, economic, and social factors should be analyzed and an appraisal made of the informal and formal supports, social functioning, economic and housing issues, and cultural and religious factors.

### ❏ Management Skills

Rapp and Poertner (1980) and Wolk, Sullivan, and Hartman (1994) stress the managerial aspects of case management. Decision-making skills and interpersonal skills to work with a wide range of people are critical for effective case managers. The child-welfare case manager must be able to relate to children and adults of differing ages and behaviors and from different cultural and ethnic groups as well as professionals, volunteers, and administrators from a range of community services.

### ❏ Confidentiality

Confidentiality is critically important with regard to interagency cooperation and cross-systems service delivery. Case managers must understand the confidentiality rules under which they are operating and be able to inform families about their rights with regard to sharing information. Arrangements can be made to guarantee confidentiality and to allow several agencies to work together; legal assistance may be needed to develop such an arrangement (Melaville & Blank, 1991). Case managers must also address issues of confidentiality when working from a family systems perspective. Because several members of a family, and sometimes several generations, are part of the service delivery system, care must be taken to ensure confidentiality.

## ❏ Culturally Competent Practice

A disproportionate number of children of color are in the child-welfare system, and the cultural-specific needs of minority children, except for native American children, have not been taken into consideration (Everett, 1991). Shortages of supportive services and lack of cultural-specific policies and practices have exacerbated the problems of minority children, especially African American children, in the foster-care system. Children and families must be considered in their sociocultural context, and the supportive nature of the extended family must be taken into consideration. Skilled case management must ensure understanding and recognition of the ecological and environmental context of children and families and work with the families to develop an optimal plan of care to support family functioning. Chipungu (1991) advocates for a family services policy and practice framework that incorporates African American cultural values, including involving the extended family and recognizing collective identity and spirituality issues.

## ❏ Supporting Strengths

A service-delivery philosophy and practice based on identifying and supporting family strengths, including incorporating cultural-specific values, is imperative. Case managers must enter into a problem-solving process with the family while building on family strengths throughout the assessment and planning process:

> *The inclusion of families in case planning activities remediates blaming parents for problems occurring in families, balances child safety with sufficient consideration for family support, promotes a wellness or resiliency model of service delivery and emphasizes equal access to services for all types of families (American Public Welfare Association, 1994, p. 7).*

## *Case Management Training and Preparation*

Weil (1985), Kamerman and Kahn (1989), and Melaville and Blank (1991), among others, recognize that comprehensive case management requires professional staff with the skills and abilities to work with complex families and agencies and within complex categorical and bureaucratic service systems. Skills as a counselor, broker, mediator, facilitator, advocate, administrator, and evaluator are needed.

Weil (1985) contends that social work education provides the necessary preparation for case management, although national consensus regarding required training is lacking. Requirements vary from state to state and program to program. Only approximately 28% of child-welfare services are provided by social workers with a bachelor's or master's degree (Russell, 1987), although several studies (Albers, Reilly, & Rittner, 1993; Booz-Allen & Hamilton, Inc., 1987) support social work as the most appropriate discipline for child-welfare practice. No discipline other than social work can be identified as preparing case managers for child welfare.

Collaborative efforts are being made between schools of social work and public human service agencies to enhance educational curricula and better prepare social work students to meet the needs of child-welfare clients (Terpstra, 1994; Zlotnik, 1993). These collaborations were developed for several reasons. Agencies were concerned about recruitment and retention problems as well as the need to hire and train competent staff to meet the needs of children and families with increasingly complex needs. Many schools of social work have reexamined their mission to meet the needs of society's most vulnerable and oppressed populations and are attempting to prepare students for complex service-delivery tasks. Several schools of social work are working with agencies to develop child-welfare competencies and are revising their educational programs to include these competencies. The California Social Work Education Center at the University of California–Berkeley School of Social Work is undertaking a state-wide effort to prepare social work students for work in child-welfare agencies. In many state agencies, Title IV-E training funds are being used to provide opportunities for staff to return to school to earn an MSW degree and to enhance their skills.

Several states have signed agreements among the state child-welfare agency, the social work education programs, and the state chapter of the National Association of Social Workers to undertake a multiyear effort to prepare social workers for family-focused child-welfare services (Zlotnik, 1993). The value of comprehensive case management in child-welfare settings is being recognized, and social work education programs need to enhance their ability to prepare students for this work.

In addition to preparing new workers, agency staff may need retraining to provide intensive, family-focused case management services. The National Resource Center on Family-Centered Practice, based at the University of Iowa School of Social Work, offers training programs for agency staff in family-focused case management (Allen, 1990).

Child-welfare agencies are also attempting to increase the number of staff who are bilingual or persons of color so that the ethnic diversity of staff better matches the ethnic diversity of clients. In some states, staff and clients differ greatly in ethnic makeup. For example, in Delaware, 81% of the staff are white and 18% black; clients are 49% white and 44% black (Harris, Kirk, & Besharov 1992).

## Standards

Although NASW offers standards for both case management practice and child protective services, these standards are guides, not requirements. The NASW 1981 Standards for Child Protection remain a model for quality child protective services. In 1992, NASW presented revised Standards for Case Management that promote adherence to a comprehensive case management model. For example, NASW's case management standards are used to guide case management practices in the Comprehensive Child Development Program (P. Pizzalongo, personal communication, October 1994) but are not followed with regard to the education and professional affiliation of the case manager.

In the proposed rule making for the Family Preservation and Support Services (1994), states are encouraged to develop quality-assurance mechanisms, including standards developed by national organizations. The American Humane Association (1986) and the National Association of Social Workers (1981, 1989) recommend that child protective service workers have at least a bachelor's of social work degree. In several states, including North Dakota, Nevada, and New Mexico, the BSW is the minimum degree required by the state child-welfare agency (Zlotnik, 1993). The U.S. Advisory Board on Child Abuse and Neglect (1990, 1993a) has called for national standards for child protective service workers, and the National Commission on Family Foster Care recommended that all foster-care workers be certified social workers (Child Welfare League of America, 1991).

Although national standards are not available, it is becoming increasingly recognized that a well-trained staff best meets the needs of families. This recognition has stimulated collaboration between social work education programs and agencies.

## Evaluation

Case management services in child welfare have not been subjected to extensive evaluation. Evaluation of case management in child welfare is difficult because the function is defined so broadly within the child-welfare service-delivery system. Although the current trend is to define case management comprehensively, many child-welfare programs still define case management according to its minimal role of brokering and linkage. Furthermore, although studies of successful programs have identified intensive case management as a key program ingredient (Ahart et al., 1992; Kahn & Kamerman, 1992), little formal evaluation has been undertaken. The National Association of Public Child Welfare Administrators in collaboration with the American Humane Association is attempting to define child-welfare outcomes that can be used in evaluation studies.

Several studies are currently evaluating family-preservation services and family-reunification programs. Although such programs are similar in that they are family-focused and home-based and include clinical case management services, we cannot expect their outcomes to be similar (Fein & Staff, 1993). The point of intervention and the family situation differ; replacement rates are probably lower for those who are involved in family-preservation programs.

The evaluation studies supported by the Department of Health and Human Services as part of the Family Preservation and Support Initiative will be multiyear studies of both family-preservation and family-support programs. This extensive effort will provide new information regarding the effectiveness of case management with different populations and in different service-delivery domains. Foundation-funded efforts are also helping states establish service-delivery outcomes and program evaluation.

Additional research is needed to determine whether a particular case management structure is more effective with particular populations or within different types of programs. In addition, we need to learn more about case management roles in complex systems. What areas do case managers need more training in? Are minimum educational requirements necessary for case management practice? Case-load size is another area that needs further study.

Research and skill building is needed to facilitate the conjoint work of case managers and families. Empowering families and working with them to set goals and find solutions can be challenging for child welfare workers who wish to "do for" rather than "do with." Scarcity of resources is another challenge. Case management practice cannot substitute for lack of needed services (Kamerman & Kahn, 1989).

## *Conclusion*

Case management is intrinsic to child-welfare practice. It is a core service in helping families develop and implement a plan that will allow them to achieve optimal functioning. Case management in child welfare should be characterized holistically to include therapeutic intervention as well as advocacy and brokerage services (Kamerman & Kahn, 1989).

As child-welfare reform and service integration initiatives take hold in many states, comprehensive services provided by competent professionals are a critical need. Resources must be committed to support quality family-focused case management services throughout family-support, family-preservation, child-protection, foster-care, and adoption services. Such resources will help "protect children from abuse and neglect, improve opportunities for optimal child development, help establish and fortify family structures, and improve the level of family functioning" (Child Welfare League of America, 1993).

## References

Administration on Children, Youth and Families. (1994, January 18). *Family preservation and support services program instruction.* Washington, DC: Department of Health and Human Services.

Ahart, A., Bruer, R., Rutsch, C., Schmidt, R., & Zaro, S. (1992). *Intensive foster care reunification programs.* (Final Report to the Assistant Secretary for Planning and Evaluation, U.S. Department of Health and Human Services). Silver Spring, MD: Macro International, Inc.

Albers, E., Reilly, T., & Rittner, B. (1993). *Children in foster care: Possible factors affecting permanency planning.* Unpublished paper, School of Social Work, University of Nevada-Reno.

Allen, M. (1990, Spring). Why are we talking about case management again? In *Prevention report.* National Resource Center on Family-Centered Practice, School of Social Work, University of Iowa.

Allen, M., & Knitzer, J. (1983). Child Welfare: Examining the policy framework. In B. McGowan & W. Meezan (Eds.), *Child welfare: Current dilemmas, future directions.* Itasca, IL: F. E. Peacock.

American Humane Association. (1986). *Professionalism, take a stand* (policy statement no. 3). Denver, CO: Author.

American Humane Association. (1991). *Helping in child protective services: A casework handbook.* Englewood, CO: Author.

American Humane Association. (1993, May). *America's children: How are they doing?* (fact sheet no. 8). Englewood, CO: Author.

American Public Welfare Association. (1990). *Factbook on public child welfare services.* Washington, DC: Author.

American Public Welfare Association. (1991). *Commitment to change: Report from the National Commission on Child Welfare and Family Preservation.* Washington, DC: Author.

American Public Welfare Association. (1992). *Status report on JOBS case management practices.* Washington, DC: Author.

American Public Welfare Association & National Association of State Mental Health Program Directors. (1994). *Child welfare, children's mental health and families: A partnership for action.* Washington, DC: Authors.

Behrman, R. (Ed.) (1992) *The future of children: School-linked services.* Los Altos, CA: Center for the Future of Children, Packard Foundation.

Booz-Allen & Hamilton, Inc. (1987). *The Maryland social services job analysis and personnel qualifications study.* Baltimore, MD: Maryland Department of Human Resources.

Briar, K. H. (1994, September). Collaboration for child welfare. In *Partnership Newsletter.* National Child Welfare Partnership Project, Institute on Children and Families at Risk, Florida International University.

Bruner, C. (1990). *Strengthening service delivery through integration and cross-system collaboration: Two readings.* Des Moines, IA: Child and Family Policy Center.

Center for the Study of Social Policy/Children's Defense Fund. (1994). *Making strategic use of the family preservation support services program.* Washington, DC: Author.

Child Welfare League of America. (1982). *Child welfare as a field of social work practice* (2nd ed.) New York: Author.

Child Welfare League of America. (1991). *A blueprint for fostering infants, children, youth in the 1990s.* Washington, DC: Author.

Child Welfare League of America. (1993). *Start me up: Discussion guide.* Washington, DC: Author.

Chipungu, S. S. (1991). A value-based policy framework. In J. E. Everett, S. S. Chipungu, & B. R. Leashore (Eds.), *Child welfare: An Africentric perspective* (pp. 290–305). New Brunswick, NJ: Rutgers University Press.

Cole, E. S. (1993). A view of permanency planning in the United States. In L. Abramczyk & J. Ross (Eds.), *International reunification symposium* (pp. 4–13). College of Social Work, University of South Carolina, Columbia.

Commission on Families. (1991). *NASW family Support principles.* Washington, DC: National Association of Social Workers.

Compher, J. V. (1983). Home services to prevent child placement. *Social Work, 28,* 360–364.

Costin, L., Bell, C., & Downs, S. (1991). *Child welfare: Policies and practice* (4th ed.). New York: Longman.

Emlen, A. (1975). *Is this child likely to return home?* Portland, OR: Regional Institute for Human Resources.

Everett, J. E. (1991). Children in crisis. In J. E. Everett, S. S. Chipungu, & B. R. Leashore (Eds.), *Child welfare: An Africentric perspective* (pp. 1–18). New Brunswick, NJ: Rutgers University Press.

Family Impact Seminar. (1994). Services reform initiative: Governor's subcabinet for children, youth and families, Maryland. In *Implementation of the family preservation and support services program: A series of roundtables–resource book.* Washington, DC: American Association of Marriage and Family Therapists.

Family Partnership Project. (1994). *Developing linkages between family support and family preservation services.* Washington, DC: Child Welfare League of America.

Family preservation and support services. (1994, October). Notice of proposed rulemaking for the Family Preservation and Support Initiative. *Federal Register, 59,* 50646–50673.

Fein, E., & Staff, I. (1993). Last best chance: Finding from a reunification services program. *Child Welfare, 72,* 25–39.

Friedman, R. S. (1991). Practice skills and knowledge: View from the field–key ecological attitudes and skills. In A. Sallee & J. C. Lloyd (Eds.), *Family preservation: Papers from the Institute for Social Work Educators 1990.* Riverdale, IL: National Association for Family-Based Services.

Hardin, M. (1992). Typical participants in child protection cases. In *Implementation of* the family preservation and support services program: A series of roundtables–resource book. Washington, DC: American Association of Marriage and Family Therapists.

Harris, N., Kirk, R., & Besharov, D. (1992). *State child welfare agency staff survey report.* Washington, DC: National Child Welfare Leadership Center.

Harris, S. (1987). *Investing in independence across the generations.* Silver Spring, MD: National Association of Social Workers.

Hegar, R. L. (1992). Monitoring child welfare services. In B. Vourlekis & R. R. Greene (Eds.), *Social work case management* (pp. 135–148). Hawthorne, NY: Aldine de Gruyter.

Joe, T., & Farrow, F. (1992). Financing school-linked services. In R. Behrman (Ed.), *The future of children: School-linked services* (pp. 56–67). Los Altos, CA: Center for the Future of Children, Packard Foundation.

Kadushin, A. (1987). Child welfare services. In *Encyclopedia of social work* (18th ed., pp. 265–275). Silver Spring, MD: National Association of Social Workers.

Kadushin, A., & Martin, J. (1988). *Child welfare services* (4th Ed.). New York: Macmillan.

Kahn, A., & Kamerman, S. (1992). *Integrating services integration: An overview of initiatives, issues and possibilities.* New York: National Center for Children in Poverty, Columbia University.

Kamerman, S., & Kahn, A. (1989). *Social services for children and youth and families in the United States.* Greenwich, CT: Annie E. Casey Foundation.

Little, R. (1982). The public welfare connection. In E. Saalberg (Ed.), *A dialogue on the challenge for education and training: Child welfare issues in the '80s* (pp. 25–31). School of Social Work, National Child Welfare Training Center, University of Michigan.

Lloyd, J. C., & Sallee, A. L. (1994). The challenge and potential of family preservation services in the public child welfare system. *Protecting Children, 10* (3), 3–6.

Maluccio, A., Fein, E., & Olmstead, K. (1986). *Permanency planning for children: Concepts and methods.* New York: Routledge, Chapman and Hall.

Mannes, M. (1993). Seeking the balance between child protection and family preservation in Indian child welfare. *Child Welfare, 73*, 141–151.

Melaville, A., & Blank, M. (1991). *What it takes: Structuring interagency partnerships to connect children and families with comprehensive services.* Washington, DC: Education and Human Services Consortium, Institute for Educational Leadership.

Melaville, A., & Blank, M. (1993). *Together we can.* Washington, DC: U.S. Government Printing Office.

National Association of Public Child Welfare Administrators, & State Mental Health Representatives for Children and Youth. (1991). *The child welfare/children's mental health partnership: A collaborative agenda for strengthening families.* Washington, DC: Author.

National Association of Social Workers. (1981). *NASW standards for social work practice in child protection.* Washington, DC: Author.

National Association of Social Workers. (1989). *Public child welfare. Professional policy statement.* Washington, DC: Author.

National Association of Social Workers. (1992). *NASW standards for social work case management.* Washington, DC: Author.

National Commission on Children. (1991). *Beyond rhetoric: A new American agenda for children and families.* Washington, DC: Author.

Nelson, J. (1984). *An experimental evaluation of a home-based family-centered program model in a public child protection agency.* Doctoral diss., School of Social Work, University of Minnesota.

Ooms, T., Hara, S., & Owen, T. (1992). *Service integration and coordination at the family/client level (part three: Is case management the answer?).* Washington, DC: Family Impact Seminar, American Association of Marriage and Family Therapists.

Ooms, T., & Owen, T. (1992). *Coordination, collaboration, integration: Strategies for serving families more effectively (part two: State and local initiatives).* Washington, DC: Family Impact Seminar, American Association of Marriage and Family Therapists.

Pecora, P., Briar, K., & Zlotnik J. (1989). *Addressing the program and personnel crisis in child welfare: A social work response.* Silver Spring, MD: National Association of Social Workers.

Pecora, P., Whittaker, J., & Maluccio, A. (1992). *The child welfare challenge: Policy, practice and research.* Hawthorne, NY: Aldine de Gruyter.

Rapp, C. A., & Poertner, J. (1980). Public child welfare in the 1980s: The role of case management. In K. Dea (Ed.), *Perspectives for the future: Social work practice in the 1980s* (pp. 70–81). Silver Spring, MD: National Association of Social Workers.

Rome, S. H. (1994). *Choosing child welfare: An analysis of social work students' career choices.* Washington, DC: National Association of Social Workers.

Russell, M. (1987). *1987 national study of public child welfare job requirements.* Portland, ME: National Child Welfare Center for Management and Administration, University of Southern Maine.

Saalberg, E. (Ed.). (1982). *A dialogue on the challenge for education and training: Child welfare issues in the '80s.* School of Social Work, National Child Welfare Training Center, University of Michigan.

Services Reform Initiative. (1994, July). *HomeBase case management software guidelines.* Baltimore, MD: Author.

Stagner, M. (1993). Who comes into foster care? How has the population changed? In L. Abramczyk & J. Ross (Eds.), *International reunification symposium* (pp. 21–29). College of Social Work, University of South Carolina, Columbia.

Stein, T. (1982). Child welfare: New directions in the field and their implications for education. In E. Saalberg (Ed.), *A dialogue on the challenge for education and training: Child welfare issues in the '80s* (pp. 5–23). School of Social Work, National Child Welfare Training Center, University of Michigan.

Tatara, T. (1993, August). *U.S. child substitute care flow data for FY 92 and current trends in the state child substitute care populations.* VCIS research notes (no.9). Washington, DC: American Public Welfare Association.

Terpstra, J. (1994, September). Reprofessionalizing child welfare. In *Partnership Newsletter.* National Child Welfare Partnership Project, Institute on Children and Families at Risk, Florida International University.

U.S. Advisory Board on Child Abuse and Neglect. (1990). *Child abuse and neglect: Critical first steps in response to a national emergency.* Washington, DC: U.S. Department of Health and Human Services.

U.S. Advisory Board on Child Abuse and Neglect. (1993a, April). *The continuing child protection emergency: A challenge to the nation.* Washington, DC: U.S. Department of Health and Human Services.

U.S. Advisory Board on Child Abuse and Neglect. (1993b, September). *Neighbors helping neighbors: A new national strategy for the protection of children.* Washington, DC: U.S. Department of Health and Human Sevices.

U.S. Department of Health and Human Services. (1994). *Comprehensive child development program: A national family support demonstration* (interim report to Congress). Washington DC: Administration on Children, Youth and Families, Head Start Bureau.

U.S. House of Representatives, Select Committee on Children, Youth and Families. (1989). *No place to call home: Discarded children in America.* Washington, DC: U.S. Government Printing Office.

Weil, M. (1985). Key components in providing efficient and effective services. In M. Weil & J. Karls (Eds.), *Case management in human service practice* (pp. 29–71). San Francisco: Jossey-Bass.

Wells, S. J. (1985). Children and child welfare system. In M. Weil & J. Karls (Eds.), *Case management in human service practice* (pp. 119–144). San Francisco: Jossey-Bass.

Wiltse, K. T. (1982). Education and training for child welfare practice: The search for a better fit. In E. Saalberg (Ed.), *A dialogue on the challenge for education and training: Child welfare issues in the '80s* (pp. 5–23). School of Social Work, National Child Welfare Training Center, University of Michigan.

Wolk, J. L., Sullivan, W. P., & Hartmann, D. J. (1994). The managerial nature of case management. *Social Work, 39*, 152–159.

Young, T. M. (1994). Collaboration of a public child welfare agency and a school of social work: A clinical group supervision project. *Child Welfare, 73*, 659–671.

Zlotnik, J. L. (1993). *Social work education and public human services: Developing partnerships.* Alexandria, VA: Council on Social Work Education.

Chapter **4**

# Aging and Long-Term Care

*Carol D. Austin*

P rovision of long-term care for our nation's elderly has become a
topic of paramount importance as a result of dramatic growth of
the long-term-care population and escalating costs for providing care.
Efforts to increase options for long-term care include expansion of
community-based care and an attempt to integrate better the in-home,
community, and institutional delivery systems. Such efforts reflect attitudes and beliefs that, within financial limits, individuals should have
the opportunity to receive long-term care in a setting of their choice.

The elderly population has grown dramatically. In 1980, 25.5 million Americans were older than 65, constituting 11% of the population.
By 2020, this age group will constitute 18% of the population. Every
day approximately 5,000 persons reach their 65th birthday, and every
day approximately 3,600 persons in this group die, thus increasing the
elderly population by 1,400 individuals each day (Keenan, 1989).

One of the most striking demographic trends is the rapid growth
of persons older than 85. Whereas the number of persons 65 and older
has increased eightfold since 1900, the group older than 85 is 22 times
larger. Their population is expected to reach 4.6 million by 2000 and 8
million by 2030. By 2050, those older than 85 will number 15 million,
or 5% of the total U.S. population (Keenan, 1989). The impact of these
demographic changes on the health-delivery system, hospitals, and
nursing homes in particular will be dramatic. Federal, state, and local
resources will be severely strained.

Older adults are the primary users of health care services. Annually, nearly 80% of older adults visit a physician, 40% receive dental
care, 20% are hospitalized for short stays, and 5% live in nursing
homes. In 1980, approximately 25% of the "oldest-old"—persons 85
years old and older—were living in nursing homes, and 40% of nursing
home residents were 85 or older (Neugarten, 1982). Projections indicate that by 2020 the oldest-old group will constitute 51% of the nurs-

ing home population. Twenty-five percent of this group will have Alzheimer's disease.

Seniors consume a considerable amount of home-health services. In 1979, they received 77% of all home-health visits. By 2020, senior consumption of health care services could increase to 50% of all hospital days, 25% of physician visits, and more than 90% of nursing home beds. The implications for financing, cost, structure, and accessibility of the health care system are awesome (Keenan, 1989).

In the early 1970s innovative community-based, long-term-care service-delivery models were designed, implemented, and evaluated. At that time, long-term care was provided almost exclusively in nursing homes. Policymakers knew that it would not be fiscally possible or responsible to serve the growing population of elders in need of long-term-care services in institutions. Furthermore, elders overwhelmingly expressed their preference for remaining in their own homes. As community-based long-term care projects were developed, case management was a standard and significant component of community-based long-term-care programs. Case management continues to be a central element in the expansion and the integration of long-term care services. Case management is provided in a diverse range of long-term-care programs under federal, state, and private auspices.

## *Defining Case Management*

What is case management? Various definitions have been advanced. Professionals agree about the steps involved in the case management process: outreach, screening, assessment, care planning, plan implementation, monitoring, and reassessment. However, these steps are implemented with considerable variation. An accurate observation is that if you've seen one case management program you've seen one case management program. Case management service in any particular programmatic context reflects specific characteristics of the client population as well as the structure of program funding.

> *Case management is therefore neither inherently nor definitively defined. It derives its definition in large part from the nature and needs of a system whose component parts it will be coordinating and integrating. . . . It must be a creature of its environment, tuned to the specific characteristics and needs of its host system, if it is to be effective (Beatrice, 1981, p. 124).*

Kane (1988) defines case management broadly as "the coordination of a specified group of resources and services for a specified group of people" (p. 5). Quinn (1993) offers a definition that includes three critical process characteristics.

> *Case management for long term care is based on three tenets: it is a holistic approach to the client; it is a problem solving strategy for the client; and it is a dynamic process involving the interactions among the case manager, the client and the providers of care (including the family, and other informal supporters, formal agencies and physicians if necessary) (p. 3).*

The National Advisory Committee on Long Term Care Case Management defines case management as a "coordinating service that helps frail elders or others with functional impairments and their families identify and secure cost effectively administered services appropriate to the consumers' needs" (Connecticut Continuing Care, Inc., 1994, p. 5). These definitions are based on a common set of steps in the case management process: outreach, screening, assessment, care planning, plan implementation, monitoring, and reassessment. Various authors have written extensively about these components (Applebaum & Austin, 1990; Austin, 1983; Capitman, Haskins, & Bernstein, 1986; Carcagno, Applebaum, Christianson, Phillips, Thornton, & Will, 1986; Cline, 1990; Grisham, White, & Miller, 1983; Kemper, Applebaum, & Harrigan, 1987).

## *Components of Case Management*

Outreach activities comprise the first efforts to reach the program's target population by identifying persons likely to qualify for and need case management and supportive services. Case-finding efforts help ensure that eligible individuals are served.

*Screening* is a preliminary assessment of the client's circumstances and resources to determine presumptive eligibility. Potential clients are screened by means of standardized procedures to determine whether their status and situation meet the program's target population definition. For programs seeking to divert clients from institutional placement, the common screening criterion has been risk of institutionalization. Accurate screening is critical. If individuals who do not meet screening criteria nevertheless slip through the crack and enter the program, they will eventually receive a comprehensive assessment, which is time consuming, labor intensive, and costly. Effective outreach and screening are necessary for efficient program operation and management. Outreach and screening are important gatekeeping tasks that directly affect the accuracy of the program's targeting efforts.

*Comprehensive assessment* is a "method of collecting in-depth information about a person's social situation and physical, mental and psychological function which allows identification of the person's problems and care needs" (Schneider & Weiss, 1982, p. 12). Frail elderly often have multiple health problems, functional disabilities, and social losses—complex situations that require comprehensive multidimensional assessment for effective care planning and services. Typically, comprehensive assessment focuses on physical health, mental functioning, ability to perform activities of daily living, social supports, physical environment, and financial resources. Comprehensive assessment is client centered in that it encourages consumer involvement and input. Many states have standardized their assessment instruments and require their use statewide. Although some programs continue to develop their own assessment instruments, many programs have adopted rigorous standardized multidimensional instruments.

Information collected during the assessment process is used to develop the care plan. *Care planning* requires clinical judgment, creativity, and sensitivity as well as knowledge of community resources and the ability to create a care plan within the constraints imposed by limited resources. Schneider (1988) identified components that should be present in every care plan:

> a comprehensive list of problems; a desired outcome for each problem; the types of help needed to achieve each desired outcome; a list of the services and providers that will be supplying help; an indication of the amount of each service to be provided; a calculation of the costs of providing the listed services for specific periods of time and an indication of the sources of payment; an indication of agreement by the client and, where appropriate, the informal caregiver (pp. 16–17).

Case managers consider the willingness and availability of informal caregivers to provide care. In fact, the balance between formal and informal services is a major consideration in the care-planning process. The client and his or her caregivers participate in the process. The care plan specifies services, providers, and frequency of services. The costs of the care plan are also determined during the care-planning process. Case managers perform a resource-allocation function in the care-plan development.

*Service arrangement* involves contacting formal and informal providers to arrange services specified in the care plan. Case managers often must negotiate with providers for services when making referrals to other agencies. Case managers also order services directly from providers when they have the authority to purchase services on their client's behalf. A key aspect of service arrangement involves sharing client-assessment information and the care plan with relevant family members and formal care providers. Accurate and clear communication is essential to successful implementation of the care plan. Persons involved in the implementation of a care plan must be informed of their roles. Successful implementation of care plans is related directly to case managers' authority to purchase services on behalf of their clients.

*Monitoring* the client's status is critical in that changes in clients' needs can significantly affect service costs. Clients may experience changes in their functional capacity, their living arrangements, the availability of caregivers, and their health status. The case manager systematically monitors such changes and alters care plans to meet clients' current needs. Ongoing monitoring combined with timely modification of care plans help ensure that program expenditures reflect current client needs and are not based on outdated assessment data.

The purpose of *reassessment* is to determine whether changes in the client's situation have occurred since the most recent assessment. Systematic and routine reassessment also helps in evaluating the extent to which progress has been made toward accomplishing outcomes specified in the care plan. Reassessments can be triggered by various events, including major events in the client's life, deterioration in the client's physical or mental status, relocation to another residence, resolution of the initial problem, termination from the program, or assignment of a new social worker.

## *Models*

Three features distinguish long-term-care case management from other models: intensity, breadth of services, and duration of services. Applebaum and Austin (1990) state,

> *Intensity refers to the amount of time case managers spend with their clients. . . . Breadth of services refers to how broadly case managers view the problem of clients. . . . Duration refers to how long case managers remain involved with clients (pp. 5–6).*

This definition targets long-term-care case management services to frail clients who might be diverted from nursing home placement.

Cline (1990) identified three case management practice models: medical care case management (hospital based), catastrophic care case management (insurance company based), and long-term-care case management (community based). The location from which case management services are provided represents the defining variable in these models. Applebaum and Austin (1990) also specified three models: broker, service management, and managed care. These models reflect the kind and level of authority case managers have over resource-allocation decisions. Quinn and Burton's (1988) models are based on various combinations of funding mechanisms and resource controls: broker, prior authorization screening, and consolidated direct service. Merrill (1985) offered a comprehensive typology of models: social, medical, and medical/social. He observed that medical case management services "share an interest in cost containment, utilization review, and risk sharing and treat the provider rather than the client as their primary constituency" (p. 14).

## *Goals*

Although the core components of case management are widely agreed upon, there is little consensus about case management goals. In examining case management goals, serious role conflicts are evident. Case management goals and tasks fall into two categories: those that are primarily client focused and those that are aimed at changing the delivery systems. Although these goals are discussed separately, they are interdependent. Case management goals are summarized in Table 1.

At the client level, individuals' needs and circumstances are considered throughout the case management process, from assessment to care planning and reassessment. Care plans, in theory, are individual-

---

***Table 1.*** *Goals Associated with Case Management*

---

*Client-Oriented Goals*
1. To assure that services given are appropriate to the needs of the particular client
2. To monitor the client's conditions in order to guarantee the appropriateness of services
3. To improve access to the continuum of long-term-care services
4. To support client's caregivers
5. To serve as bridges between institutional and community-based care system

*System-Oriented Goals*
1. To facilitate the development of a broader array of noninstitutional services
2. To promote quality and efficiency in the delivery of long-term-care services
3. To enhance the coordination of long-term-care service delivery
4. To target individuals most at risk of nursing-home placement in order to prevent inappropriate institutionalization
5. To contain costs by controlling client access to services, especially high-cost services

---

Adapted from Austin, C. (1987). *Improving access for elders: The role of case management.* Seattle, WA: Institute on Aging, University of Washington.

ized service prescriptions. Case managers are responsible for enhancing clients' access to long-term-care services. The sheer complexity of programs and agencies combined with bureaucratic procedures present daunting barriers for frail clients and their caregivers. Case managers serve as a single point of contact in a complex and fragmented delivery system. For many frail clients, the factor determining whether they will remain in their own home or be placed in a nursing home is the presence of an able and willing caregiver. In some instances, caregivers also become clients. Case managers may intervene on behalf of caregivers whose resources have become depleted. Continuity is critically important in the provision of quality case management services. Ideally, a client will work with one case manager.

System change and development is the other primary focus of case management. In the care-planning process, the case manager identifies service gaps in the community, facilitates the development of new services, and may discover the presence of costly service duplication. Case managers are also able to foster coordination among providers in the local delivery system. In many communities, system development is directed toward expanding the scope and volume of community-based services, which provides a significant opportunity for case managers to influence the quality and efficiency of newly developed and existing services.

The combination of case management and community-based services has been advanced as a strategy for preventing or delaying premature or unnecessary admission to nursing homes. Effective and efficient targeting of clients, as well as close attention to cost in care planning, are necessary if case managers are to fulfill their cost-containment responsibilities.

> Case management, whatever setting in which it is applied, should be accountable so that costs are as streamlined as possible and that public and private financing of case management is spent in a way that protects consumers, payers of case management and direct services and the general public (Connecticut Continuing Care, Inc., 1994, p. 69).

## History

Baker and Vichy (1989) state, "Case management is one of the most popular current 'new' approaches to organizing care, especially for long term care populations" (p. 205). Demographic realities and the cost of nursing home care have created concern about the institutional bias of the long-term-care system. It has been claimed that many nursing home residents are provided with inappropriate and/or unnecessary care. The rising cost of nursing home care has been a growing concern since the early 1970s. In an attempt to respond to increasing costs, community-based long-term-care services have been advanced as a potentially cost-effective way to provide care for elders in their own homes, thereby preventing or delaying institutional placement.

Expansion of community-based care was fueled by two major trends. First, funding for in-home and community-based services has increased, stemming from the expansion of existing federal funding sources. Growth in Medicare, Medicaid, Title III of the Older Americans Act, social services block grants, and ACTION programs have further fragmented delivery systems. The purpose of additional *increased* funding was to expand benefits or reprioritize services. Financing operations and service-delivery approaches were tested and evaluated in a series of demonstration projects starting in the early 1970s.

The second major trend in system expansion has been the presence of case managers responsible for arranging and monitoring long-term-care services for program clients. Fragmentation and complexity in the long-term-care delivery system are well documented. Vulnerable elders and their families find it difficult to obtain needed information and to gain access to programs and services. Case management also can be inserted into an already existing delivery system without altering relationships among the providers of the system (Austin, 1983; Beatrice, 1981).

Various models of case management have been tested and evaluated in long-term-care demonstration projects. In these projects, case managers functioned as clients' single contact with the delivery system. Case managers were expected to ensure appropriate, timely, coordinated, and cost-effective care and thus overcome fragmentation in the service-delivery system (Austin, 1987; Miller, Clark, & Walter, 1984; Rubin, 1987; Vourlekis & Greene, 1992; Weil, Karls, & Associates, 1985). "Case management has become popular precisely because society recognizes that fragmentation, lack of coordination and profit-driven rather than need-based decision making are often characteristics of service delivery" (Vourlekis & Greene, 1992, p. 189). Over time, case management practice has evolved in scope and complexity, and today case management includes authority to purchase services on behalf of clients. Coordinated service delivery and cost containment will be important goals for the foreseeable future.

## Demonstration Projects

The evolution of case management approaches can be traced through federally supported demonstration projects. Since the early 1970s, the Health Care Financing Administration (HCFA), in collaboration with states, counties, local agencies, and several foundations, have funded 18 community-based long-term-care demonstrations (Table 2) (Austin, Roberts, & Low, 1985; Capitman, 1986; Greenberg, Doth, & Austin, 1981; Kemper et al., 1987). These projects were designed to test different approaches to financing, developing, and providing community-based long-term-care services. The basic question was whether community-based services could be a cost-effective substitute for nursing home care. These demonstration efforts incorporated three main reform strategies: (1) to develop, coordinate, and improve

**Table 2.** *Long-Term-Care Demonstration Projects*

| | |
|---|---|
| On Lok (California) | 1971–present |
| Wisconsin Community Care Organization | 1973–1979 |
| Triage (Connecticut) | 1974–1979 |
| Washington Community-Based Care | 1975–1979 |
| ACCESS (New York) | 1975–present |
| Alternative Health Services (Georgia) | 1976–1981 |
| PROJECT OPEN (California) | 1978–1983 |
| San Diego Long-Term-Care Project | 1979–1984 |
| FIG Waiver (Oregon) | 1979–1981 |
| Multiservice Senior Project (California) | 1979–present |
| Texas Intermediate Care Facility II | 1980–1985 |
| New York Nursing Without Walls | 1980–present |
| South Carolina Long Term Care | 1980–present |
| New York Home Care Project | 1980–1984 |
| Florida Pentastar | 1981–1983 |
| Channeling—Basic Sites (Baltimore, MD, Eastern Kentucky, Houston, TX, Middlesex County, NJ, Southern Maine) | 1982–1985 |
| Channeling Financial Control Sites (Cleveland, OH, Greater Lynn, MA, Miami, FL, Philadelphia, PA, Rensselaer County, NY) | 1982–1985 |
| Social/HMO (Brooklyn, NY, Portland, OR, Minneapolis, MN, Long Beach, CA) | 1985–present |

the long-term-care delivery system; (2) to control entry to and utilization of nursing home services; and (3) to create consolidated long-term-care delivery systems. The demonstration projects shared two primary goals: to improve quality of life and reduce costs.

In 1971 no mechanism for funding in-home and community-based services was available. Although these demonstration projects differed in various ways (e.g., services covered, funding sources, location of organization, and delivery system), they all included case management and an expanded array of in-home and community-based services (Capitman et al., 1986; Greenberg et al., 1981; Haskins, Capitman, & Bernstein, 1984; Kemper et al., 1987). In fact, in some of the demonstrations, case management became the primary method through which project staff attempted to maintain vulnerable elders in their own homes (Kemper et al., 1987). More recent demonstration projects incorporate more complex case management functions (Applebaum & Austin, 1990). In the earlier demonstrations, case managers functioned primarily as brokers, making referrals and advocating for their clients with providers.

Millions of dollars were spent on these projects, yet only the South Carolina Long Term Care project produced cost savings. Cost savings could not be produced if a program did not efficiently reach its target population. Evaluators of one early demonstration, the Wisconsin Com-

---

***Table 3.*** *Program Context Variables*

---

*Financing/Reimbursement*
The financial base of the program: Its source, form, and amount. For example, client cost-sharing waivers, capitation, fee for service.

*Targeting Criteria*
The definition of the target population that specifies the type of client to be served and those who will not be served. For example, at risk of nursing-home placement, functionally impaired, having frail support system, persons with unmet needs.

*Gatekeeping*
Gatekeeping mechanisms designed to control the number and types of services that clients have access to, particularly high-cost services. For example, cap on individual expenditures, authorization power, provider risk.

*Organizational Auspices*
The organizational location for case management activities. For example, provider agency, freestanding case management agency, hospital, day care.

---

Adapted from Applebaum, R., & Austin, C. (1990). *Long-term-care case management.* New York: Springer.

munity Care Organization, concluded that the project served the wrong population. Project clients were not at risk of institutionalization, and provision of community services produced no cost savings. Less expensive community care did not substitute for more costly institutional care because the clients were not likely to be admitted to a nursing home. The demonstration project lacked a very important feature: It did not have the authority to intervene in the nursing-home-admission process by accurately targeting those persons at risk of institutional placement. Subsequently, the South Carolina project determined eligibility for community services by administering a nursing-home preadmission screening tool. Only persons who were assessed as nursing-home certifiable received community services.

Case managers do not work in a vacuum. The programs' structure and process establish the boundaries within which case managers function. Community-based long-term-care programs include both in-home services and case management. Case management services are constrained by four primary program characteristics: financing/reimbursement, targeting criteria, gatekeeping mechanisms, and organizational auspices (Table 3).

## ❏ Financing/Reimbursement

The scope and character of the case management role is constrained by the program's financing. Early demonstration projects incorporated cost-based financing. Reimbursement followed the provision of service. Caps on the cost of an individual care plan and pooled funding were also tested during the demonstration period. Funds from several sources (Medicare, Medicaid, Title III of the Older Americans Act, private premiums) were pooled for the entire case load, and care plans were developed within specified limits. Most of the demonstrations relied on Medicare (section 222 of the Social Security Act–1972 and/or Medicaid waivers (section 1115 of the Social Security Act–1975) for financing. These waivers allowed more flexible use of Medicare or Medicaid funds to expand home and community-based services for their clients.

> *Case managers could use expanded services to reach more individuals for a longer time than programs normally allowed. . . . The case manager could at last manage a client's services instead of being just a broker or an advocate on the client's behalf (Quinn, 1993, p. 27).*

Prior to waiver financing, community-based services could not be purchased with Medicare or Medicaid funds. Medicare and Medicaid funded institutional care. Thus, Medicare and Medicaid waivers were critical for payment of in-home and community-based services. Over time, financing became more structured and controlled.

Medicaid waiver financing (section 2176 of the Omnibus Budget Reconciliation Act of 1981) is the fiscal foundation for community-based long-term-care services in 40 states. The waiver program made it possible to substitute home- and community-based services for more costly institutional services to persons who were Medicaid eligible and nursing-home certifiable.

Two programs (On Lok and Social/HMO) have incorporated prospective reimbursement or capitated financing. These programs receive a capitated amount for each client. If costs across the entire case load exceed the capitated amount' the provider incurs a loss. If costs fall below this capitated amount, the provider realizes a surplus. Prospective financing and provider risk are the next steps in the developmental process. The capacity of providers to work within the constraints of a prospective payment system will in part depend on provider confidence that high-quality case management is reliably implemented, including eligibility determination, the development of care plans, costs of care plans, and timely modification of care plans. Capitman (1986) observes that "increasingly, the scope of case management and the use of other cost control mechanisms, while constraining the costs of the administrative service, appear to be important ingredients in the design of successful community long term care programs" (p. 403).

## ❏ Targeting

Accurate targeting of individuals at risk of nursing-home placement is an important objective of community-based long-term-care services. Eligibility criteria were developed to assess levels of frailty and the risk of institutional admission.

In most of the long-term-care demonstrations, few clients actually entered nursing homes (Haskins et al., 1984; Kemper et al., 1987). Various targeting criteria have been used in community-based long-term-care programs (Table 4). Some criteria were objective (e.g., age, residence, Medicare or Medicaid eligibility), whereas others were verifiable (nursing-home certified, about to be discharged from a hospital or nursing home), and still others required professional judgment (activities of daily living, extent of informal support system, at risk of institutionalization).

The presence, willingness, and capacity of caregivers is a critical consideration in targeting and care planning. A consistent goal in community-based long-term-care programs has been to support, not supplant, the care provided by the informal delivery system (i.e., family, friends, neighbors, volunteers, church members). Some seniors are fortunate to have extensive support networks. Others are isolated and vulnerable. The presence of a caregiver can be used as a criterion for screening potential clients out of the program. For the purposes of targeting, the presence of an apparently capable and willing caregiver may not be an accurate targeting criterion. Not all caregivers are capable of providing care for a needy relative. Further assessment of caregiver capacity and client needs is needed.

Nursing-home preadmission screening provides a convenient and consensual approach to targeting. Persons who are not determined certified for nursing home admission are not eligible for community-based services. Persons who are determined nursing-home certifiable can be targeted as being at risk of institutional placement. However, not all persons assessed as nursing-home certified are actually admitted to institutions. Nevertheless, they have been screened and have met targeting criteria for community services.

Effective targeting directly influences program costs. Clarfield (1983) stated that the cost of home care varies according to level of disability. For clients with mild disabilities, home care costs less than insti-

---

**Table 4.** *Targeting Criteria*

---

Residence
Age
Medicare eligible
Medicaid eligible
Certified for intermediate or skilled nursing-home care
At risk of nursing-home placement
Functionally impaired: Needs ADL assistance
Mental functioning problems
Community-based care plan cost limit
Major loss or crisis
Unmet needs, fragile support system
Potential for nursing-home discharge
About to be discharged from hospital
Recently hospitalized
At risk of frequent hospital admissions
Lack of community services
Monitoring and education needed to maintain stable state

---

Adapted from Austin, C., Roberts, L., & Low, J. (1985). *Case management: A critical review.* Seattle, WA: Institute on Aging, University of Washington.

tutional care. When the level of disability increases, a point is reached where home care becomes as expensive as or more expensive than nursing home or hospital care. Weissert, Cready, and Pawelak (1988) studied the results of community-care demonstrations during the previous two decades. Home care did not produce expected cost-containment outcomes, because services were inaccurately targeted on clients who were not at risk of institutional placement. In these programs, home- and community-based long-term-care services raised the overall health care service use and costs.

## ❏ Gatekeeping

Targeting and gatekeeping are closely related. Targeting determines who is eligible, and gatekeeping controls the number and types of services clients receive. Gatekeeping is particularly important for controlling access to high-cost services. Effective and efficient targeting influences the kinds of gatekeeping mechanisms in a given delivery system. Both targeting and gatekeeping can significantly affect the cost of long-term-care service delivery. Gatekeeping has taken various forms.

A major advance in gatekeeping occurred when case managers were given authority to purchase services on behalf of their clients. This authority is the defining characteristic of the service-management model of case management. The case manager is fiscally accountable, and his or her authority to purchase services is constrained by the range of services provided and the supply of those services in the local delivery system. Purchase authority changes the nature of the relationship between the case manager and the service provider, giving the case manager greater leverage with providers. As brokers, case managers make referrals, which frequently means that clients are put on waiting lists. Brokers cannot guarantee that services will actually be delivered.

Budgetary control involves setting a maximum amount or "cap" on expenditures. One approach is to cap case-load costs based on the average expenditures for the program's entire case load. In the financial-control model of the National Channeling Demonstration, for example, expenditures for the entire case load were limited to 60% of the costs of nursing-home care. Under this system, care plans for individual clients could vary as long as the total project budget remained under the 60% cap. Another approach involves cost caps on individual care plans. Frequently, cost caps are based on a percentage of the cost of nursing-home care. The service-management model usually involves both purchase authority and cost caps, which means that case managers must become competent in budget management and maintain expertise in the skills and knowledge that form the foundation of case management practice.

Provider risk as a gatekeeping mechanism has been recently introduced in the case management process. It involves a clear shift in financial responsibility and liability for expenditures to provider organizations. Provider risk is a central feature of the Social/HMO, On Lok, Patient Appraisal and Care Evaluation (PACE, a replication of the On Lok Model), and other prospectively reimbursed programs. Provider organizations can remain financially afloat within a prospective payment system if they keep costs below the negotiated capitation rate. This financial arrangement creates incentives for providers to control total costs by promoting preventive self-care and substituting lower-cost services (home care) for higher-cost services (nursing home care). Prospective payment systems require gatekeeping. Case managers are needed to manage the risks. Care planning is at the heart of resource allocation and is crucial for effective risk management.

Centralizing authority for allocation of resources is another gatekeeping method. Case managers have discretion to use a broad scope of resources and related funding sources. Maximum centralized authority is found in programs in which a case manager authorizes, funds, and terminates a wide range of services for clients. The Social/HMO, On Lok, and PACE sites incorporate this consolidated approach to case managers' authority. Case managers' capacity to contain costs is largely dependent upon the kind and degree of gatekeeping authority they possess. With authority comes accountability as well as increased awareness of the costs and effects of the services they authorize.

## ❏ Organizational Auspices

Case managers who are responsible for targeting function as gatekeepers and have the power to authorize purchase of services. This case manager determines whether potential clients meet targeting criteria and develops care plans within the limits set by gatekeeping procedures and cost caps. The case manager influences the distribution of resources within the delivery system by selecting providers from whom to purchase services. The agency that administers the case management program is a key player in the local delivery system. Determining the organizational location for case management is an extremely political process in some communities.

Case management services can be provided by various organizations. The case management role and performance are directly influenced by the organizational setting. Case management can be delivered from diverse organizational settings, including hospitals, community agencies, independent case management organizations, adult-day-care centers, or Area Agencies on Aging. It can also be provided at various bureaucratic and geopolitical levels: state, regional, and local.

Ongoing debate has focused on the relative benefits of locating case management in provider agencies or freestanding case management organizations. It has been argued that case management is most appropriately provided by a freestanding agency and that this arrangement provides a measure of autonomy and avoids conflict-of-interest problems that can arise when case management and direct services are offered by the same agency (Kane, 1988; National Association of Area Agencies on Aging, 1984). A concern is that case managers would be pressured to include services provided by their employer in case plans and that they would not objectively assess the quality of services.

On the other hand, representatives of provider agencies argue that they are already functioning as case managers. They argue that provider staff are close to clients' needs and concerns because they are frequently in the home. From this perspective, freestanding case management is an unnecessary and costly duplication of services. Combining case management with direct provision of services is viewed as being more efficient and less costly.

The costs involved in creating a freestanding case management agency are difficult to justify. It takes time for a new agency to find its niche and to become known and accepted by local providers and clients. This situation is particularly challenging because the case management program will control distribution of resources in the local delivery system. Providers are likely to resist such authority. Furthermore, providers may claim that the creation of another agency merely duplicates capacities that already exist.

The location of the organization that performs case management functions may be dictated by program funding. Medicare and Medicaid certification may be required. Area Agencies on Aging may be designated as regional planners. On Lok and the Social/HMO involved considerable provider risk and could not delegate case management to an external organization. Insurance companies provide case management to policy holders by contracting with selected community agencies or employing their own staff. Insurers want to minimize their potential risk and exposure. Case managers working in this environment are tied to the insurers either through direct employment or contract.

## ❏ Cost

Seidl, Austin, and Greene (1977) offered a framework for examining costs. Five primary issues were raised: How are home-care clients identified? What is the structure of case management? What are the efficiency and quality of the direct services provided? Who bears the cost?

It would have been difficult to stimulate the growth of community-based long-term-care services without claiming that these services were less costly than nursing-home care. However, evidence has shown little savings, and it has been argued that the cost-saving tactic created expectations that could not be met. On the other hand, at the beginning of the demonstration phase, not enough funds were available to pay for in-home and community-based services. In the early 1970s, federal officials decided to permit greater flexibility in the Medicaid program by making it possible for demonstration projects to spend Medicaid money on services other than nursing-home care. This stimulated a series of demonstration projects and set the stage for subsequent growth of a community-based long-term-care system. It was necessary to anticipate cost savings in order to establish Medicaid as a funding source for community-based services.

What is known about case management costs? It's difficult to separate the costs of case management from the costs of direct services provided through the care plan. The National Long-Term-Care Channeling Demonstration Project isolated the cost of case management in 10 sites operating from 1982 to 1985. Evaluators divided monthly case management costs into three categories: initial functions (screening, assessment, care planning); administrative, overhead, and clerical; and ongoing case management. They found that the average cost of providing initial, one-time-only case management was $206 per month. Average administrative, overhead, and clerical monthly costs were $134 per month. The monthly costs of ongoing case management, consisting of activities conducted after the completion of initial functions, averaged $89. Costs of ongoing programs are likely to differ from the costs of demonstration projects. Nevertheless, these figures indicate that long-term-care case management is an intensive effort with identifiable costs.

Although case management costs represented a relatively small proportion of the total service dollars spent in the Channeling Demonstration Project, these costs suggest that case management intervention nevertheless requires significant resources. Accurate targeting is critically important in keeping costs down. However, case management costs should not be the primary determinant of program structure. Cost-driven systems may sacrifice quality and reward undeserving clients. As Seidl and colleagues (1977) state, "If nursing homes were cheaper, would it make sense to have a public policy to send everyone there? . . . The least expensive program, in dollar terms, would be to do nothing" (pp. 15, 18).

## Clinical Issues

Relationship is a core concept in case management practice. In theory, case management practice is a linear, sequential process whereby tasks smoothly follow one another (Burack-Weiss, 1988). In practice, however, "smooth" is perhaps the least accurate description of case managers' experiences. Clients may be noncompliant and uncooperative even when they are involved in the development of their care plans. Clients may resent the authority of the case manager or desire services that are not available. Clients accept some parts of the care plan and reject others. Families may not always facilitate the process. Some families may be willing but not capable of caring for their relatives, whereas others may be capable but not willing. Some clients may not have family caregivers.

Individualized case management practice is a core commitment. Unfortunately, some case managers are forced to serve unmanageably large case loads. These case managers find it difficult to individualize services and to develop relationships with their clients.

> The depth of the interaction and the intensity of the case management effort will be in inverse proportion to the number of individuals to be processed through the system—as client load (scope) increases, the intensity and depth of the intervention will decline (Beatrice, 1981, p. 127).

Client self-determination and individualized care plans may be sacrificed in programs that are not committed to quality service delivery. Quality case management practice requires reciprocal, facilitative relationships among the elder, caregivers, and the case manager. Burack-Weiss (1988) astutely noted that "with the advent of case management, practice with the aged has inexorably moved from looking at the person-in-situation to looking for the situation in the person" (p. 24). The danger is that assessment and care planning will focus on how clients fit into the system rather than on the clients' individual needs and the development of an individualized care plan. Even when care plans are developed from a client-centered perspective, the relationship between the case manager and the client is not guaranteed to motivate the client to follow the care plan.

Recent books on case management practice devote little discussion on clinical mental health issues (Applebaum & Austin, 1990; Quinn, 1993). Instead the focus has been on pragmatic problem solving and coordination of services within the context of community-based care planning. Radol Raiff and Shore (1994) note that clinically oriented case management is relationship oriented from a psychotherapeutic perspective:

> *Clinical case management has a two-pronged thrust: it is more focused on the changes, options and pacing of relationships than the "broker" models and it weaves clinical understandings throughout the process of dispositions planning, service referral, advocacy and follow-up (p. 85).*

Case management theory is articulated in technical terms, but its practice has an emotional orientation. Case management terminology includes comprehensive assessment, providers, care plans, budgetary caps, systems, and monitoring, whereas the language of practitioners is affective and includes terms such as anxiety and depression. Burack-Weiss (1988) observed,

> *reflections upon the clinical aspects of the process is a reminder that the elder is the pivotal point in any system. Practitioners forget it at their clients' expense—and their own (p. 25).*

## What Is Quality Case Management?

In the field, discussion has shifted from what is case management to what is quality case management (Applebaum & McGinnis, 1992; Kane, 1988; Kane & Kane, 1987). To a large extent, quality case management depends on how one views the tasks.

> *Can the case manager show the highest degree of respect for a person— acknowledging and responding to that individual's needs and dignity— and still be a manager, balancing the needs of the many (Dubler, 1992, p. 85)?*

The question of what constitutes quality case management has been addressed in two ways: (1) the specification of normative practice standards or guidelines against which the quality of case management practice can be assessed and (2) the development of quality-assurance systems designed to monitor the provision of case management services provided in the context of a specific program.

Although case management programs have specified professional requirements for training and timely service delivery, until recently no formal standards for state and federally funded programs that provide case management were available. Since 1990, three professional organizations have developed standards to guide long-term-care case management services: the National Institute on Community-Based Long-Term Care (1990), the National Association of Social Workers (1992), and the National Association of Private Geriatric Case Managers (1990). Efforts to certify case managers are also under way (National Academy of Certified Case Managers, 1994). In 1993, the Connecticut Community Care, Inc., Connecticut's statewide case management agency, received funding from the Robert Wood Johnson Foundation to develop guidelines for case management practice. This project produced a set of basic principles for developing a framework for practice guidelines:

- Case management is a consumer-centered service that respects consumer rights, values and preference.
- Case management coordinates all and any types of assistance to meet identified consumer needs.
- Case management requires clinical skills and competencies.
- Case management promotes the quality of services provided.
- Case management strives to use resources efficiently. (Connecticut Community Care, Inc., 1994, pp. 8–9).

Detailed guidelines were developed based on these basic principles. Individual guidelines were promulgated for consumer rights, preferences, and values; comprehensive assessment; care plan; implementation, monitoring, reassessment, discharge, and termination; quality of case manager and provider services; and the efficient use of resources.

Despite the increase in case management services, little information is available about how to monitor and evaluate their effectiveness. Increasing attention is being focused on specifying quality criteria and on the design and implementation of quality-assurance systems. As a distinct service, case management must meet quality criteria. In addition, the direct services provided as a part of the care plan must also meet standards of quality.

Applebaum and Phillips (1990) noted that evidence of good quality care, for both case management and direct services, is provided through the combined functions of evaluation and quality assurance. Evaluation determines whether delivered services have intended effects. After it is determined that a particular service or product does, indeed, result in expected outcomes, the issue of quality assurance can be addressed. Quality-assurance systems are designed to address how this beneficial outcome can be assured across time and across various settings and case managers. Quality assurance means compliance with standards.

A comprehensive quality-assurance program is based on consensus regarding desired outcomes of case management services at both the client and community levels. Quality goals include attention to multicultural realities and demonstrate commitment to comprehensive quality outcomes in the agency's functions and activities. Consumer empowerment, through direct participation in care planning as well as feedback through client-satisfaction surveys, is critical to quality. Case managers' competencies and clinical skills are also routinely assessed in order to determine how well they are performing core case management tasks.

Quality-assurance efforts have focused on structural measures to ensure that quality services are delivered. For example, the Ohio Department of Aging funded a comprehensive quality-assurance system through Title 3 of the Older Americans Act (Applebaum, Atchley, McGinnis, & Bare, 1988). In this project, random home visits of clients were conducted each month. If a client's condition was deemed substandard (poor physical condition, personal care not performed, homemaking tasks not completed), care services were examined.

## *Ethical Issues*

Client autonomy and self-determination are critical ethical issues in the provision of case management services. Ethicist Bart Collopy (1988) defines autonomy as

> *a cluster of notions including self-determination, freedom, independence, liberty of choice and action. In its most general terms, autonomy signifies control of decision making and other activity by the individual (p. 10).*

Autonomy is generally considered at the "agency" level, that is, freedom to decide among options, and "action" level, that is, freedom to carry out a particular course of action. In many instances, vulnerable older adults are dependent on others to implement or assist them with their decisions. Caring for vulnerable clients without controlling them is a delicate and complex task.

Protecting and enhancing personal autonomy can be a complicated process. Case managers who "overrespect" an individual's autonomy run the risk of engaging in benign neglect and underserving the client. Autonomy may be constrained by cognitive impairment—a common reason for excluding older persons from care decisions. The line between persuasion and manipulation can be particularly tenuous in work with vulnerable, dependent clients.

Protection of autonomy and concern for noncompliance are two sides of the same coin. At what point does an elder's autonomous decision making become inappropriate, noncompliant behavior? Case managers often struggle with cases in which clients do not comply with their care plans, even when they have participated in care planning. What constitutes dangerous noncompliance? When should adult protective services become involved? Dealing with noncompliant clients puts case managers in complex ethical situations that challenge their professional skills and wisdom.

In a recent study of 251 case managers, Kane, Penrod, and Kivnick (1994) asked respondents to identify ethical issues that they have dealt with in their practice. The largest group of respondents reported that conflicts between the family or the case manager and the client regarding nursing home placement was the ethical issue that they encountered most often. The second most frequently encountered ethical concern was family and client's differing views on how to put a community-care plan in place. Case managers' most frequently reported solution was to support client preferences if the client was competent.

This study also addressed ethical problems with regard to client needs and wants. The most frequently mentioned issue was "the client wants unsafe or unhealthy life-style," and the second most frequently reported conflict was "client needs home care and does not want [it]" (Kane et al., 1994, p. 7).

In care planning, the central question is "who is the client?" Case managers and agencies preferences regarding the extent to which families and clients should be involved in decision making can differ significantly. Client participation in decision making is seldom the only consideration in the development of care plans. Decision making is a complex process that often involves provider agencies as well as clients and their families.

Sometimes case managers find that their personal and professional ethics are in conflict with agency policies and that the best interests of the client conflict with agency goals or policies. In addition, case managers may experience tension between the amount of time devoted to direct service and administrative tasks. Realities of agency life may inhibit case managers' flexibility and authority in developing care plans that meet clients' assessed needs. Is it possible for case managers to advocate for clients and represent the agency's interests at the same time? This basic role conflict can create considerable ethical ambiguities for case managers.

> *Conflict will always be present when difficult resource allocation deci-*
> *sions must be made. . . . However, case managers function best within*
> *their own professional ethics. . . . They are keenly aware of the need to*
> *reserve resources for the next needy client they will see, they are suffi-*
> *ciently motivated by their own personal and professional desire to help*
> *people that their efforts to meet each client's needs are not diminished.*
> *. . . This all requires a balanced approach (Browdie, 1992, p. 89).*

Client-centered case management is replete with ethical challenges that
require a high degree of professional knowledge and skills. Ethical concerns often appear layered, each layer revealing another set of dilemmas that challenge the case manager's judgment, skills, and integrity.

## *Challenges*

Case management has become a permanent part of the long-term-
care landscape. Although much has been learned, much remains to be
learned. For example, the impact of race and ethnicity on case management practice has not been adequately addressed. Targeting in case
management programs has focused on levels of disability and capacity
to perform activities of daily living, not on race or ethnicity. Yet competent assessment and care planning, in particular, require careful attention to cultural diversity. Combining formal case management and
informal family-based caregiving is a particularly salient issue in care-
plan development. How do race and ethnicity affect care planning? We
don't know. Drawing on her work in the Puerto Rican community,
Schensul (1993) states that case management requires

> *cultural brokering skills—understanding the family and community con-*
> *text and medical aspects of the problem and ways of seeking care for the*
> *problem. Further, it requires sensitive coordination, communication, and*
> *crisis management skills [and] functions as an instructional program for*
> *the family, strengthening the family's capacity to negotiate service sys-*
> *tems for future as well as for current problems (p. 25).*

Case managers who work with various cultural groups are more effective
if they understand the dynamics of the communities that they serve. In
multicultural settings, competent case management requires the incorpo-
ration of resources and strategies from within and outside the client's culture. Quality case management is culturally competent case management.

Several practice-related issues are important to the future development of case management. How do costs and consumer outcomes vary
with the intensity, duration, and scope of case management service?
Who needs what level of case management services? How do care plans
affect cost and consumer outcomes? How does case management prac-

tice vary across program and agency settings? How should case managers be trained and what content should be included? How should case management be practiced in managed-care systems? How should the structure and financing of the delivery system be organized to support the case management function?

It is easy to lose perspective when the larger picture is not as visible as the daily needs of clients and demands of agencies. If community-based services are not available, case managers will not be able to develop care plans that meet their clients' assessed needs. Case managers cannot provide in-home and community-based services that do not exist. Thus case management alone cannot reform the structure and financing of the delivery system. The overwhelming funding bias toward nursing-home care continues. It is less disruptive and less expensive to provide case management services than to fund an adequate supply of services.

## References

Applebaum, R., Atchley, S., McGinnis, R., & Bare, A. (1988). *A guide to ensuring the quality of in-home care.* Columbus, OH: Ohio Department of Aging.

Applebaum, R., & Austin, C. (1990). *Long-term care case management; Design and evaluation.* New York: Springer.

Applebaum, R., & McGinnis, R. (1992). What price quality? Assuring the quality of case-managed in-home care. *Journal of Case Management, 1*(1), 9–13.

Applebaum, R., & Phillips, P. (1990). Assuring the quality of in-home care: The "other" challenge for long-term care. *Gerontologist, 30,* 444–450.

Austin, C. (1983). Case management in long-term care: Options and opportunities. *Health and Social Work, 8,* 16–30.

Austin, C. (1987). *Improving access for elders: The role of case managers.* Seattle, WA: Institute on Aging, University of Washington.

Austin, C., Roberts, L., & Low, J., (1985). *Case management: A critical review.* Seattle, WA: Institute on Aging, University of Washington.

Baker, F., & Vichy, T. (1989). Continuity and care and the control of costs: Can case management assure both? *Journal of Public Health Policy, 10,* 204–213.

Beatrice, D. (1981). Case Management: A policy option for long-term care. In J. Callahan & S. Wallack (Eds.), *Reforming the long-term care system* (pp. 121–161). Lexington, MA: D.C. Heath.

Browdie, R. (1992). Ethical issues in case management from a political and systems perspective. *Journal of Case Management, 1*(3), 87–99.

Burack-Weiss, A. (1988). Clinical aspects of case management. *Generations, 12*(5), 23–25.

Capitman, J. (1986). Community-based long-term-care models, target groups and impacts on service use. *Gerontologist, 26,* 389–397.

Capitman, J., Haskins, B., & Bernstein, J. (1986). Case management approaches in coordinated community-oriented long-term-care demonstrations. *Gerontologist, 26,* 398–404.

Carcagno, G., Applebaum, R., Christianson, J., Phillips, B., Thornton, C., & Will, J. (1986). *The evaluation of the national channeling demonstration: Planning and operation experience of the channeling projects.* Princeton, NJ: Mathematica Policy Research.

Clarfield, A. (1983). Home care: Is it cost-effective? *Canadian Medical Association Journal, 129,* 1181–1183, 1199.

Cline, B. (1990). Case management: Organizational models and administrative methods. *Caring, 9*(7), 14–18.

Collopy, B. (1988). Autonomy in long-term care: Some critical distinctions. *Gerontologist, 28,* 10–17.

Connecticut Continuing Care, Inc. (1994). *Guidelines for long-term-care case management practice.* Bristol, CT: Author.

Dubler, N. (1992). Individual advocacy as a governing principle. *Journal of Case Management, 1*(3), 82–86.

Greenberg, J., Doth, D., & Austin, C. (1981). *A comparative study of long-term care demonstrations.* Minneapolis, MN: Center for Health Services Research, University of Minnesota.

Grisham, M., White, M., & Miller, L. (1983). Case management as a problem-solving strategy. *Pride Institute Journal of Long-Term Health Care, 2*(4), 12–28.

Haskins, B., Capitman, J., & Bernstein, J. (1984). *Final report, evaluation of coordinated community-oriented long-term-care demonstration projects.* Berkeley, CA: Berkeley Planning Associates.

Kane, R. (Ed.). (1988). Introduction. *Generations, 12*(5), 5–6.

Kane, R., & Kane, R. (1987). *Long-term care: Principles, programs and policies.* New York: Springer.

Kane, R., Penrod, J., & Kivnick, H. (1994). Case managers discuss ethics. *Journal of Case Management, 3*(1), 3–12.

Keenan, M. (1989). *Changing need for long-term care: A chartbook.* Washington, DC: American Association of Retired Persons.

Kemper, P., Applebaum, R., & Harrigan, M. (1987). *A systematic comparison of commuity-care demonstrations.* Madison, WI: Institute for Research on Poverty, University of Wisconsin–Madison.

Merrill, J. (1985). Defining case management. *Business and Health, 2*(8), 5–10.

Miller, L., Clark, M., & Walter, L. (1984). *The comparative evaluations of the Multipurpose Senior Services Project, 1981–1982. Final report.* Berkeley, CA: University of California, Berkeley.

National Academy of Certified Case Managers. (1994). Certified case managers directions. *Case Manager, 5*(1), 41–48.

National Association of Area Agencies on Aging. (1984). *Models of community-based long-term care systems.* Washington, DC: Author.

National Association of Private Geriatric Case Managers. (1990). *Towards certification.* Tucson, AZ: Author.

National Association of Social Workers. (1992). *NASW standards for social work case management.* Washington, DC: Author.

National Institute on Community-Based Long-Term Care. (1990). *Case management guidelines for practice.* Washington, DC: National Council on the Aged.

Neugarten, B. (1982). *Age or need?* Beverly Hills, CA: Sage Publications.

Quinn, J. (1993). *Successful case management in long-term care.* New York: Springer.

Quinn, J., & Burton, J. (1988). Case management: A way to improve quality in long-term care. In K. Fisher & E. Weissman (Eds.), *Case management: Guiding patients through the health care maze* (pp. 9–14). Chicago: Joint Commission on Accreditation of Health Care Organizations.

Radol Raiff, N., & Shore, B. (1994). *Advanced case management*. Newbury Park, CA: Sage Publications.

Rubin, A. (1987). Case management. In *Encyclopedia of social work* (Vol. 1). Silver Spring, MD: National Association of Social Workers.

Schensul, J. (1993). Approaches to case management in Puerto Rican communities. *Journal of Case Management, 1*(4), 18–25.

Schneider, B., (1988). Care planning: The core of case management. *Generations, 12*(5), 16–19.

Schneider, B., & Weiss, L. (1982). *The channeling case management manual.* Prepared for the National Long-Term-Care Channeling Demonstration Program, Institute on Aging, Temple University, Philadelphia.

Seidl, F., Austin C., & Greene R., (1977). Is home care less expensive? *Health and Social Work, 2*(2), 5–19.

Vourlekis, B., & Greene, R. (1992). *Social work case management.* New York: Aldine de Gruyter.

Weil, M., Karls, J., & Associates. (1985). *Case management in human service practice.* San Francisco: Jossey-Bass.

Weissert, W., Cready, C., & Pawelak, J. (1988). The past and future of home care and community-based long-term care. *Milbank Quarterly, 66,* 359–388.

# Chapter | 5 |

# Case Management with Severely Emotionally Disturbed Children and Adolescents

*John Poertner*

S pecialized case management for seriously emotionally disturbed children and adolescents did not exist prior to 1980. It is not surprising then that many questions, debates, and differences of opinion surround case management definitions, clients, service providers, and effectiveness. Because case management for this population is a relatively new specialty, we know very little from a research perspective about its effectiveness. This chapter presents a brief history of children's mental health case management and identifies various perspectives on the elements of case management such as goals and roles as well as who may be best equipped to be a case manager and the ways that case management differs for children and parental caregivers.

## *History*

The roots of children's case management lie in mental health services for adults with severe and persistent mental illness, particularly the Community Support Program. One can also find roots of case management for children in other child-serving systems, such as children with developmental disabilities, child welfare, and juvenile justice. Knitzer's (1982) *Unclaimed Children* awakened the nation to the plight of children and adolescents in need of mental health services. In this seminal work, Knitzer estimated that "two thirds of the 3 million seriously disturbed children and adolescents in this country do not get the mental health services they need, while many more get inappropriate care" (p. 3). She also demonstrated the difficulties that families experience in their attempt to obtain care for their emotionally disturbed child. Case management received little attention in her work primarily because so few case management services existed. One reference to therapeutic case advocacy noted that only two states reported defining and funding specialized case management services for this population.

Two years later, in 1984, Congress authorized the Child and Adolescent Service System Program (CASSP). As part of the National Institute of Mental Health (NIMH), this program provided grants to states to improve services for children and their families. Among the principles adopted to guide CASSP efforts, one stated:

> *Children with serious emotional problems should be provided with case management or similar mechanisms to ensure that multiple services are delivered in a coordinated and therapeutic manner and that they can move through the system of services in accordance with their changing needs (Friesen, 1993, p. 17).*

The combined efforts of parents, advocacy groups, and policymakers initiated a great deal of activity that resulted in case management becoming a common element of state and community mental health systems. More recent legislation such as the Omnibus Health Act (P.L. 99-660) requires states to submit plans to NIMH describing their case management services and, since 1991, specifically addressing services for children and adolescents. In a recent study of states' implementation of case management for children under P.L. 99-660, Jacobs (1995) reported that 74% of the 35 states surveyed had defined case management for children as a service that was generally acceptable throughout the states' mental health system. Using a set of criteria to assess the level of development of case management within these states, Jacobs found that only 26% of the states had considerable or extensive development. From Knitzer's work in 1982 to this 1991 assessment, considerable interest and activity have focused on development of case management services. However, states clearly have a long way to go to fulfill the CASSP principle of providing access to case management services for all children with serious emotional disorders.

## Goals of Case Management

One difficulty with case management for children and adolescents with serious emotional disorders is the range of perspectives on goals. Discussions with health insurance professionals (including Medicaid) indicate that their primary goal is cost containment. Because mental hospital stays for children can be lengthy and costly, the goal of case management is to identify a less costly means of treating children. Because state and federal funding mechanisms like Medicaid are probably the largest funders of children's case management, it is likely that cost containment will be a central feature of most children's case management models (Fox & Wicks, 1995).

Case management is also frequently discussed as the most appropriate response to a fragmented, categorical, and overburdened child-serving system (Boyd, Clark, & Panacek-Howell, 1989). Most communities have a child-welfare system, a juvenile-justice system, a mental health system, and an education system—all of which play a role in the lives of children and families. However, it's not always clear which system is supposed to do what with which children: A child who acts out and breaks the windows of an automobile has broken the law (juvenile justice), may be beyond the control of his or her parents (child welfare), may be experiencing an outburst related to an emotional disorder (mental health), and may be exhibiting problem behaviors in school that identify the child as behavior disordered (special education). In other words, the difficulties of children cannot be neatly categorized. All too frequently, categorization of youth leads one system to determine that the case of a particularly difficult child or family is not in their domain but should be served by another system. In reality, the interaction of several community institutions may be needed to assist the child and family. This multisystem complexity leads to the conclusion that a case manager is needed to work between the systems. In this case, the goal is coordination of services.

A difficulty with regard to service coordination as a goal in the children's mental health field is the lack of precision about the meaning of service coordination. Does the case manager simply communicate among key actors in the system? Does the case manager bring key actors together to develop a plan? Does the case manager have the authority and/or responsibility to commit the resources of the various systems?

Within the special-education and disability fields, it has become common to replace the term "case management" with "service coordination." Families and children are not labeled as "cases," but as "people who need services." Therefore, service coordination is a more acceptable term. Within the disability movement, service coordination is the mechanism that assures that a person with a disability is included in mainstream society; the goal is inclusion in society. It is not unusual to hear activist parents saying, "Whatever it takes to keep the child safely within the family and community," which perhaps is a clearer statement of the service-coordination goal. If this is the goal of service coordination, it may be possible to replace the term "case management" with "service coordination" with minimal confusion about the purpose of services.

When working with children and adolescents, the goal of inclusion in the community and society fits with other public policy, for example, the Education for All Handicapped Children's Act (P.L. 94-142), the

Individuals with Disabilities Education Act (P.L. 99-457), and the Foster Care and Adoption Act (P.L. 96-272). Inclusion in mainstream society means that children with serious emotional disorders ought to be living with families in the community, educated with their peers, and participating in community activities such as Boy or Girl Scouts, girls/boys clubs, and recreation programs. Children thereby obtain the skills they need to function in the community. Although this goal is not the exclusive realm of case managers or service coordinators, it serves as a powerful force directing the activities of case managers.

Although this chapter focuses on children and adolescents, families are important participants in this endeavor. Parents of children with serious emotional disorders report that they have often been viewed by professionals as part of the problem or the cause of their child's problem. Case managers sometimes report role confusion regarding their work with a child *vis-à-vis* their work with parents. However, if the goal of case management is inclusion of the child within the family and community, case managers can join more effectively with parents. The inclusion goal may be more useful than the cost-cutting or service-coordination goals.

## Case Management Models

Robinson and Toff-Bergmann (1990), in an examination of case management models for working with adults with serious mental illness, identified four models: an expanded broker model, personal strengths, rehabilitation, and full support. Early and Poertner (1995), in their review of case management models for working with children and families, identified four current approaches: outpatient therapist, interdisciplinary team, broker, and strengths. Brokerage and strengths are common to both lists. The inclusion of outpatient therapist in the children's mental health field most likely reflects the recent development of this field and probably does not warrant a separate designation. The interdisciplinary team model is fairly common in children's mental health and is not evident in the adult area. Although the emphasis of the rehabilitation model on skill building can be seen in some children's case management approaches, it does not seem to be directly applied in children's mental health. Similarly, the full-support model identified by Robinson and Toff-Bergman (1990), which combines teaching coping skills with clinical management, is not directly applied in children's mental health.

The book in which Early and Poertner identify children's case management models includes descriptions of innovative programs from

Vermont and New York as well as a program aimed at older youth making the difficult transition to adulthood (Poertner & Friesen, 1995). Although the various models are described in terms of case management functions, distinctions are not clear, probably because the field of case management in children's mental health is in an early stage of development.

Nevertheless, case management models in children's mental health are being developed. Therefore, comparing and contrasting a set of existing models with a reasonable degree of clarity is difficult. By describing some common case management models within generally agreed-upon roles and functions, it is possible to see major differences in approaches. This chapter uses the functions of case management to describe the brokerage, strengths, and interdisciplinary team models as examples of differing and common practices.

Early and Poertner (1995) define brokerage in terms of the linking function of case managers:

> In the brokerage approach, the main responsibility of a case manager is to make arrangements for clients to receive services. The notion is that the service delivery system is not well coordinated or flexible. . . . By definition, a broker is one who acts as an agent to procure something for someone who employs the broker (p. 47)

In the case of children's mental health, the case manager is to procure services that have been defined as needed by the child or other family members.

The interdisciplinary team is a set of professionals with expertise in particular areas. The situation of children with serious emotional disorders is so complex that it is thought to be beneficial for professionals from a variety of disciplines to examine the situation of the child and family, for each professional to do an assessment from his or her disciplinary perspective, and for each to make certain that the child and family receive the indicated services.

Robinson and Toff-Bergman (1990) define the strengths model as follows: "The case manager identifies a client's strengths and attempts to create situations where these can be enhanced and where success can be achieved" (p. 4). Poertner and Ronnau (1989) define the strengths approach in terms of service components: focus on family strengths, assessment, relationship building, advocacy, identification and achievement of objectives, and resource acquisition. As indicated by these definitions, it isn't easy to define any of the models clearly. The individual approaches with their similarities and differences become clearer when examined according to their common roles and functions.

## *Case Management Roles and Functions*

Case management roles include assessment, planning, linking, monitoring, and advocacy (Early & Poertner, 1995). One of the difficulties in differentiating case management approaches according to function is that not all models or approaches clarify their difference in function from the same function in another model. Such lack of clarity may leave the reader wondering if a difference actually exists. An additional complexity in children's mental health involves the distinction of roles and functions for working with children in contrast with work with adult family members.

Case management with children and adolescents is fundamentally different and complementary to working with parents or family caregivers. Unfortunately, these differences are often obscured or ignored in practice. Petr (1992) identifies what he terms "adultcentrism" in work with children–"the tendency of adults to view children and their problems from a biased, adult perspective" (p. 408). According to Petr, this bias can be seen in various ways, including our theories of child development that essentially view children as incomplete and incompetent. This is often seen in children's mental health whereby case management is perceived as something service providers do to, with, or for parents rather than to, with, or for youth. Too often, the child is seen as a passive recipient of services as opposed to a partner. In an effort to bring children into this field, the following sections discuss case management functions first in terms of working with children, then in relation to working with families.

### ❑ Case Management Functions in Work with Children and Youth

Case management with children and youth with serious emotional disorders are described here according to the standard functions of assessment, planning, linking, monitoring, and advocacy (Brown, 1989). However, two additional dimensions not frequently discussed are also included. Because different models of case management are directed with different values, the value base is discussed. In addition, relationship building, which is often subsumed under assessment, is discussed separately.

*Values.* The values underlying a case management model, although infrequently explicated, do make a difference. For example, the seldom stated value underlying the broker model is that children should receive needed services. Therefore, a task of the case manager is to determine what services the child needs and ensure that he or she receives them. This leads to services that are generally thought of as professionally delivered, which includes various therapies and treatments. However, this perspective may exclude other ways to meet needs that may fall under clinical or professional services, such as various volunteer, library, peer-group, or community recreational activities.

The interdisciplinary team is another dominant model in children's mental health. This model implies that various professional disciplines assessing the child from their perspectives will yield useful information that translates into service needs. It then becomes the case manager's job to make sure that the child and family receive the needed services. These examples are offered nonjudgmentally for the purpose of demonstrating that values do have consequences for workers, children, and family caregivers.

It is not possible to list all the values underlying different case management models because models generally do not make their value base explicit. The model described by Poertner and Ronnau (1992) describes its value base as being drawn from the disability field and includes the following:

1. The emotional disability is only one of the youth's characteristics. The individual and the disability are not one and the same.

2. Youth with disabilities also have abilities (strengths).

3. Youth with disabilities can learn and grow.

4. Youth with disabilities are the primary informant on how they experience the disabilities.

5. A youth with a disability should be part of society, not out of the main stream.

6. Society should make reasonable accommodations for youth with disabilities.

7. Families are the primary caregivers (p.115).

This list is presented for purposes of illustration only. The disability analogy may not be the most appropriate or effective. Certainly, it is possible and desirable to develop other models based upon different values. The value base that directs a particular case management model is an underdeveloped area. It would be easier to compare and contrast case management models if the value base of each were explicitly identified.

***Relationship development.*** In practice, case management functions are not linear. It is not unusual for several or all of these functions to be occurring at the same time. However, for purposes of explication, case management functions will be discussed sequentially.

Relationship development with children and youth is fundamentally different from that with adults. As Petr (1992) points out, one does not interview children in the same way as one interviews adults. A case manager may sit at the kitchen table with an adult caregiver, drink coffee, and develop a working relationship while obtaining the adult's perspective on caring for a child. Such a strategy does not work with children. But because this limitation in children's mental health case management is virtually not discussed, variations across case management models cannot be explored.

Following Petr's advice would be helpful regardless of the case management model. Petr suggests entering the world of the child to find ways of working with him or her. When one enters the world of the child, one finds at least two important characteristics. First, the child's age makes a big difference. Infants, preschool children, early elementary-school-age children, junior high school youth, and older adolescents all develop relationships differently. Second, although children and youth develop relationships differently, participating in activities is a common characteristic. Children and youth develop relationships, express their preferences, and learn and grow through activities. Engaging in age-appropriate activities is an important case management task if a relationship with a child is to be developed.

When one begins to consider age-appropriate activities, it becomes easier to find ways to enter a child's world and develop a relationship with a child. With younger children, games and other "play" activities work well. As children become older, their activities change. Sewing, basketball, walking, riding, and "hanging out" at the mall are normal relationship-building activities for teens. It must be remembered, however, that case managers are more than "big brothers" or "big sisters." Engaging in activities with youth has a specific purpose; shared activities are ways to engage the youth in the other case management activities of assessment and goal setting. Increasingly, case managers are getting out of the office to meet families in the home. The next challenge is to take the youth for a drive, go shopping, play baseball, or participate in some other appropriate activity.

***Assessment.*** Going to a mall with an adolescent allows the case manager and adolescent to get to know each other. To enter the world of the youth is to begin to learn about the youth as an individual rather than as a diagnosis. Shared activities facilitate the assessment process, and the information one obtains while participating in such activities is critical to the assessment process. The dominant case management models are often vague in their descriptions of the assessment process. They tend to approach assessment from one of three perspectives: focus on problems, needs, or strengths.

Identifying problems that a youth is experiencing is common to the interdisciplinary team model and some applications of the brokerage model. One such approach is to identify the problem type or diagnosis that fits the child. Although the educator may identify the youth in general terms as behavior disordered, mental health professionals may further identify the youth as schizophrenic. These labels are determined through the methods used in the education and mental health fields.

Another approach is to identify problems in the child's functioning. The task is to identify problems that the youth is having in various domains. Each multidisciplinary team member looks for problems in her or his area of expertise. Hearing, sight, school behavior, learning, chemical imbalances, and relationships with family members are a few examples. This assessment might lead to observations that the youth has a slight visual impairment, is behind his or her grade level in reading skills, and has difficulty staying on task. Of course, this is an oversimplification, but it illustrates the kind of information one receives with this type of assessment.

Another assessment approach frequently practiced in the brokerage model is identifying needs. The assessment process includes an examination of the normal developmental needs of a child and a comparison of them to the needs of the child being assessed. One such assessment process evaluates life domains, such as physical, social, and psychological needs, then identifies the child's needs relative to normal development. This may result, for example, in an adolescent needing a best friend, to learn some specific independent living skills, or access to counseling.

This assessment might be done by a single case manager, a multidisciplinary team, or a group of people who know the child and family. Some recent approaches emphasize the use of a group of people who know the child well. Although such an approach can provide useful information, the needs of the child or youth can easily be lost in the process. It is extremely difficult for most youth to state their point of view in groups dominated by adults. However, a case manager and a youth who get to know each other well are frequently able to produce a useful assessment.

The strengths approach assumes yet another perspective on assessment. In this approach, strengths are seen as resources, and the assessment process focuses on helping the youth identify his or her strengths according to four categories: skills and abilities that the youth has demonstrated, goals the youth would like to accomplish, people with whom the youth has a relationship, and desirable characteristics.

Through examination of these categories in the normal life domains of a youth, strengths can be identified. Considering a range of life domains such as education, socialization, self-definition, affection, physical health, and economic well-being provides a large base from which to identify strengths.

The process occurs in the context of mundane activities. As the case manager and the youth are shopping, for example, the case manager may ask about school activities and daily routines. Through this conversation about what is going well, whom the youth relates to among school staff and peers, and what the youth would like to achieve in school, the case manager obtains a list of strengths. The youth may also identify areas he or she would like to change. In this way, the assessment and goal-setting processes blend together in a natural way.

Consider the following example of a youth labeled by his school as being behavior disordered, who had recently been released from a state hospital, and was working with a case manager. The case manager found out that he was interested in helicopters (an interest/strength). They went to the library to find books on helicopters and explored where in the community they might find someone who was a helicopter pilot. Through this process, the case manager discovered that the youth liked to draw futuristic helicopters (an ability/strength). His best subject in school was mathematics (an ability/strength), and his mother was willing (a resource person/strength) to approach the school about incorporating his interests into his individual educational plan. This example demonstrates how the relationship and assessment processes blend together.

No research to date compares case management approaches in terms of outcomes for youth. Similarly, research indicating which assessment approach is most effective is not available. Consequently, it is not possible to advocate for an assessment method based upon empirical evidence. At this stage in children's case management development, the selection of an assessment method is directed more by goal setting and values than by demonstrated effectiveness.

***Case planning.*** Case planning with youth ranges from determining the services that the youth should receive to identifying specific behaviors the youth must demonstrate to indicate that he or she no longer requires services. The broker model clearly implies that the youth needs and ought to receive specific services. For example, a youth is determined to need counseling, medication, and attendant care. Therefore, the case management plan lists these services, along with information about service providers and "who will do what" to provide the necessary services.

The interdisciplinary team case plan is very similar. The team is represented by different professionals, each of whom determines the service needs of the youth. The case plan lists a collection of services covering the range of specialties represented by the team, for example, monthly visits with a psychiatrist, counseling at a mental health center, placement in a behavior-disordered classroom, and recreational activities after school and on the weekends.

In some case management approaches, case planning for the youth is behavioral in focus. That is, the plan lists specific behaviors expected of the child. For example, the youth will attend school every day, when the youth becomes agitated in school he or she will request permission to go to a designated safe place with an attendant, and after school the youth will go to the YMCA for recreational activities.

The strengths model also uses a behavioral focus, but with a different focus. Goal setting in this approach arises out of the youth's strength assessment. To return to the example of the youth with an interest in helicopters, after his interest and drawing activities were identified as strengths, the case plan built upon this interest and positive activity to set a relevant goal and identified the steps required of the case manager and youth to accomplish this goal. A short-term goal along the road to designing helicopters might be locating an aeronautical engineer who could talk with the youth about the field and the educational background needed to become a designer of helicopters. In other words, the individualized case plan identifies the actions or steps that the youth and case manager will take toward achieving this goal, along with specific dates for task completion. In this approach, case planning develops individual objectives that build on strengths and exploit opportunities for learning.

***Linking.*** The linking function generally refers to steps that the case manager takes to ensure that the youth receives needed services. Most case management models are not explicit about these activities. They seem to vary according to how active or passive the case manager is with regard to the advocacy function.

In the interdisciplinary team model, after the various team members determine what services are needed, a member of the team may be selected to serve as the case manager in terms of linking services. Depending on the philosophy of the team or the individual view of the designated case manager, he or she may be more or less active in performing the linking function. If the case manager is not actively engaged in the linking function, services are identified, and it is the family's or youth's responsibility to take the steps necessary to connect the youth with the service. For example, the youth may have to take responsibility to go to the YMCA and enroll in an after-school recreation program, or the parental caregiver may be expected to make this connection.

Similarly, the broker model varies widely as to how actively the case manager serves as a link between the youth and services. In agencies and approaches in which the case manager is more active in the linking process, he or she takes responsibility for contacting service providers, demonstrating that the youth is eligible for the service, assisting with forms, and checking to make sure that the youth receives the service. In some cases, the broker case manager may accompany the youth to make these arrangements.

The strengths model attempts to tailor the linking function to the abilities of the youth. For example, the case plan identifies a recreation program in which the youth would like to participate as well as identifies the steps required to initiate participation. A joint decision is then made regarding who (case manager or youth) will do which tasks. Consequently, the case manager may be very active and the youth less active or *vice versa*.

***Advocacy.*** Advocacy as a case management function is closely connected to the linking function. In some approaches, advocacy refers to the level of activity that the case manager assumes in arguing for or obtaining services. Some case management approaches include the term "advocacy" in their title to emphasize the importance of this function.

In the interdisciplinary team model, advocacy is considered less important than other functions. The rationale is that since all of the disciplines are at the table and participating in the decision-making process, the various professionals will agree on the required services. Some professionals who have participated in these teams still see the need for a designated case manager to advocate for the case plan developed by the team.

The emphasis on the advocacy function varies widely across brokerage models. Some broker models view advocacy as critical because the service system is fragmented and categorical and the mental health case manager's role is to ensure that children with mental disorders receive the services they need from the various systems. In this regard, they advocate for flexible eligibility criteria and creative ways to pay for needed services. They may even work toward service providers creating new services to meet the needs of a particular child. This level of advocacy requires a very special set of skills to accomplish the desired tasks without alienating service systems. Many parents report that in their individual advocacy efforts for their children they sometimes inadvertently alienate a service system and therefore fail to obtain what they need. Consequently, considerable discussion in the field has focused on defining the most appropriate skills, authority, and responsibility of case managers in the community (Friesen & Briggs, 1995; Roberts & Poertner, 1995).

One systems response to questions of advocates' authority and responsibility is the protection and advocacy system. The Protection and Advocacy for Mentally Ill Individuals Act (P.L. 99-319) established independent agencies in each state to pursue legal, administrative, and other remedies to ensure the protection of the rights of individuals receiving treatment, services, or habitation through the state. This was an extension of the original protection and advocacy system established for people with disabilities under the Developmentally Disabled Assistance and Bill of Rights Act of 1975 (P.L. 94-103). A consideration in creating this system was how to locate the advocacy function so that it would be most effective. Consequently, these agencies are required to be independent of service provision, and advocacy is the only case management function they perform. Some people believe that this independence is necessary for effective advocacy. Therefore, advocacy needs to be a separate system, or the advocacy efforts of parents need to be encouraged.

The strengths model takes a slightly different approach to advocacy. Although the case manager in this approach may perform individual advocacy in the same manner as a broker, emphasis is also on assisting the youth to learn self-advocacy skills. This assistance may occur in various ways. First, the steps required to obtain a service are identified in the case plan, and a discussion occurs about who will complete which tasks. In this discussion difficulties that may occur are identified. If the youth and the case manager do not feel that the youth has the skills needed to accomplish a task, they may agree that the case manager will undertake the task and that the youth will be present and observe task completion. In this way, the youth learns self-advocacy skills through modeling. In other situations, the youth and case manager may agree that the youth will undertake the task but needs to practice the task. In such instances, the youth and the case manager might role play a conversation between the youth and the person who is the target of the advocacy effort, a coach, for example. In other situations, the youth may advocate for him- or herself.

***Monitoring and evaluation.*** Monitoring and evaluation is commonly thought of as periodic evaluation of the progress of the youth and the case plan. Little discussion across children's case management models focuses on the most effective way to monitor or evaluate. Consequently, differences among the models may be minimal.

The interdisciplinary team model sometimes assigns the monitoring and evaluation function to the designated case manager, then receives periodic reports on the progress of the child. The team may also collectively evaluate the progress of the youth by individual assessments. In this approach, monitoring and evaluation of services are determined by evaluating desired outcome for the youth.

The broker model operates similarly, although in this case the individual broker is responsible for assessing the effect of services, usually by acquiring the perspectives of the individuals involved with the child. This assessment is based on feedback from the youth, the family caregiver, the extended family, school personnel, and others in the community who are involved with the case plan. Their combined feedback is then used to reinforce or modify the case plan.

The strengths model uses the collaborative case plan to complete the monitoring and evaluation function at the case level. In this model, emphasis on goal and task accomplishment drives monitoring and evaluation. The case plan is the ongoing working document between the youth and the case manager. During each meeting, they jointly review their separate responsibilities and their experiences while completing the tasks and accomplishing the goal. The completion of each task or goal is cause for celebration. When the youth accomplishes the task or goal, it is recognized as another strength, and the case manager makes an attempt to find opportunities to encourage the youth to continue to demonstrate this strength. Failure to accomplish a task or goal is seen as an opportunity to review obstacles and chart another path, be it a new set of tasks or a new goal.

It is not uncommon for a case manager and a youth in the early stages of working together to err on the degree to which a task needs to be broken down into its component parts. Consequently, when a task is not completed, it may just need to be broken down into smaller parts. For example, a task might initially be identified as going to the YMCA to sign up for a swimming class. If the youth agrees to do this but is unable to accomplish it by the date agreed upon, it may signal a need to identify smaller steps that will result in becoming enrolled in swimming classes. It may also indicate that the youth does not really want to participate in swimming. In either case, the task that is not accomplished serves as an opportunity for joint learning. Therefore, monitoring and evaluation is part of the learning process.

Evaluation at the case level is a critical part of the interactive learning process, as is evaluation at the agency and case-load levels. Evaluation is guided by the goal of case management, which for children is inclusion. Evaluation beyond the case level focuses on the degree to which children and youth live in family situations and are included in community activities such as education and recreation.

## ❏ Case Management Functions in Working with Parents or Family Caregivers

Case management with parents or family caregivers is fundamentally different from and complementary to case management with youth. The goal for children with emotional disorders includes living in a family setting, defined as a household with a biological parent, an adoptive parent, a relative, or another adult who has connected with the child on an emotional caring level. This broad definition of family reflects the goal of inclusion in the community and unifies case management work with children and families. Consequently, the term "family caregiver" or simply "caregiver" designates this broad group of adults who help troubled youth function in the community.

Case management models do not frequently distinguish differences in working with youth and family caregivers. Therefore, it is less useful to describe different models and the ways in which they vary. However, because working with caregivers and working with youth differ significantly, the case management function is used to describe the differences in working with family caregivers rather than to describe the variations among models. A recent qualitative study of a group of parents receiving case management services identified caregivers' expectations of case managers (Donner et al., 1995). This set of expectations is used here across case management functions to demonstrate important differences from the parents' point of view (Table 1).

One major difference is in the focus of case management services. Case managers often experience confusion with regard to the focus of case management when working with caregivers rather than youth. Figure 1 suggests one way to assist case managers maintain focus.

In this figure, the vertical axis represents the time a case manager has available. The horizontal axis represents age of the youth. For very

**Figure 1.** Case manager time.

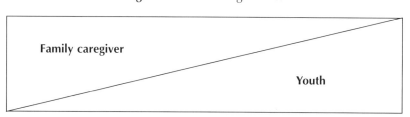

**Table 1.** Caregivers' expectations of case managers.

*Attitudes that parents seek in case managers*
Give caregivers hope and a vision of the future
Believe that children should be with families
Believe that families are the experts on their caregiving needs
Be nonjudgmental and value free regarding parents' life-styles

*Commitment to establishing a relationship with families*
Ask parents what they need to care for their child
Translate family concerns into resources and services
Permit families to determine what tasks they will do and what tasks they want the case manager to do
Identify and build on family strengths
Be comfortable moving in and out of families' lives
Reach out to parents
Participate in the successful things that happen in families
Be comfortable in being informal and sharing information about themselves
Know one's limits

*Assistance with the service system*
Be in touch with all people involved with the family and child
Know community resources and have ability to acquire and influence them
Have the capacity and authority to make decisions
Act as a liaison with programs

*Creating a supportive network of informal resources*
Assist and advocate for the youth to be involved in normal age-appropriate activities
Create resources when they do not exist
Have flexible funds available to acquire informal resources
Introduce caregivers to other families, support and advocacy groups

*Organizational variables that support parents and case managers*
Small case loads
Flexible work schedules
Regular daily contact with caregivers and their child
Someone always available
Parent-centered policies
Getting parents involved in the development and implementation of case management services, policies, and training

young children the case manager devotes most of his or her time to working with the caregiver in meeting the caregiving demands of the child. As the age of the child increases, however, the case manager must spend more time with the youth. This time focuses on assisting the youth to acquire skills necessary for appropriate functioning in the community. For a 17- or 18-year-old youth, nearly all of the case manager's time is devoted to working with the youth. The figure further suggests that for children 9–12 years old, the case manager spends approximately equal amounts of time with the child and the family caregiver. Case managers report that this strategy is helpful in maintaining focus.

*Values.* Case management models rarely identify their value base. However, in a recent analysis of what parents expect from case managers, caregivers identified a set of family-friendly values (Donner et al., 1995). Included in this set of values was giving caregivers hope and a vision of the future, believing that children should be with families, and perceiving that families are experts on their child's caregiving needs. The demands of caring for a child with a serious emotional disorder are great, and a longer-term view of what is possible is extremely difficult to maintain. According to parents, identifying and building upon the child's strengths is one way to demonstrate the success of the child as he or she grows and develops, thus giving caregivers hope. Another way to give hope is through sharing the successes of other children and families. Each child who has successfully negotiated school, family, and community is a role model for others.

Another value that parents expressed was the expectation that case managers believe that families are experts on their caregiving responsibilities and needs. Parents frequently view professionals as denying this caregiving reality. For example, one parent related a story about calling the child's doctor about the apparent side effects of a new medication, only to be told by the physician that this *side effect was not possible.* Although the physician may have been correct, the parent perceived this response as a denial of what she said. Another caregiver, who was questioned about what she did while she was being provided respite care, perceived this interrogation as implying that she used the time off for some purpose other than respite. She felt that the professional was not genuinely interested and failed to recognize her need for respite in order to continue to provide care for her children.

Various case management models are capable of operating according to a set of values that coincide with values of parents. Nothing inherent in the design of the interdisciplinary team, brokerage, or strengths models facilitates or inhibits operating from this value base. One case management service hung a poster on the wall that listed the family-centered values of the agency. Such a strategy is likely to be equally effective with case managers across various case management models.

*Relationship.* The parents' list of expectations of case managers made clear that commitment to establishing a relationship was essential

(Donner et al., 1995). These parents went a step further in describing the attitudes and activities that would most likely result in the establishment of such a relationship. Parents want case managers to be informal in working with them and to share information about themselves. They want case managers to be comfortable as they move in and out of the family's life. Caregivers recognize the cyclical nature of their struggles and need the case manager to be available when they are struggling and to be less involved when they are not. At the same time, they want case managers to reach out to them and participate in their successes as families, even as parents recognize that case managers also have limits. Finally, these parents said they wanted case managers to identify and build upon family strengths.

These responses represent a reasonable list of attitudes and activities likely to result in a mutually satisfying working relationship. Again, no item in this list appears to be specific to a particular case management model, although how a case management program is structured might make it easier or more difficult to develop the type of relationship envisioned by parents. For example, it is not unusual for an interdisciplinary team to be structured in such a way that the child and family must go to the team. In addition, these teams are sometimes structured in ways that make it difficult for family caregivers or youth to express their desires, needs, or points of view. Without the capability of reaching out to the family and asking about their caregiving needs, it is difficult to establish the kind of relationship desired by family caregivers.

Some applications of the broker model and the strengths model include features that explicitly address the ideal relationship as identified by family caregivers. For example, outreach and intensive involvement with families appear in both broker and strengths case management approaches. Parental expectations about working relationships also transcend the categories of assessment, case planning, and advocacy. From a parental caregiver's point of view, relationship development is not a separate stage but is a product of all the interactions between a case manager and a caregiver.

*Assessment.* In addition to the difficulty of separating relationship development from other case management functions such as assessment, differences between case management models are not always evident. Because case managers work with family caregivers as a result of some "problem" presented by the youth, assessment in terms of working with family members is most often reflected through assessment of the youth, as previously discussed. Unfortunately, caregivers frequently report feeling blamed for the youth's problem. In such situations, the case manager tends to engage in problem identification with the family or family system.

In the past, the difficulties experienced by youth were commonly perceived as being caused by or linked to parental behavior (Early & Poertner, 1993). Severe abusive behavior, for example, sexual abuse, can obviously cause severe behavior problems among some youth. However, the etiology of mental health diagnoses is often unclear. If the goal of children's mental health case management is inclusion of the youth in a family and community, it is more useful to engage caregivers on the subject of caregiving tasks rather than to search for parental problems. The case manager who suspects abusive behavior has the responsibility of reporting his or her suspicions, and another service system is responsible for responding.

Regarding relationship development, parental caregivers noted that they want case managers to ask caregivers about their needs in caring for their child, then translate these requests into services (Donner et al., 1995). These tasks are clearly central to the assessment process. Some case managers report that asking parents what they need to care for their child sometimes results in responses such as: "I need Johnny to stop doing . . ." or "I need Johnny to be good." Such responses are understandable among caregivers who are tired and frustrated after many years of providing care for a child with severe problems. There are both informational and emotional components to such responses.

Although the reality of the child's troublesome behavior is addressed under case planning, the emotional component of the message needs to be addressed as well. Validating the parents' experiences with the child as well as with the system is important. Again, this reflects one of the core values identified by parents—that families are experts on their caregiving needs and demands.

The strengths model attempts to make strengths identification a central part of the assessment process. With this approach, the identification of family strengths uses abilities, desires, people involved with the family, and personal characteristics together with a family system model to identify family strengths (Ronnau & Poertner, 1993). Family systems are complex and include many different components; thus one can look for strengths in many places. Ronnau and Poertner identify 24 components in their family systems model. With 4 categories of strengths and 24 family system components, strengths are easy to find.

Other case management models include identification of strengths as a component in the assessment process. The importance of strengths identification lies in the ways in which they are used. Ronnau and Poertner (1993) discuss three different applications of strengths. One application suggests that case managers tell the caregivers their specific caregiving strengths. This approach helps caregivers view themselves as competent parents and encourages them to include caregiving strengths in their self-definitions. This strategy is also useful in developing a relationship. It provides hope and helps caregivers sustain the energy needed to provide care. Another use of strengths is to help define caregiving to others in the community. Case managers can also help caregivers identify and use their strengths in providing care.

*Case planning.* The parental expectation that case managers translate family concerns into resources and services and build on strengths represents a clear statement of how parents perceive case planning. This view is consistent with recent developments in the field, for example, case planning ideas identified as "wrap-around" services. In these developments, services respond to parental caregiving demands by "wrapping" services around the youth rather than making the family and youth "fit" the service. Although no empirical evidence is available to support these approaches, many good case examples are available. Carl Dennis, for example, has used these ideas in creative and apparently effective ways (Goetz, 1994). In his examples, the key element is talking with the caregiver about the 24-hour caregiving day. If the caregiver has difficulty getting the child up in the morning in time for school, wrap-around services might provide someone to come into the home and assist with these tasks. If the youth is having difficulty during the school day, the case manager might advocate for needed support in the school. If the caregiver has difficulty supervising the youth after school, wrap-around services might provide someone to meet the youth after school and help him or her stay active and safe until parental supervision is available. If the caregiver has difficulty with behavioral outbursts in the evening, wrap-around services might provide someone to respond to the youth on an emergency basis. These examples demonstrate the various ways that case planning is managed from a wrap-around perspective and the ways in which caregiver expectations of case managers might be fulfilled.

To some, this approach may appear to replace parental caregiving rather than supplement it. However, the harsh reality is that the severe behavior problems of some youth require such services. Building on caregiver strengths can be used with wrap-around services to ensure balance as well as validate caregiver efforts. To build on caregiver strengths, these strengths must be identified, and caregivers need to find additional avenues to use these strengths in providing care. For example, a case manager who discovered that a mother was a practicing nurse prior to giving birth to a child with multiple problems identified things that she was doing that were related to her nursing background.

Her knowledge of medicines was extremely useful over the years in communicating with physicians about her son's difficulties and responses to various medications. The case manager identified this strength and encouraged her to use this ability more forcefully in communicating with a psychiatrist. The case manager also showed the mother the similarity between working with physicians and advocating with school personnel for appropriate services in her son's individual educational plan. Thus, the mother's self-identity as a nurse was used more broadly in her care for her son.

*Linking.* In the Donner et al. (1995) study, one set of parental expectations related to linking but not in the way most case managers might think. Linking is frequently perceived as obtaining needed services from formal service providers. Parents clearly want this outcome, which they perceive as an advocacy function. At the same time, however, they want assistance in creating a supportive network of informal services (Donner et al., 1995), which represents a different type of linking.

In this area, parental caregivers assist the youth in their involvement in normal age-appropriate activities, create resources when they are not available, and find flexible means with which to acquire informal resources. Such activities might include linking youth with recreational and developmental programs such as scouts, YMCAs, swimming or martial-arts lessons; linking caregivers with identified friends and neighbors who can assist with specific tasks; and linking caregivers with other parents who are experiencing similar difficulties. Such activities represent normal community functioning and fit nicely into the goal of assisting youth to fit into family and community life.

Family caregivers also identified permitting families to determine what tasks they will do and what they want the case manager to do (Donner et al., 1995). Although families included this value in relationship development, it clearly transcends this category and is relevant to case planning, linking, and advocacy. Jointly identifying responsibilities within all case management functions is critical to case management practice. Families experience this cooperative effort as empowering. One parent reported that she was completing the case-planning document before the case manager arrived for their appointment. Clearly, she was able to take over the case planning and thus allow the case manager to move on to other problem situations. Another parent marched into the governor's office to obtain an explanation of an occurrence in a state hospital. It is extremely unlikely that a case manager could undertake such an action. Case managers are typically public employees who must "respect" agency boundaries and hierarchy. Parental caregivers, however, are constituents and, perhaps more important, voters.

*Advocacy.* As the example described above indicates, parents may be the most effective advocates. At the same time, caregivers expect assistance with the service system. Because so many caregivers have difficulties with the system, obtaining such assistance is often considered an advocacy function. From a parental perspective, advocacy includes being in touch with everyone involved with the family and child, knowing community resources, having the ability to acquire and influence resources, having the capacity and authority to make decisions, and acting as a liaison with programs. This set of tasks is large and time-consuming.

These advocacy tasks raise questions about system design. For case managers to be able to deliver on these expectations, they need to spend considerable time with each family, which translates into the need for small case loads. Advocacy-oriented case managers need to have the authority to make decisions across systems, and the child- and family-serving system in the community must provide case managers with this authority. Such issues have not yet been adequately addressed.

*Monitoring and evaluation.* Although monitoring and evaluation were not explicitly addressed in the list of parental expectations, caregivers clearly view their perspective of caregiving as extremely important. The fact that caregivers stated that it is important for case managers to believe that families are the experts on their caregiving needs suggests that this strategy needs to be a central point of evaluation. It is also critical to ongoing work with caregivers. The interaction between the caregiver and the case manager about the reality of caring for the child must be part of the ongoing process of monitoring and evaluation.

The ultimate goal of case management is also a central focus of monitoring and evaluation. When the goal of case management in children's mental health is for the child to be living in a family situation and participating in normal activities in the community, the ultimate evaluation of the program is facilitated. It is not difficult to establish a system that tracks where youth are living and the number of noninclusive services and activities in which the youth is engaged, including special-education classes as well as services such as day treatment. Through tracking of living arrangements and noninclusive services, the ultimate success of case management is evaluated from a program point of view.

## Conclusion

Children's mental health case management is in its infancy. Since it first gained attention in the early 1980s, the body of literature on case management programs and ideas has proliferated. Unfortunately, little is known about the success of case management from an empirical point of view. A research base is critical for the ongoing development of the field. This research should take into account differing models of case management with their variously defined roles and functions. However, the research agenda should also include a host of policy considerations. Burns, Gwaltney, and Bishop (1995) and Friesen and Poertner (1995) identify an important research agenda for the field.

From a practice point of view, case management approaches have evidently developed by borrowing ideas from various sources. In conjunction with the research agenda, learning from other fields and from case managers is essential for generating new ideas and practices. Children's mental health case management will become more effective with the development and exploitation of practice wisdom as well as research knowledge.

Practice and policy also need to consider thoughtfully the perspectives of children and family caregivers. Family caregivers and youth have different and complementary points of view that are important to achieving the goal of case management. Mental health case management seems to be moving toward work with family caregivers and not with youth, apparently driven by the notion that meeting the needs of family caregivers will simultaneously meet the needs of children. This idea is only partially true. Working with parents to the exclusion of youth is also being driven by cost-containment objectives. An administrator stated that he liked the way case management addressed the needs of family caregivers but that under managed care it was simply not cost effective to work also with youth. Although no data support or refute this position, it nevertheless is a short-sighted position. The perspective of youth must be incorporated; as Petr (1992) noted, adultcentrism must be overcome if we are to achieve the goal of keeping children with serious emotional disorders in family settings and in the community.

Children's mental health case management has also learned a great deal from parental caregivers. The transition from blaming parents to collaboration with them has not been easy, swift, or universal. However, as the list of parents' expectations of case managers suggests, this perspective is helpful and realistic. In fact, the expectations of parents are strikingly similar to the original CASSP principles that served as the basis for the children's mental health case management movement.

The reality is that children need a parental caregiver to help them navigate the difficult road to adulthood. From a practice point of view, taking advantage of caregiver resources requires case managers to find ways to fulfill caregiver expectations. From a policy point of view, we need to engage with parental caregivers, or the costs to society to address the needs of troubled youth is likely to be more than any community can reasonably afford. This is an exciting time in children's mental health case management. If the attention that this field has enjoyed continues, we will make great strides in including children with serious emotional disorders into the community.

# References

Boyd, L. A., Clark, H. B., & Panacek-Howell, L. (1989). Evaluating case management in systems of care for children: A pragmatic approach. In A. Algarin, R. M. Friedman, A. J. Duchnowski, K. M. Kutash, S. Silver, & M. K. Johnson (Eds.), *Children's mental health services and policy: Building a research base* (pp. 120–137). Tampa, FL: University of South Florida Research and Training Center for Children's Mental Health, Florida Mental Health Institute.

Brown, J. (1989). Case management and services for other at-risk children. In A. Algarin, R. M. Friedman, A. J. Duchnowski, K. M. Kutash, S. Silver, & M. K. Johnson (Eds.), *Children's mental health services and policy: Building a research base* (pp. 138–141). Tampa FL: University of South Florida Research and Training Center for Children's Mental Health, Florida Mental Health Institute.

Burns, B., Gwaltney, E., & Bishop, G. K. (1995). Children's mental health case management research: Issues and direction. In B. Friesen & J. Poertner (Eds.), *From case management to service coordination for children with emotional, behavioral, or mental disorders: Building on family strengths* (pp. 353–372). Baltimore, MD: Paul H. Brookes.

Donner R., Huff, B., Gentry, M., McKinney, D., Duncan, J. Thompson, S., & Silver, P. (1995). Accountability of case management for children with emotional problems. Parent perspectives. In B. Friesen & J. Poertner (Eds.), *From case management to service coordination for children with emotional, behavioral, or mental disorders: Building on family strengths* (pp. 27–36). Baltimore, MD: Paul H. Brookes.

Early, T. J., & Poertner, J. (1993). Families with children with emotional disorders: A review of the literature. *Social work, 38,* 743–764.

Early, T. J., & Poertner, J. (1995). Mental health case management with children with emotional disorders and their families. In B. Friesen & J. Poertner (Eds.), *From case management to service coordination for children with emotional, behavioral, or mental disorders: Building on family strengths* (pp. 37–59). Baltimore, MD: Paul H. Brookes.

Fox, H., & Wicks, L. (1995). Financing care coordination services for children and adolescents with severe emotional disorders under Medicaid. In B. Friesen & J. Poertner (Eds.), *From case management to service coordination for children with emotional, behavioral, or mental disorders: Building on family strengths* (pp. 95–131). Baltimore, MD: Paul H. Brookes.

Friesen, B. J. (1993). Overview: Advances in child mental health. In H. C. Johnson (Ed.), *Child mental health in the 1990s.* Washington, DC: U.S. Department of Health and Human Services.

Friesen, B., & Briggs, H. (1995). The organization and structure of case management services. Implications for service quality and effectiveness. In B. Friesen & J.

Poertner (Eds.), *From case management to service coordination for children with emotional, behavioral, or mental disorders: Building on family strengths* (pp. 63–94). Baltimore, MD: Paul H. Brookes.

Friesen, B., & Poertner, J. (Eds.). (1995). *From case management to service coordination for children with emotional, behavioral, or mental disorders: Building on family strengths.* Baltimore, MD: Paul H. Brookes.

Goetz, K. (1994). Kaleidoscope: Chicago's pioneer in wrap-around services. In *Report: Building bridges: Supporting families across service systems, 13*(1–2), 20–21.

Jacobs, D. F. (1995). States' policy response to the need for case management. In B. Friesen & J. Poertner (Eds.), *From case management to service coordination for children with emotional, behavioral, or mental disorders: Building on family strengths* (pp. 373–385). Baltimore, MD: Paul H. Brookes.

Knitzer, J. (1982) *Unclaimed children.* Washington, DC: Childrens Defense Fund.

Petr, C. G. (1992). Adultcentrism in practice with children. *Families in Society, 73,* 408–415.

Poertner, J., & Friesen, B. (1995). Service coordination in children's mental health: A vision for the future. In B. Friesen & J. Poertner (Eds.), *From case management to service coordination for children with emotional, behavioral, or mental disorders: Building on family strengths* (pp. 387–400). Baltimore, MD: Paul H. Brookes.

Poertner, J., & Ronnau, J. (1989). The family advocacy case management model: An innovative approach to meeting the needs of families caring for youth with emotional disabilities. In A. Algarin, R. M. Friedman, A. J. Duchnowski, K. M. Kutash, S. Silver, & M. K. Johnson (Eds.), *Children's mental health services and policy: Building a research base* (pp. 142–150). Tampa FL: University of South Florida Research and Training Center for Children's Mental Health, Florida Mental Health Institute.

Poertner, J., & Ronnau, J. (1992). A strengths approach to children with emotional disabilities. In D. Saleebey (Ed.), *The strengths perspective in social work practice* (pp. 111–121). New York: Longman.

Roberts, C., & Poertner, J. (1995). Creating and maintaining support and structure for case managers. Issues in case management supervision. In B. Friesen & J. Poertner (Eds.), *From case management to service coordination for children with emotional, behavioral, or mental disorders: Building on family strengths* (pp. 257–274). Baltimore, MD: Paul H. Brookes.

Robinson, G. K., & Toff-Bergman, G. (1990). *Choices in case management: Current knowledge and practice for mental health programs.* Washington DC: Mental Health Policy Resource Center.

Ronnau, J., & Poertner, J. (1993). Identification and use of strengths: A family system approach. *Children Today, 22,* 20–23.

# Chapter | 6

## Beyond the Twenty-Eighth Day: Case Management in Alcohol and Drug Treatment

*W. Patrick Sullivan*

Recent trends in the treatment of alcohol and drug problems reflect a host of historical forces that have had an impact on the health care field. Alcoholism and drug abuse are no longer perceived as problems faced solely by adult males but as major health concerns of women and children as well. Furthermore, these problems are not restricted to a small segment of society but cut across class lines and directly and indirectly affect the lives of millions of individuals. These phenomena, in conjunction with stronger legal consequences for problematic usage, have increased demands on the treatment system and, concomitantly, escalated the costs to society. To illustrate, Wilson (1993) reported that between 1980 and 1986 admissions to private psychiatric hospitals for the treatment of substance abuse increased by 64%, fueled in part by a growing market for services for adolescents. Additionally, Pacione and Jaskula (1994) noted that the costs for substance-abuse treatment rose by 27% between 1987 and 1988, with an additional 18% increase by 1989.

These skyrocketing costs come at a time of greater demands for accountability in the behavioral health field. The explosion of managed care firms vying for market share and the adoption of the managed care paradigm in the public sector reflect a growing desire to curb costs while providing quality care (Broskowski & Eaddy, 1994). It is no surprise that the face of substance-abuse treatment is also changing in a manner consistent with these social trends.

Given the pressures on the addictions field to hold down costs yet produce desired outcomes, the expansion of case management practice in treatment settings is not surprising. Austin (1990) noted that case management is intuitively appealing in those fields of practice where the target problems are complex and psychosocial in nature. When focusing on community-based care, the use of natural resources, and least restrictive alternatives to address consumer needs, case management holds promise as a service mechanism that can also reduce expenditures (Ridgely & Willenbring, 1992).

This chapter begins by outlining a rationale for the expansion of case management services in alcohol and drug treatment and reviews historical trends that predate the emergence of this specialty service. This is followed by an examination of specific issues that must be addressed when implementing case management systems, including necessary funding mechanisms and intraorganizational supports and behaviors needed to sustain the effort. Finally, outcome evaluations of case management in the addictions field are summarized, followed by focused discussions on specific practice issues, including cultural competence, and potential ethical conflicts that arise in applied settings.

## The Case for Case Management

While case management has proliferated in fields of practice such as mental health and aging, this specialty service has been less prominent in alcohol and drug treatment (Rapp, Siegal, & Fisher, 1992). Various factors account for this disparity, one of which may be the illness/medical paradigm that has characterized the alcohol/drug treatment field. Societal acceptance of alcoholism and drug dependence as a condition worthy of social action has been augmented by the portrayal of these conditions as illnesses. Accordingly, any discussion of the environmental and extrabiological imprint on the course and maintenance of abuse behavior is often viewed with skepticism and even scorn. Frans (1994) suggests that "competing views [between the disease and behavioral models] are generally characterized as irresponsible, and their sponsors summarily dismissed as dangerously uninformed by disease view proponents or accused of being in 'denial' themselves" (p. 71).

Yet, objective review of evaluation studies of alcohol and drug treatment, particularly when focused narrowly on abstinence as the criterion for success, is cause for concern. Although it can certainly be argued that program success is directly associated with the chronicity of substance abuse, in an era of fiscal restraint the efficacy of treatment must be demonstrated. How might case management improve treatment outcome?

Sullivan, Wolk, and Hartmann (1992) reviewed a range of factors reported to influence the resiliency of treatment and suggested that explanatory models of dependency and recovery should adopt a psychosocial perspective. Indeed, various indicators of social stability appear to support or erode the long-term impact of treatment. These factors include stability and cohesion in personal relationships, residential tenure, and employment. Additional factors that influence adjustment include interpersonal and environmental stress as well as individual competence and problem-solving capabilities. Therefore, the presence or absence of stressful and chaotic life situations, the relative availability of social support, and the capacity effectively to negotiate life challenges and use positive coping skills are toggles that can buffer or trigger drug and alcohol use and influence the abuse career.

Cultural factors can also modify and amplify substance use and are worthy of investigation. Fine, Akabas, and Bellinger (1982) suggested that workplace environments are critical to understanding substance use and abuse of an individual and that interventions must be designed to consider this important factor. Increases in substance abuse among women and adolescents and the exceedingly high rate of dependence among gay and lesbian individuals must also be understood from a cultural context.

It would be foolish to suggest that case managers can have a dramatic impact on sexism and racism and single-handedly alter the culture of complex organizations. In fact, case management interventions are rarely designed to affect major system change, and case managers rarely wield the power necessary to alter institutional arrangements (Austin, 1990; Moore, 1992). Ridgely and Willenbring (1992) recognize the potential frustration of case managers, given that they are "assigned the impossible task of making organizations behave differently toward their clients or making and implementing rational care plans within irrational systems of care" (p. 22).

Nonetheless, most models of case management reflect a holistic perspective by examining the "goodness of fit" between people and their situations. Such inquiry is also geared to uncover client and environmental strengths and deficits. Therefore, case managers' natural inclination is to assess the range of dynamics that support problematic as well as healthy behaviors and to intervene accordingly. Case managers in substance-abuse treatment view illness and recovery through a wider lens and work toward a diverse range of goals in collaboration with consumers. The strengths model of case management reflects this expansive view of treatment and desired outcomes (Rapp et al., 1992; Sullivan et al., 1992). From this perspective, "case management is a creative and collaborative process involving skills in assessment, counseling, teaching, modeling, and advocacy that aims to enhance the social functioning of clients" (Sullivan et al., 1992, p. 198).

On first blush, focus on enhanced social functioning does not appear to depart from traditional models of care. However, case managers in substance-abuse treatment may offer services that do not focus directly on the abuse behavior but instead attend to those areas of social functioning described above as contributing to or maintaining dependency. It is equally important to note that efforts to help consumers with their problems in living while in treatment are viewed by some professionals as an example of professional enabling, which highlights a potential source of resistance to case management in the substance-abuse field. It will be argued later in this chapter that the holistic focus embodied in case management is particularly suited to addressing the needs of diverse populations that have been historically underserved by treatment programs.

## *Historical and Current Trends in Case Management*

As noted earlier, case management is a relatively recent addition to the array of services commonly offered in drug and alcohol treatment programs. It would be an oversight, however, not to recognize historical trends within the treatment industry that predate the current use of case management as a distinct specialty service.

Willenbring (1994) reflected on the range of providers who have historically provided services now identified as case management functions. Included in this group are persons who have worked in inner-city missions, including street workers and the clergy. These individuals play a pivotal role in linking individuals with support services and basic resources. Professionals in the criminal-justice system, primarily probation and parole officers, have also served as case managers even while simply providing triage functions.

Specialized treatment services that prefigured case management included early employee assistance programs (EAPs) and industrial social work programs. In these programs, poor work performance was often identified initially as a problem, but sensitive employers recognized that substance abuse was often a cause of such problems. Given the prevalence of alcohol and drug problems in the workplace, along with other distracting personal issues, EAPs became an institutionalized feature in many organizations. Early identification and intervention is viewed as a method to reduce absenteeism, increase productivity, and retrain valuable employees (see Trice & Schonbrunn, 1981).

The EAP model has been subjected to criticism for focusing too narrowly on the pathological behavior of workers without simultaneously focusing on the contribution of the host organization to employees' difficulties (Balgopal, 1989). The focus on workplace culture, spearheaded by psychologists, social workers, and management theorists, has resulted in a wide range of human service interventions and the use of job sites as important laboratories for change. For example, organizational development interventions can be seen as a precursor to total-quality-management and job-enrichment programs. These trends also affected the evolution of EAPs. To illustrate, Ford and Ford (1986) offered a systems approach to EAPs, arguing that a nonlinear model underscores the need to consider individual behavior as one component within a network of interrelationships that extend into space and time. They note that

> to consider an employee's alcoholism (although this may be the key primary focus) may be to neglect family dynamics, financial entanglements, recent stressors, or health lifestyle—all of which may require planned intervention over time to establish adaptive functioning (p. 42).

This perspective lays the groundwork for an enriched EAP model that encompasses case management functions, including outreach work, individually tailored goal setting, and the use of an expanded range of interventions to achieve a wider array of outcomes.

## *Implementing Case Management in Addictions Programs*

Case management has proliferated rapidly in the human services. Indeed, case management is so widely practiced in multiple service settings that the term no longer has inherent meaning. The degree to which case managers provide direct service and control access to services and even the status they enjoy vary greatly from setting to setting. Given the relative infancy of case management in addictions services, history indicates that case managers will initially be forced to fight for status and resources within organizations. This tendency is exacerbated when case management interventions are at variance with the standard operating principles and philosophy of host agencies. The early experience of Missouri's Comprehensive Substance Abuse Treatment and Rehabilitation (C-STAR) program is used throughout this section as a basis for illustration.

Despite conceptual and operational confusion surrounding case management in general, fundamental agreement exists with regard to the key functions of case management. These core functions are usually described as assessment, care planning, linking or brokering, monitoring or follow-along, and advocacy. These standard case management roles have surfaced in the addictions field as well. These roles are emphasized differently in a range of case management models across various fields of practice.

Broker models of case management, for example, view the professional as the human link between the consumer and the overall system of care. Brokering functions have been commonly employed in some settings that serve persons with alcohol and drug problems. The adoption of broker models requires little alteration in organizational culture or operations, particularly when the case manager serves as a link between the host organization and standard providers such as vocational rehabilitation offices or the public welfare system.

Clinical models of case management, in contrast, accent the therapeutic relationship. Adoption of this model may not require additional professional staff if case management practice simply mirrors traditional counseling approaches. However, if clinical case management links standard therapeutic roles with new helping activities, such as outreach and resource acquisition, then significant organizational alterations are required. For example, outreach work, by nature, does not allow the establishment of back-to-back one-hour appointments throughout the day and requires different patterns of communication and supervision.

The above discussion does not provide an exhaustive look at case management models but merely introduces how case managers' functions are shaped by the overall service delivery system or, conversely, how case management can modify organizations (Moore, 1992; Sullivan, Hartmann, Dillon, & Wolk, 1994). Failure to anticipate and plan for these issues can doom the viability of a case management system from the outset. Therefore, the explicit and implicit assumptions of case management models must be examined to analyze its relative fit within a host organization and to ascertain the kinds of revisions in procedure and culture that are needed.

Ridgely and Willenbring (1992) examined the relationship between the functions of case management, or what case managers do, and operational features of systems that influence how case managers perform their role. Among the important operational features that distinguish the delivery of case management are duration of services, intensity of contact, focus of service, availability of service, site of the intervention, consumer direction, professional training, authority, and team structure.

To demonstrate the use of this schema, the strengths model of case management will be used as an illustration. The strengths model, which was developed for work with the severely and persistently mentally ill, has recently been introduced in addiction services. The principles that undergird the model, as well as guidelines for the actual behaviors required of case managers, have been clearly articulated. Matching the discriminators offered by Ridgely and Willenbring (1992), the strengths model is designed as a long-term helping process featuring intensive contact (at least weekly) between the case manager and consumer; is customer driven; is focused on resource acquisition, with normalization as the overarching goal; and employs an assertive outreach approach. By definition the strengths model of case management requires that case loads remain light and that the case manager be an equal partner in a multidisciplinary team. This advanced generalist does not necessarily have to be university trained, although such is the norm, and in most applications an individual as opposed to a team approach is employed (Rapp et al., 1992; Sullivan et al., 1992).

An early effort to examine the implementation of the strengths model of case management in alcohol- and drug-treatment programs revealed that the model was compromised in significant ways (Sullivan et al., 1994). For example, outreach services and resource acquisition activities, cornerstones of the strengths approach, were performed less frequently than was anticipated. Timney and Graham (1989), drawing from a sample of case managers serving alcohol- and drug-treatment programs in Ontario, Canada, reported similar findings. They stated that *in vivo* helping was less common than on-site visits and that activities focused on providing practical help (employment issues, etc.) were far less common than counseling-related interventions.

Research in the area of technology transfer and the diffusion of innovations indicates that deviations from an original model, or reinventions, can be anticipated in early phases of development. It is critical to understand the forces that modify an innovation to discern how to make the product better or to ensure greater fidelity to the original design. Accordingly, studies that report significant gaps between the ideal and actual behaviors of case managers demand close attention.

Staffing pattern is a preliminary issue requiring careful consideration, including the required credentials and experiences of case managers and case management supervisors. For example, should case managers be required to hold a college degree or is personal life experience equally important? Raiff and Shore provided a simple schema that can be used to decipher background and preparation necessary for staff who are given case management responsibilities. When the framers of the Missouri C-STAR program promoted the expansion of case management services (referred to as community support), it was decided that workers should hold a bachelor's degree, preferably in social work. It was assumed that this cadre of helpers should be well-trained in the area of holistic assessments and treatment planning as well as unfettered by a paradigm that might view case management activities as superfluous. Case managers were asked to perform functions in community settings that required a high level of professional skills. A minimalist model of case management that primarily involves basic brokering activities requires less stringent educational requirements. Although arguments that support the need for experience over educational background can certainly be presented, national trends emphasize the importance of professional credentials and licenses in addictions programming, particularly as the field moves toward managed care.

The experience of the C-STAR program in Missouri, although varying by site, revealed potential for significant friction between veteran staff members who entered the addictions field on the basis of their personal experience and newly employed college-educated staff. Veteran staff appeared to view case management skeptically and some case managers clearly were not well-versed in addictions practice, particularly in their understanding of the dynamics of manipulation and denial.

In this context, the performance of the case management supervisor or multidisciplinary team leader is critical to the success of the program. In the early phase of the C-STAR program, it appeared that case management supervisors occupied their positions because of their overall clinical ability, not because of their understanding of the emerging community-support role. This clinical knowledge was even at variance with the assumptions embodied in the strengths model, which was the model used by case managers. Not surprisingly, in case conferences, the perspectives of the case managers rarely held sway, and the final treatment plan seldom reflected the interventions and goals of case management. In this environment, outreach activities, as well as interventions that directly targeted the problems in living faced by consumers, were commonly undervalued and underused.

To illustrate the issues outlined above, consider the fact that case managers often help consumers obtain jobs and secure stable housing. Although such efforts fit well under case management functions, addictions counselors may view these efforts as premature and as an example of professional enabling. Thus, the case manager striving to ensure that basic needs are met may be working at odds with a treatment staff who feel strongly that a client must "hit bottom" before he or she can benefit from treatment. If the organization or treatment team is not supportive of case management, it is unlikely that case managers will continue to provide these unappreciated services. Over time these same professionals tend to drift away from case management perspectives and toward the clinical orientation (Sullivan, 1990).

These forces place the organization on the horns of a dilemma. One response is to create distance between case management and traditional clinical activities. Here, supervisors who are familiar with case management may be specifically recruited and enlisted to create independent, autonomously operating teams. Unfortunately, this isolationist approach rarely embodies the holistic focus needed to assist the recovery process or affect change in the organizational culture. The continuous-treatment-team model, whereby professionals represent a range of disciplines including medicine/psychiatry, nursing, social work, vocational rehabilitation, recreation, and case management, can be effectively employed. This approach requires agreement on a broad set of goals (beyond abstinence) and on a range of interventions to accomplish them. Here, the team leader must orient and reorient members to the basic philosophy of community-based care. It is also likely that a great deal of anxiety and tension will surface in team meetings, requiring sensitive management by the supervisor. Some existing staff members may be unable to adapt to the new mission, and the organization should be prepared to receive resignations (Raiff & Shore, 1993; Sullivan et al., 1994). This factor underscores the importance of the recruitment process and the need to be clear about the desired characteristics of new hires.

The most effective treatment programs are likely to be those that can blend characteristics of traditional treatment programs with the psychosocial methods embraced by case managers. Here, case management is viewed as a treatment enhancement, not a stand-alone intervention (Siegal, Rapp, Kelliher, Fisher, Wagner, & Cole, 1995). Siegal and associates developed an innovative project in which strengths-based case management was introduced in a Department of Veterans Affairs medical center addictions program that relied on more traditional treatment methods. A key ingredient to the success of this effort was the ability to forge operational agreements between the substance-abuse counselors and case managers.

Regardless of whether individual or team models of case management are adopted, case loads must remain light and manageable if services are to be effective, especially when the program is committed to a model based on individualized treatment planning, outreach, and resource acquisition. Ashery (1994) has reviewed a series of reports and suggested that effective case management programs feature a 1 to 15 staff–client ratio. Supervisors must pay close attention to the mix of consumers that a team or individual is asked to carry. When individuals are new to treatment, the threat of relapse and associated problems in living is likely to be high. Likewise, consumers with coexisting psychiatric disorders present significant challenges to staff. A supervisor should ensure that these clients are interspersed with those who appear to be in a period of relative stability and who require less intense supervision. Unfortunately, in applied settings it appears that maintaining an optimum case-load mix is difficult (Ashery, 1994). Failure to attend to the composition of a team or individual case load will result in high levels of professional burnout and turnover.

This discussion should serve as a caveat for those who view the addition of case management as a relatively simple and positive supplement to existing addiction services. Using a framework developed by Patti (1974), it is clear that the introduction of case management in addictions programs is likely to engender resistance. First, system-wide change affects the daily work of the organization and requires at least some reallocation of institutional resources (including power). Everything from billing procedures, staffing patterns, and how case reviews are conducted must be modified if the program is to be efficiently executed. Second, adding case management to an existing mix of services is likely to transform the mission and goals of the program. The expanded focus on problems in living, reflected by the establishment of program goals in the area of vocational activity, recreation, and housing, moves services beyond abstinence as the sole criterion for success.

If case management is to gain more than a toehold in the addictions field, financial incentives must be in place to support it. One sure way to revolutionize the human service landscape is to revamp funding streams and mechanisms. Wilson (1993) reflects that when private insurance companies began paying for 28 days of inpatient treatment in the early 1970s, this method of care became a "clinical commandment." Not surprisingly, the prevailing intervention paradigm became "remove from society, repair the problem, and replace in society" (p. 100). If funding streams shaped a substance-abuse treatment system anchored by the 28-day inpatient model, it may well be that the current fiscal climate is providing the impetus for the emergence of case management and community-based care. The expansion of managed-care organizations, behavioral health-care carve-outs and reduced dedicated federal and state budgets reflect efforts to hold down costs in the human services. One simple way to reduce costs, particularly under capitated and prospective-payment models, is to substitute less expensive community-based care for inpatient and other expensive forms of treatment. Intensive outpatient services, for example, are increasingly recognized as a viable alternative to inpatient care.

The C-STAR program illustrates how a state division of alcohol and drug abuse reshaped the provider community. This program developed a unique system to ascertain the intensity of services needed by consumers. Explicit in this concept is the notion that intensive outpatient services can be provided in a manner that simulates the level of structure offered in inpatient settings. Community support services (case management) are a centerpiece of this effort. It was also ascertained that many of the consumers served, particularly mothers with children, were Medicaid eligible. A variety of Medicaid waiver programs, such as the Medicaid Rehabilitation Option (MRO), can be used specifically to reimburse most aspects of case management services.

This effort alone has resulted in unforeseen growth in the C-STAR program (Leslie Jordan, personal communication, April 20, 1995).

Recent developments in Indiana (including use of MRO) are also likely to result in the expansion of case management services. In past years, a plethora of providers have been funded, many of whom offer one discrete specialty service. In the future, contracts will be awarded only to those organizations or networks that offer a full continuum of care. Case management is one service included in this continuum.

How case managers will perform in the field of addictions will become clear only as the role is more universally embraced. Existing case management models merge clinical concerns with the fiscal realities that confront providers. In some settings, case managers are afforded major fiscal and clinical responsibility by exercising control over the purchase of services needed by the individual client. In this model, referred to by Austin (1990) as the service manager role, case managers serve as gatekeepers to various resources and exercise significant leverage through their purchasing power. Although this model of case management is clearly ascending in the for-profit behavioral health care field, in nonprofit and public settings case managers enjoy far less power.

Even in those settings where case managers do not have direct purchasing power, they still remain a vital element in an evolving addictions-treatment arena shaped by the new realities of managed care. When operating in a pure capitation model or when blended funding and prospective payment place providers in an at-risk or shared-risk environment, case management is a crucial service. In this model, the provider must manage the total pool of funds available from public and private sources, moving the system away from a fee-for-service reimbursement pattern. Here the traditional functions offered by case managers, including *in-vivo* support, close monitoring and follow-up, and service-brokering activities, become invaluable to the long-term health of the managed-care provider. Relapse prevention, extensive aftercare, and long-term care models of addictions treatment will join case management as dominant themes in the next decade. As managed care continues to expand in the behavioral health field and with the increased use of Medicaid superwaivers and carve-out programs, case management will become a prominent specialty in alcohol and drug treatment.

## *The Impact of Case Management*

Explicating the functions and assumptions of a case management model and the characteristics of the system in which a case manager functions is a critical first step in ascertaining the fidelity of implementation. It is necessary to explore these issues in order accurately to evaluate the outcome of services. Unfortunately, case management services in alcohol and drug treatment are at a nascent stage, and clear discussions of the actual behaviors of case managers in applied settings are lacking.

Chamberlain and Rapp (1991), in their review of a decade of evaluation studies of case management in mental health, found few outcome data, despite the popularity of this intervention. It's hardly surprising, given the fact that this innovation in alcohol and drug treatment is relatively new, that few hard data exist to support its use (Ashery, 1994). By definition, focus on overall quality of life enlarges the set of outcome indicators that can be used to assess the efficacy of this intervention. Rhodes and Johnson (1994) argued that when sobriety is viewed as the only criterion for success, an either–or dichotomy may lead a person to experience failure with each relapse. In contrast, psychosocial models "offer the possibility of growth from a continuum from disease to wellness and, therefore, recognize incremental growth" (p. 151). Additionally, case management's greatest promise in the addiction field may lie in the area of treatment retention and relapse prevention after an individual has completed a traditional treatment program.

Certainly, the beneficial effect of treatment retention cuts across all population groups and has been highlighted as a critical factor in improved treatment outcomes (Hartmann, Wolk, & Sullivan, 1993; Siegal, Rapp, Fisher, Cole, & Wagner, 1993). Although treatment retention may reflect the readiness of people to accept help, preliminary evidence suggests that case management services appear to have a positive impact on treatment-retention rates with particularly difficult groups, including methadone-maintenance clients and intravenous drug users (Dennis, Karuntzos, & Rachal, 1992; Rapp, Siegal, Fisher, Wagner, Kelliher & Bechtolt, 1993). Siegal and associates (1995) have had promising preliminary results employing a strengths-based case management model in conjunction with traditional services offered at a veteran's treatment program. Like most strengths models, this project uses a systematic goal-setting method focused on key life domains. They report that more than two-thirds of the objectives established by participants were completed, a finding consistent with the use of this method with consumers of mental health services.

Those adults and children with dual problems of mental illness and addictions are difficult to serve. Case management services, however, have been successfully employed with these populations as well. Evans and Dollard (1992) described an intensive case management program for emotionally disturbed children, many of whom (22%) had chemical-use problems. Although no comparison group was available, results indicated that case-managed youth had reduced incidents and days of care in a psychiatric institution postintervention.

Sullivan and Maloney (1992) described an innovative program for adults facing substance abuse and mental illness that offered case management as a primary service. They reported that consumers expressed generally high levels of satisfaction with services and that tangible help was offered in the areas of housing, vocational needs, medical assistance, and interpersonal relationships as well as with the target problems. However, a subgroup of the clients studied appears to gain no benefit from case management, which suggests that we need to learn how to match consumers with service packages. Dennis and associates (1992) studied a cohort of intravenous drug users and found that attention to vocational concerns of clients was one of the best predictors of reduced intravenous drug use by consumers. Unfortunately, these same researchers discovered that counselors rarely made referrals outside the host agency to address such concerns, suggesting again the vital role of case managers. Finally, Bokos, Mejta, Mickenberg, and Monks (1992) indicated that case managers who had some control over the use of service dollars were able to expedite the consumers' entrance to treatment. The ability to help clients receive the care needed is consistent with broker models of case management and can be considered a reasonable impact measure.

Case management demonstration projects are currently being offered to homeless individuals, those who are HIV-positive, and young mothers who face chemical addictions. Over the next several years the data generated from such projects will be useful for ascertaining the usefulness of case management and community-care models. However, at this point it can only be suggested that case management shows great potential to strengthen addictions programs—a promise with only a smattering of empirical support.

## *Future Directions in Case Management and Addictions Practice*

Other factors, beyond fiscal incentives, have provided the impetus for increased focus on community-based care in alcohol and drug treatment. Although it is popular in some circles to refer to case management as old-fashioned case work, this analogy is far too simplistic. Early alcohol and drug treatment was geared toward white males. Persons entering treatment today, however, reflect the diversity of the treatment population, calling into question the one-size-fits-all approach of many helping programs. Furthermore, various particularly nettlesome problems are now routinely seen in community settings. For example, case managers must deal with coexisting disorders such as severe mental illness and addictions or addicted HIV-positive consumers. A new generation of popular drugs requires differential treatment. Many consumers are involved with several different human services, including the legal system. Such complexity requires a specialized helper who is conversant in clinical and environmental interventions, systems access, and advocacy.

Raiff and Shore (1993) noted that culturally competent practice is one hallmark of an advanced case management practice system. Likewise, addictions services have matured alongside a greater sensitivity to the needs of diverse populations who receive or should receive treatment services. Case management services offered in such settings should be subjected to the same level of scrutiny.

The studies presented above suggest that the problems-in-living focus of case management has appeal to this new cadre of individuals presenting for treatment. Specifically, a treatment model based on psychosocial principles may be particularly well-suited for nontraditional treatment populations. For example, Beckman (1984) argued that to serve women adequately in treatment programs we must first get them to treatment, persuade them to stay there, and offer effective gender-sensitive programming. Various barriers must be overcome to get women to enter and remain in treatment, not the least being concerns about child care and fear of losing custody of children. Moreover, other problems of living caused by poverty present significant impediments to treatment as well. Case management services focus on problems and goals in living and thus may offer consumers the tangible help they need to stay in treatment. Systematic goal-setting and resource-acquisition activities, a common method of teaching problem-solving skills, are particularly beneficial to women in treatment (Marr & Fairchild, 1993). Even leisure activities, often viewed as a trivial focus of case management, have been identified as an important component of recovery (McCracken, 1991).

Gomberg (1982) argued that substance abuse among women cannot be adequately understood without recognizing the effects of sexism. Likewise, chemical dependence in the gay and lesbian population has roots in social stigma, oppression, and isolation (Saunders & Valente, 1987). Such themes also affect persons of color who enter treatment programs or go unserved.

Knowledge that real or perceived barriers to treatment exist for many specialized populations requires us to devote serious attention to case-finding and case-coordination efforts. Inaccurate statistics on the prevalence of substance abuse among these populations negatively affect funding and the development of services. Outreach case managers, particularly those with a mandate to serve on the street, are in a prime position to make contact with those who need services. Recovered counselors with similar life experiences can be extremely useful in working with these populations. Case managers in this environment must be well versed in both social networks and street culture.

The assessment process ideally establishes the parameters of consumers' unique needs and thus is the critical first step in establishing the type and intensity of services that are needed. In the managed-care environment, assessment must establish risk factors and determine treatment needs, especially in the capitation model. It is important, however, that the assessment process remain sensitive to the real pressures faced by diverse populations and assess consumer strengths as well as deficits (Rapp et al., 1992; Sullivan et al., 1992). Many assessment methods, particularly those that focus narrowly on deficits and pathology, dwell so heavily on past difficulties that consumers may become discouraged or even resistant to treatment. In contrast, those assessments that also focus on consumer accomplishments, strengths, and aspirations can have a positive impact on self-esteem and enhance motivation for recovery (Siegal et al., 1995).

Freeman and Landesman (1992) offer a unique assessment tool that builds upon the cultural ecomap. This assessment tool allows the practitioner to uncover the sources of empowerment and powerlessness while exploring individuals' experience of their immediate culture and interracial world. Such assessment methods capture the realities of minority group members who must develop bicultural perspectives to survive and thrive. The forces of oppression and discrimination must be considered in the assessment process. This requires critical evaluation of the tools of assessment, including the verbal interchange between consumer and helper, and attention to the pace and temporality of the process.

Consumers' history with professional helpers and other authorities, tension created by racial dynamics between consumer and helper, and the natural suspicions generated by substance usage must be considered in the engagement process. Outreach workers who work with homeless individuals report spending weeks and even months building a simple relationship. Even after case managers have developed a bond with consumers, they should anticipate that the consumer will continue to test the relationship and frequently retreat from the treatment process (Raiff & Shore, 1993). This reality alone signals the need for community-based helping that uses case management as a key service.

Although much of the preceding discussion focuses on street work, case managers must consider a host of other issues when providing in-home services. Specifically, case managers must be cognizant of the traditions and customs of consumers. For example, definitions of family must be clearly ascertained in situations in which fictive kin and family friends are viewed as key members in the support network. Goddard (1993) found that social organization in the traditional African American community suggests that social relatives are nearly indistinguishable from biological family. Furthermore, it's important to recognize that in these cultures the total community is responsible for the individual. Case managers must become familiar with and knowledgeable about these mores. For example, case managers may view families that turn to indigenous healers or that use nonmedical remedies to treat problems as being in denial or lacking in education. It is more beneficial to view such behaviors as signs of strength, not pathology. In many cultural traditions spirituality is extremely important. Pinkett (1993) notes that substance abuse in the African American community can be viewed as "spiritual manifestations or misguided attempts at spiritual expression" (p. 80). The traditional church and clergy in such communities are a potential source of strength and support.

Given the powerful forces at play in the lives of diverse populations, the realities of poverty and feelings of powerlessness and hopelessness must be confronted daily by case managers. Case managers who toil on the streets every day understand that clients' basic needs must be met first. Lengthy assessment processes and concern with intrapersonal dynamics must give way to the needs for food, shelter, and safety. If these issues are adequately addressed, the case-planning process can be empowering. The strengths model, for example, highlights the importance of consumer-directed treatment. The goal-planning process is very effective in work with women. Such problem solving models life skills that consumers can adapt to their daily life. Many women, gays, lesbians, and people of color routinely use substances as a way to overcome their feelings of powerlessness and confusion and as a way to bring order to their lives. The goal-planning process in case management offers consumers the opportunity to bring order and rational actions into their lives. Indeed, the entire case management process models a proactive and rational approach toward dealing with life struggles and personal goals (Roach, 1993).

Finally, advocacy has been identified as a core function in most case management models. However, unless case managers are given genuine power, they have little ability to serve as effective advocates. This is particularly true when case managers are asked to be systems-level as well as client advocates. When case managers must confront administrative barriers in their own organizations, they obviously face severe conflicts. Moreover, if case managers are viewed as entry-level workers, they will be ineffective in their efforts to advocate on behalf of clients (Willenbring, 1994). Case managers' ability to advocate for clients at the policy and political levels is vital. In this light, Ashery (1994) promotes the concept of community advocacy, recognizing the barriers case managers face in compensating for system-wide problems. Community advocacy requires the establishment of collaborative relationships between the network of addictions providers and policymakers in order to identify the gaps between consumer needs and available services and to explore creative ways to improve the existing system.

A host of potential ethical issues must be considered when case management is introduced into substance-abuse treatment. Perhaps no issue requires greater scrutiny than the danger of running headlong to embrace a service-delivery mechanism that has yet been proven effective. Ashery (1994), on a somber note, reflects that "case management has had only limited success, has not lived up to its promises, and has not yet been proven to contain costs" (p. 179). The studies presented above, however, suggest some basis for guarded optimism.

Perhaps more than in any other field in which case management is practiced, several key ethical issues must be confronted with regard to case management in the addictions field. Specifically, case managers in the addictions field routinely encounter individuals who engage in illegal activity. Case managers may even witness this behavior and, with team members, struggle to deal with the tension between treatment issues and responsibility to the larger society. This is especially troubling when case managers work to help consumers receive goods and services that can be sold to satisfy their addictions or when they help to place clients in jobs or volunteer positions in which their poor performance could negatively affect others. How do case managers work to help consumers obtain housing and jobs while negotiating the requirements of confidentiality? More discussions on these topics will surface as the field matures.

Beyond these issues, various clinical concerns, including treatment matching and the timing of intervention, must be confronted. Sullivan and Maloney (1992) reported that a subset of consumers appear to receive no treatment benefit from case management. In a time of fiscal constraint, scarce resources must be used wisely. The timing of case management is also a key consideration. Should case management occur simultaneously with traditional interventions or should a period of stability be demonstrated before services begin? One school of thought suggests that problems in living and substance use operate synergistically and that improvements or decrements in either area affect the other. On the other hand, it is quite possible that case managers may buffer the wide-ranging impact of substance abuse by easing the problems in living consumers face. Therefore, it may be wise that consumers hit bottom, face the reality of their predicament, and gain some measure of control over their addiction before case management services are offered. Again, we need studies that explore these issues; the effectiveness of treatment programs may ultimately hinge on these focused explorations.

## Conclusions and Implications

Austin (1990) noted that case management is an incomplete intervention. In the substance-abuse field, it appears that case management can be an important adjunct to standard treatment protocols, resulting in a comprehensive treatment package that benefits consumers. Although case management may be kindred to social casework practice, the reality is that professionals are seeing people with multiple problems in a time of fiscal restraint and with less luxury to rely on institutional safety nets. Clearly, research is needed to assess the potential impact of case management; services should not proliferate on the basis of faith alone.

Important questions remain unanswered. When and to whom should case management be offered? What ethical issues must be considered in providing services to persons who continue to abuse substances? When should services be discontinued? As case management matures and becomes an integral part of the total service package in substance-abuse treatment, these questions will demand attention. The face of substance-abuse treatment is clearly changing. The emergence of the behavioral health care industry has begun to challenge old paradigms of doing business. In these heady times, it's important we continue to strive to develop services that will have the greatest possible benefits to our customers.

## References

Ashery, R. (1994). Case management for substance abusers: More issues than answers. *Journal of Case Management, 3,* 179–183.

Austin, C. (1990). Case management: Myths and realities. *Families in Society, 71,* 398–405.

Balgopal, P. (1989). Occupational social work: An expanded clinical perspective.

*Social Work, 34,* 437–442.

Beckman, L. (1984). Treatment needs of women alcoholics. *Alcoholism Treatment Quarterly, 7*(1), 101–114.

Bokos, P., Mejta, C., Mickenberg, J., & Monks, R. (1992). Case management: An alternative approach to working with intravenous drug users. In R. Ashery (Ed.), *Progress and issues in case management* (pp. 92–111). Rockville, MD: U.S. Department of Health and Human Services.

Broskowski, A., & Eaddy, M. (1994). Community mental health in a managed care environment. *Administration and Policy in Mental Health, 21,* 335–352.

Chamberlain, R., & Rapp, C. A. (1991). A decade of case management: A methodological review of outcome research. *Community Mental Health Journal, 27,* 171–188.

Dennis, M., Karuntzos, G., & Rachal, J. V. (1992). Accessing additional community resources through case management to meet the needs of methadone clients. In R. Ashery (Ed.), *Progress and issues in case management* (pp. 54–77). Rockville, MD: U.S. Department of Health and Human Services.

Evans, M., & Dollard, N. (1992). Intensive case management for youth with serious emotional disturbance and chemical abuse. In R. Ashery (Ed.), *Progress and issues in case management* (pp. 289–315). Rockville, MD: U.S. Department of Health and Human Services.

Fine, M., Akabas, S., & Bellinger, S. (1982). Cultures of drinking: A workplace perspective. *Social Work, 27,* 436–440.

Ford, J., & Ford, J. (1986). A systems theory analysis of employee assistance programs. *Employee Assistance Quarterly, 2,* 37–48.

Frans, D. (1994). Social work, social science, and the disease concept: New directions for addictions treatment. *Journal of Sociology and Social Welfare, 21,* 71–89.

Freeman, E., & Landesman, T. (1992). Differential diagnosis and the least restrictive environment. In E. Freeman (Ed.), *The addiction process: Effective social work approaches* (pp. 27–42). New York: Longman.

Goddard, L. (1993). Natural resistors in AOD abuse prevention in the African-American family. In L. Goddard (Ed.), *An African-centered model for prevention for African-American youth at high risk* (pp. 73–77). Rockville, MD: U.S. Department of Health and Human Services.

Gomberg, E. (1982). Historical and political perspective: Women and drug use. *Journal of Social Issues, 38,* 9–23.

Hartmann, D., Wolk, J., & Sullivan, W. P. (1993). Inpatient and outpatient outcomes in Missouri's alcohol and drug treatment programs. *Journal of Health and Social Policy, 5*(2), 67–76.

Marr, D., & Fairchild, T. (1993). A problem solving strategy and self-esteem in recovering chemically dependent women. *Alcoholism Treatment Quarterly, 10*(1–2), 171–186.

McCracken, J. (1991). Creativity and leisure for recovering alcoholics. *Alcoholism Treatment Quarterly, 8*(3), 83–89.

Moore, S. (1992). Case management and the integration of services: How service delivery systems shape case management. *Social Work, 37,* 418–423.

Pacione, T., & Jaskula, D. (1994). Quality chemical dependency treatment in an era of cost containment: Clinical guidelines for practitioners. *Health and Social Work, 19,* 55–62.

Patti, R. (1974), Organizational resistance and change: The view from below. *Social Services Review, 48,* 367–383.

Pinkett, J. (1993). Spirituality in the African-American community. In L. Goddard (Ed.), *An African-centered model of prevention for African-American youth at high risk* (pp. 79–86). Rockville, MD: U.S. Department of Health and Human Services.

Raiff, N. R., & Shore, B. (1993). *Advanced case management.* Newbury Park, CA: Sage Publications.

Rapp, R., Siegal, H., & Fisher, J. (1992). A strengths model of case management/ advocacy: Adapting a mental health model to practice work with persons who have substance abuse problems. In R. Ashery (Ed.), *Progress and issues in case management* (pp. 79–91). Rockville, MD: U.S. Department of Health and Human Services.

Rapp, R., Siegal, H., Fisher, J., Wagner, J., Kelliher, C., & Bechtolt, J. (1993, November–December). A strengths-based approach to enhance treatment compliance. *Addiction and Recovery, 13*(6), 22–25.

Rhodes, R., & Johnson, A. (1994). Women and alcoholism: A psychosocial approach. *Affilia, 9,* 145–156.

Ridgely, M. S., & Willenbring, M. (1992). Application of case management to drug abuse treatment: Overview of models and research issues. In R. Ashery (Ed.), *Progress and issues in case management* (pp. 12–33). Rockville, MD: U.S. Department of Health and Human Services.

Roach, J. (1993). Clinical case management with severely mentally ill adults. In M. Harris & H. Bergman (Eds.), *Case management for mentally ill patients* (pp. 17–40). Langhorne, PA: Harwood Academic Press.

Saunders, J., & Valente, J. M. (1987). Suicide risk among gay men and lesbians: A review. *Death Studies, 11,* 1–23.

Siegal, H., Rapp, R., Fisher, J., Cole, P., & Wagner J. (1993). Treatment dropouts and noncompliers: Two persistent problems and a programmatic remedy. In J. Inciardi, F. Timms, & B. Fletcher (Eds.), *Innovative approaches in the treatment of drug abuse* (pp. 109–122). Westport, CT: Greenwood Press.

Siegal, H., Rapp, R., Kelliher, C., Fisher, J., Wagner, J., & Cole, P. (1995). The strengths perspective of case management: A promising inpatient substance abuse treatment enhancement. *Journal of Psychoactive Drugs, 27,* 67–72.

Sullivan, W. P. (1990). Becoming a case manager: Implications for social work educators. *Journal of Teaching in Social Work, 4,* 159–172.

Sullivan, W. P., Hartmann, D., Dillon, D., & Wolk, J. (1994). Implementing case management in alcohol and drug treatment. *Families in Society, 75,* 67–73.

Sullivan, W. P., & Maloney, P. (1992). Substance abuse and mental illness: Social work practice with dual diagnosis clients. *Arete, 17*(2), 1–15.

Sullivan, W. P., Wolk, J., & Hartmann, D. (1992). Case management in alcohol and drug treatment: Improving client outcomes. *Families in Society, 73,* 195–203.

Timney, C., & Graham, K. (1989). A survey of case management practice in addictions programs. *Alcoholism Treatment Quarterly, 6*(3–4), 103–127.

Trice, H., & Schonbrunn, M. (1981, spring). A history of job-based alcoholism programs: 1900–1955. *Journal of Drug Issues, 11,* 171–197.

Willenbring, M. (1994). Case management applications in substance use disorders. *Journal of Case Management, 3,* 150–157.

Wilson, C. (1993). Substance abuse and managed care. In W. Goldman & S. Feldman (Eds.), *Managed mental health care* (pp. 99–105). San Francisco: Jossey-Bass.

# Chapter 7

# Case Management in Health Care

*Candyce S. Berger*

C ase management, a relatively new intervention in health care, continues to expand in influence and gain attention for achieving cost-effective and quality improvements in the delivery of health care services. Some describe it as a great contribution to health care; others believe it will be the demise of health care. How is it that one intervention generates such diverse opinions regarding its contribution to practice? The debate over the value of case management is a source of conflict and confusion in the field, much of it stemming from lack of clarity about its goals, professional domain, and value.

This chapter describes how case management has evolved in the health care field as well as its implications for social work practice. The contextual factors shaping the development of case management are presented in an effort to clarify the goals and models of case management in health care. The case management process is explored and case manager's skills delineated.

The influence of case management in the health care field is likely to grow in the next decade, and social work practitioners must come to terms with this new approach to service delivery. Social workers will need to determine how to integrate case management into their practice repertoire both as a provider and as a collaborator as well as proactively shape their role to ensure that case management services enhance patient care.

## Social Casework in Health Care

Case management is rooted in social work methods. In fact, the case management process is described throughout the literature even though the term is not always used. Social work utilizes problem-solving methods involving assessment, diagnosis, intervention, and follow-up–a process described in the social work literature as "casework" and that closely approximates case management.

Medical social work pioneer Ida Cannon (1923) recognized the important role social workers play in hospitals in fostering the relationship between the hospital and community agencies. She described the social worker's role as one of being knowledgeable about community resources in order to utilize them effectively to support the patient's care. She referred to these resources as the social worker's "social pharmacopoeia" (p. 116), depicting the social workers' role as assessing the social condition of the patient, prescribing the social elements in treatment, and finding the means to implement the social treatment required. She addressed the importance of advocacy and the need to change the environment to accomplish the treatment plan.

Bartlett (1940) emphasized the medical social worker's concern with the patient's social relationships. The social worker involved the patient, the patient's family, and the community in addressing the patient's problem situation. Bartlett listed various functions and skills that social workers need: knowledge of medical diagnosis and treatment, the ability to facilitate and interpret medical information to patients, a willingness to help patients relate constructively to the complex medical organization, and skills to facilitate discharge planning. Mirroring these pioneers in the medical social work field, Germaine's (1984) ecological perspective as well as the work of Rosenberg and Rehr (1983), Schlesinger (1985), and Miller and Rehr (1983), all describe social casework in the medical setting as maximizing the patient's ability to access and utilize health care services. Although none of these authors uses the term *case management,* their description of the casework process uses terminology such as screening for high-risk patients, assessment, intervention, evaluation, and follow-up—all of which are part of the case management process. The only significant difference between descriptions of the two is that case management focuses on containing costs and developing flexible benefits to increase care alternatives.

## State of Case management in Health Care Today

The adoption of case management in health care evolved slowly. Current interest in this intervention can be understood within the context of the sweeping changes that have bombarded the health care delivery system for the past 10 to 15 years.

### ❏ Disproportionate Distribution of Resources

Rising health insurance copayments and deductibles are eating into consumers' personal budgets without a commensurate increase in quality or access to health care services. Many U.S. citizens fall through ever widening holes in the health care "safety net." Restrictive insurance policies and coverage limitations are pushing many people into substandard levels of coverage or no coverage at all. Approximately 37 million Americans are uninsured, with 2 million losing their health care benefits every month. Women and children have been hit particularly hard. Nine million to 12 million children are uninsured, with 25% of all children uninsured at some time during the year. Finally, a disproportionately small number of individuals are consuming most of the health care dollars. Approximately 10% of the population accounts for 70% of health expenditures (Taulbee, 1991); Resnick (1992) reported that in one company, 3% of the employees accounted for 50% of the health care dollars.

## ❏ System Complexity

Another factor shaping change in the health care delivery system is the complexity of the health and human service delivery systems. Technology has driven physicians and other health care providers to specialize. In fact, professional and technical specialists have overpowered the systems of care, contributing to fragmentation, gaps in service delivery, duplication of services, and delivery of unnecessary services.

## ❏ Cost Containment

The rising cost of health care has been a major national concern for several decades. Health care costs are increasing at three times the rate of inflation, rising from $248 billion in 1980 to $646 billion in 1990. If costs continue to escalate at the present rate, they will reach $1.5 trillion by the year 2000. Spiraling costs have strained both private and public budgets, creating a strong coalition in favor of instituting containment measures in the health care industry.

Cost-cutting strategies have been introduced in an effort to regain some control over escalating costs. An increasing proportion of the costs has been shifted from the payer to the consumer and provider of services through changes in benefit structures, pricing strategies, and reimbursement systems. In addition, financial incentives have been implemented to encourage consumers to use health care delivery systems that demonstrate greater cost efficiency. For example, in most health insurance benefit plans, the health maintenance organization (HMO) option for health benefits costs the employee less than traditional indemnity options. With the HMO options, co-payments and deductibles are also less costly. Finally, insurance companies have attempted to change health care utilization patterns through implementation of techniques and strategies such as preadmission review, concurrent review, second opinion, and case management.

## ❏ The Emergence of Case Management in Health Care

Case management principles are being applied to health care to contain costs and to improve a fragmented health care delivery system. Purchasers search for mechanisms to control costs while minimizing negative effects on quality of care. Both providers and payers view case management as a promising approach.

Case management in health care has historical roots in the rehabilitation-based models of the 1940s used in workers' compensation cases (Henderson & Collard, 1992). The Health Maintenance Act of 1973 changed the way health care services were delivered and financed. The HMO model moved away from traditional fee-for-service models of care, offering instead a prepaid comprehensive service delivery system. In theory, case management was a component of the HMO model (Kane, 1992).

Case management grew rapidly in the 1980s as a result of frenzied efforts to control spiraling health care costs. Insurance companies, the government, and employers became interested in case management primarily as a way to control costs (Henderson & Collard, 1992). These key purchasers of service formed a potent coalition to bring about change. Purchasers were no longer willing to accept the uncontrolled rise in costs and called for dramatic changes in the financing and delivery of health care services.

A major move toward case management in health care programs occurred with the passage of the Omnibus Budget Reconciliation Act (OBRA) of 1981 (Henderson & Collard, 1992; Kane, 1992; Loomis, 1992; Omnibus Budget Reconciliation Act, 1981). Spitz and Abramson (1987) state:

> Under this legislation, state Medicaid programs could receive federal waivers which allowed them to "implement a case management system . . . which restricts the provider from or through whom a recipient can obtain primary care" (U.S. Code of Federal Regulations, Title 42, Section 431.55[c]). "Federal requirements prohibited case management from substantially impair(ing) access to services of adequate quality" and required "that a specific person or agency be responsible for locating, coordinating or monitoring Medicaid services on behalf of a recipient" (U.S. Code of Federal Regulations, Title 42, Section 431.55[c] [1] and [2]). In addition, the state would have to demonstrate that case management was cost effective (p. 363).

The case management component of OBRA was so successful that the Consolidate Omnibus Budget Reconciliation Act (P.L. 99-272) of

1985 extended its use by states to provide case management as an optional service in the Medicaid program without seeking federal waivers (Spitz & Abramson, 1987).

Intracorp, a national health care management firm, is generally recognized as one of the first organizations to apply case management to the medical claims area (Henderson & Collard, 1992). External case managers worked with hospital personnel to manage a client's care. Case management in the medical claims area continues to grow rapidly, fueled by outcome data substantiating the benefits of case management in controlling costs.

Medicaid programs throughout the country moved quickly to adopt case management into their programs. This movement began with the growth of Medicaid HMO programs (Spitz & Abramson, 1987). A threefold increase in Medicaid enrollees in HMOs occurred between 1970 and 1990, though the new enrollees represented a small proportion (approximately 4%) of Medicaid recipients. Other case management programs for Medicaid recipients targeted specific populations, such as prenatal care, HIV/AIDS, and rehabilitation.

Employers were quick to follow the lead of Medicaid in embracing case management. Escalating costs for employee health benefit programs were cannibalizing company profits. Business quickly recognized the benefits of case management in the medical claims area. Many large employers, such as Ciba-Geigy and Zenith Corporation, began to provide in-house case management through their occupational health or medical departments (Henderson & Collard, 1992). Shoor (1993) reported that in an annual health care benefits survey conducted by A. Foster Higgins & Co. in 1989, 50% of employers reported using case management in the medical claims area. This percentage rose to 69% by 1992. Shoor (1993) includes a report on a survey of 410 *Business and Health* readers indicating that 52% of respondents rated case management effective, compared with 32% who favored precertification for hospitalization, 34% for utilization management, and 20% for second-opinion programs.

As the financing of care moved to fixed payment systems such as diagnostic related groups (DRGs) and contractual agreements that fix reimbursement levels, providers searched for ways to bleed costs out of the system. Efforts focused on removing duplication of services and unnecessary steps in the care process to reduce costs while improving quality. Total quality management principles began to infiltrate the health care arena, focusing attention on the processes of care. Case management evolved naturally within this atmosphere of cost containment and quality assurance.

Comprehensive, effective case management benefits the entire health care field. Payers and providers as well as patient, family, and community benefit (see Table 1).

## Defining Case Management

Combining cost efficiency with effectiveness, case management in health care is growing rapidly. However, case management means different things to different people. For some, it focuses on benefits management; for others it pertains to utilization management; to still others, it allows for improved access and quality of care. This lack of a clear definition of case management fuels the debate and conflict regarding the application of case management principles in health care settings.

**Table 1.** Benefits of case management.

| Recipient of benefits | Type of benefits |
|---|---|
| Patient | • Achieve highest level of services<br>• Highest level of health status<br>• Improves communication<br>• Efficient use of health care funds |
| Family/significant other | • Shifts burden of coordinating care to a trained individual<br>• Helps sort through data in order to make critical decisions<br>• Provides emotional support<br>• Improves communication |
| Providers | • Coordinate their part of care with others<br>• Ensures continuum of care is addressed<br>• Helps monitor the quality of care<br>• Helps measure outcomes of care<br>• Improves payment for services<br>• Encourages exploration of alternatives to care<br>• Improves communication |
| Payers | • Ensures claims dollars are used appropriately<br>• Improves the insured's satisfaction with the payer<br>• Enhances the company's image<br>• Improves communication |

*Note:* Adapted from the American Hospital Association (1992). In S. Rose (Ed.), *Case management and social work* (pp. 149–159). New York: Longman.

The following sections delineate the various definitions or defined purposes of case management. It is necessary to understand the breadth of usage of the term in order to clarify how case management is being defined within specific settings and/or situations.

## ❏ Case Management versus Benefit Management

One of the first thoughts that come to mind when considering case management is that it involves changes in one's benefits package. For some people, this is all that case management means. Benefits management involves massaging a benefits package to achieve maximum flexibility of use. For example, services that are not traditionally covered by a plan may be reimbursed if doing so is cost effective. In other words, respite care may not be a covered benefit, but the insurer may approve coverage if it prevents nursing-home placement or rehospitalization. The insurance industry tends to define case management in this way because its primary focus is to reduce costs. Although benefits management is an important component of a case management program, it is not sufficient. Although it does achieve more cost-efficient use of resources, it does not necessarily address issues related to fragmentation.

## ❏ Case Management versus Utilization Management

Case management is often defined according to principles of utilization management. As discussed earlier, utilization management focuses on the most effective and efficient use of health care resource. It employs strategies such as preadmission review, second opinion, preauthorization for services, and concurrent review. Again, although utilization management is an important component of case management, it is not a sufficient definition. Utilization management focuses on the appropriate use of resources but does not necessarily manage the most effective course of care.

## ❏ System- versus Client-Centered Case Management

Kane (1992) differentiates between system-focused case management and client-focused case management. System case management is similar to utilization management and benefits management in that case management serves a rationing and priority-setting function. Client-centered case management focuses on coordinating health care services within a complex and fragmented delivery system. Kane describes it as follows:

> The client-centered rationale recognizes the complexity of the health care delivery system in all its multidisciplinary glory, the vulnerability of

> the client (who is too often the passive recipient of care), and the bewil-
> dering effects of high technology on the health care consumer. Physical,
> mental, and social factors are further intertwined in the presentation of
> many health problems and in the course of recovery. Therefore, case
> management is suggested as an antidote to a complex and inhumane
> system that consumers cannot readily manipulate on their own behalf.
> (p. 173).

Client-centered case management puts quality of service first, with cost containment as a natural by-product of this process (Koska, 1990).

Kane (1984) provides a simple definition of case management that encompasses all the critical components. Case management is a system of locating, coordinating, and monitoring a specific group of services for a defined group of people. In essence, it involves organizing and sequencing services to provide the most appropriate and highest quality care in the most timely manner, in the most appropriate setting, for the least cost. This view of case management combines cost-reduction concerns with quality issues. The major goal of case management is to achieve cost effectiveness, not merely cost reduction (American Hospital Association, 1992; Koska, 1990). This has been described as the process of "rationalizing" care rather than "rationing" care. Rose (1992) describes rationalizing care as involving coordination, continuity, and arranging appropriate care to achieve the most effective and efficient services for the patient.

## Case Management Models

The literature is replete with descriptions of case management models (Kane, 1984; Loomis, 1992; Merril, 1985; Weil, 1985). Before delving into the specific components of case management and the skills required to perform these duties, it's important to understand the various models that are currently being used within health care settings. By understanding the commonalties and idiosyncrasies associated with each model, practitioners will have a better understanding of the model being used within their own systems, be able to delineate the skills needed to implement the model, and be able to evaluate the implications of the model for social work.

The American Health Association (1992) categorized case management into five basic models. Each of these models can be found in use in various health care settings; several models can be used simultaneously. These models are primary care case management, medical case management, social case management, medical–social case management, and vocational case management.

Primary care case management is an early model in which the key player is the primary care physician, who is responsible for coordinating all aspects of patient care. Medical case management focuses on patients with severe illnesses or injuries, emphasizing intensive medical monitoring of the course of care. Social case management focuses on a nonacute population living in the community. Here, the emphasis is on coordinating social and economic resources to prevent more costly, higher levels of care. Medical–social case management synthesizes medical and social case management by integrating the use of health, social, and economic resources. Finally, vocational case management focuses on helping the disabled to achieve gainful employment.

Although these five models differ in focus and/or intensity of service, they share the common purpose to organize and sequence services to achieve the highest quality of care by the most cost-effective means. The goals are to (1) help the individual achieve the optimum outcome, (2) implement appropriate preventive measures to avoid complications, and (3) sustain the individual's best level of health (American Hospital Association, 1992).

## The Case Management Process in Health Care Settings

Although the various models of case management may differ in regard to their goals and scope of service, their processes have many common features. Moreover, case management in health care shares a process common to case management in other fields. Although terminology might vary, the intent is the same. Case management can be characterized as a problem-solving process that follows four generic steps: case finding/identification, assessment and planning, intervention, and monitoring/outcomes (American Hospital Association, 1992; Austin, 1983; Kane, 1984; Newald, 1986; Weil, Karls, & Associates, 1985).

### ❏ Case Finding/Identification

Case-finding criteria can be grouped into two major categories: illness and cost. Criteria related to illness factors can be subdivided into catastrophic events and serious, chronic, or fatal conditions. Preventive conditions have only recently emerged.

Examples of catastrophic events or injuries include spinal cord injury, head injuries, heart attacks, stroke, trauma. In the area of medical claims, case management of these populations is very effective. Early identification leading to intervention can dramatically reduce the costs of care by moving patients more quickly to lower levels of care and by ensuring coordination of services and benefit flexing to guarantee that the most effective services are implemented in the most timely fashion.

Patients diagnosed with serious and/or fatal chronic diseases include persons diagnosed with HIV/AIDS, cancer, diabetes, pulmonary disease, and the like. These patients fall into the high-risk category because of potential duration of their condition and the multiple medical events that occur over the course of the illness. The potential for fragmentation of service delivery is great, leading to unnecessary use of resources, communication breakdowns among providers, and gaps in service delivery. For example, persons with AIDS must navigate a complex maze of inpatient, outpatient, and community-based health care services. In addition, they often need to access other programs and services, including legal care, housing, food, transportation, respite care, and personal care. Case managers play a critical role in helping the patient coordinate services, facilitating the patient's access to services, and improving the patient's quality of care and quality of life. But case management with persons with AIDS is also fiscally advantageous. At the Department of Social Work at the University of Washington Medical Center, a case management program for persons with HIV/AIDS was implemented. A unique component of this program was the initiation of case management services at the second stage of the disease rather than stage 4 (as mandated by Medicaid requirements). Earlier intervention had a positive effect. The medical center population had shorter lengths of stay when compared with patients who did not receive case management services until stage 4.

High risk is associated with high costs. Most health care organizations and payers are aware of their "high-cost" cases. Some utilize DRG groupings or ICD-9 billing codes to review cost data for trends. Such analysis produces a list that serves as a guide to identify the need for early case management. This approach specifically links the criteria to the cost.

Regardless of which high-risk classification scheme is used for early identification, the important factor is to establish criteria and a routine mechanism for case finding. These techniques can vary along a continuum from repeated screening of high-risk populations to a more passive screening of people referred for service (Kane, 1992). To be effective, the screening criteria should identify cases in which poor outcomes, untoward events, under- and overutilization, and poor efficiency might occur if intervention is not implemented (Macnee & Penchansky, 1994). These cases are often referred to in the literature as the "sentinel" events (Rutstein, Berenber, Chalmers, Child, Fishman, & Perin, 1976).

## ❏ Assessment and Planning

The assessment process varies from an in-depth, multidisciplinary process to a more perfunctory eligibility determination (Kane, 1992). A more comprehensive analysis typically utilizes a biopsychosocial perspective that examines the interrelationship among physical, psychological, social, and environmental systems. The assessment process can be done by an individual, compiled from various data sources, or performed by a multidisciplinary team (Weil et al., 1985).

The assessment may also incorporate a perspective in time. The evaluation might include data on past, present, and future issues. For example, in the assessment of a patient with a spinal-cord injury, the assessment might include an analysis of past coping strategies, present support systems and resources, and potential levels of functioning in the future. This perspective will eventually create a very different picture from one that focuses only on the present. The case manager must be aware of the patient's comprehensive needs, including current and potential strengths and weaknesses (Rubin, 1992). If the individual conducting the assessment also serves as the case manager, the assessment process helps initiate a working relationship with the client.

The case management model that is employed may also influence the scope and intensity of the assessment process. For example, the social and vocational case management models emphasize the psychological, social, and environmental criteria. The medical case management model relies heavily on assessment of the physical dimension. The medical–social case management model yields the most comprehensive analysis, incorporating all four systems into its analysis.

The assessment process is a critical phase because it sets the stage for all subsequent phases. The assessment delineates the salient goals to be accomplished, which drives the plan toward intervention. It also constructs the framework for monitoring the process and outcomes of intervention. Kane (1992) delineates four key benefits of a routine assessment process: (1) comparison of clients' needs, (2) monitoring change over time, (3) determining eligibility for various services, and (4) judging the adequacy of existing support systems and determining whether they need to be shored up by formal assistance. The outcome of the assessment helps determine the type and scope of interventions needed.

## ❏ Intervention

A comprehensive intervention plan must be established for each client. Interventions can include information and referral, coordination of services, linkage and brokering, advocacy, and treatment.

The role of the case manager in providing treatment is the subject of debate. Clearly, in the primary care case management model, the primary care physician and the case manager are one and the same. In the other models, however, the role of the case manager is more ambiguous. Some models utilize the case manager as a service provider for some or most aspects of care. Others maintain a clear boundary between case manager and service provider. Research in the health care field does not speak to the advantages or disadvantages of either approach in terms of quality of care.

In the absence of data on quality-of-care outcomes, this issue is often analyzed from a financial perspective. For example, in hospital settings nurses are stepping into the role of case managers. These nurses are often highly skilled and/or trained, particularly in the use of critical pathways. Consequently, they are paid higher salaries compared with social workers and floor nurses. The hospital can maximize the knowledge and skills of these highly competent practitioners by limiting their role to coordination rather than implementation, thus increasing their availability without driving up the costs of care. In other words, the nurse care manager operates like the conductor of a symphony—directing the rhythm and timing of all the music but not stepping down to play an instrument.

Hammer and Champy (1993) describe the cost efficiency of having a case manager or case management team responsible for multiple tasks and therefore eliminating the number of steps or contacts in the process. They believe that the process should be simplified, the unnecessary steps removed, and the number of individuals involved reduced. Communication is thereby facilitated, the possibilities for gaps or slippage in the process decreased, and the potential for duplication of effort and work minimized. With this scenario, the case manager must have broad decision-making authority.

It is extremely difficult for a case manager to maintain a rigid boundary between case management and treatment activities. Through repeated interactions, the case manager develops a relationship with the patient. Crisis or immediate needs may surface for which the case manager is capable of intervening (Rubin, 1992). For example, a patient may not be able to keep a physician appointment because of transportation problems, and the case manager might arrange for transportation. Another client may be afraid to make an appointment for a test or medical procedure. The case manager may be called upon to provide support and help the client talk through the issues and/or accompany the patient. Although case managers are not necessarily expected to provide therapeutic interventions or to provide crisis intervention, they may be expected to provide personal support and/or concrete assistance (Rubin, 1992).

Although debate surrounds the role of the case manager as treatment provider, most professionals agree about the case manager's role in providing coordination and linkage services. The case manager must follow the progression of services over the continuum of care. It is not enough for the case manager to resume responsibility for coordination after the patient is discharged from the hospital; he or she must become involved with the patient at preadmission and during hospitalization and work with hospital staff to ensure that all formal and informal systems are in place and sequenced appropriately. The case manager is responsible for seeing that all aspects of the patient's care needs are met; this responsibility is at the core of the case management process (Intagliata, 1982; Miller, 1983; Rubin, 1992).

Linkage or brokering is a major intervention strategy that enables effective coordination. Linkage connects the client with the resource community to ensure that his or her needs are met. Case managers may have to assume the role of advocate. In fact, patient advocacy is a primary intervention, particularly in community-based settings (Williams, Warrick, Christianson, & Netting, 1993). Client and family resistance are also barriers to the process. Clients may not seek services because necessary supports are unavailable.

Getting all the pieces of the service plan in place so that they are carried out in logical sequence is at the heart of the process (American Hospital Association, 1992; Rubin, 1992; Weil et al., 1985). In the more comprehensive models of case management, this requires the case manager to make referrals for various levels of care appropriate to the client's medical, social, financial, and spiritual needs.

## ❏ Monitoring

The intervention plan developed from the assessment process should include a list of specific actions to achieve identified goals as well as measurable objectives to evaluate progress. Case managers need to be aware of all aspects of the process and how the plan is being implemented. They must constantly monitor the processes to determine where breakdowns occur and how to intervene to prevent problems in the present and future. The case manager must stay in contact with all service providers to ensure appropriate follow through in service delivery.

Monitoring can occur in several ways. It can consist minimally of reviewing documentation and paperwork or require face-to-face contacts with service providers and clients. Rubin (1992) discusses the importance of face-to-face contact as a good way to influence quality of service. Firsthand contact can enhance quality of feedback and improve the case manager's relationship with clients and service providers.

Monitoring may be one of the most difficult aspects of case management, especially if the case manager comes from outside the provider system. Providers do not take kindly to "outsiders" looking over their shoulder to evaluate their work. Often, the goals of the service provider conflict with those of the case management program, which tends to brand the case manager as an unwanted intruder into the patient's care. Many providers set up elaborate systems to keep case managers away from the direct-service process in an effort to circumscribe the influence. The following example illustrates this dilemma.

> *An inpatient pediatric rehabilitation unit was having problems obtaining approval for services from a particular insurance company. The case manager from the insurance company (external to the hospital) described the hospital staff as hostile and reluctant to provide adequate information about the care process and patient status. The hospital staff described the case managers as intruding into care, attempting to undermine the work of the health care team, and unresponsive to client needs. The problem escalated to the point that the insurance provider was threatening to restrict its patients from obtaining rehabilitation services from this unit. Because the social workers on the unit were informally recognized as the internal case managers, much of the conflict was laid at their feet.*
>
> *The director of social work was asked to intervene. After several meetings, it became apparent that the problem was primarily systemic. The external case managers felt they were not given sufficient access to the health care team or involved in decision making even though they were the payers of care. When case managers questioned decisions, they were deemed unresponsive to patient needs and as intruders.*
>
> *It was decided that the case managers would be incorporated into the care team and would participate in the care conferences. In this way, the payer and the provider were able to form an effective partnership to ensure appropriate levels of care. An interesting result of this agreement was that the case manager was now required to face the patient and/or family when making a decision about coverage. Members of the health care team believed that this helped "soften" the case managers and that they were more likely to approve care. The case managers believed that their involvement helped to surface alternatives to care and by flexing benefits achieved more effective and efficient care plans after discharge.*

The case management plan should always be viewed as a work in progress. The case manager should be prepared to revise the plan when information from the monitoring process indicates that it is no longer effective or is unable to address newly emerging issues and needs. Thus the plan requires constant reevaluation and renegotiations with patients and providers.

## ❏ Outcomes

Implicit in the monitoring function is an evaluation component whereby the case manager consistently records the process and rates the quality of service (Rubin, 1992). This evaluation tends to be micro focused on the process, measuring whether services occur, the quality of the service, and the achievement of defined clinical goals.

Outcome measurement at the macro level is equally important. This approach focuses on the global outcomes of the overall intervention with a client or groups of clients. Outcome evaluation can be grouped into three major categories: financial gains, improvement in health status, and improvement in quality of life. The first addresses the goal of cost containment, whereas the latter two focus on the management goal of improvement in quality of care.

Outcomes on cost containment are prevalent in the literature and are provided primarily by purchasers of health care services. The insurance industry boasts significant financial savings from case management programs in the medical claims area. Studies report an average of $5–$11 return on investment from case management, with one company reporting more than $1 million in savings in the first 10 months of their program (Resnick, 1992; Taulbee, 1991). Such positive outcomes spurred the rapid growth of case management within the medical claims area, specifically in insurance companies. Brandeis University's Bigel Institute for Health Policy found that medical case management was offered by virtually every major private insurer in the United States (Henderson & Wallack, 1987).

Other mechanisms are used to measure the cost effectiveness of case management. From an employer perspective, the duration of time a worker is away from work can translate to significant costs or savings. Various measures address efficient utilization of resources. Costs can also be measured by prevented hospitalizations, decreased length of stay, or unnecessary use of resources. For example, hospitals report reduced lengths of stay after implementing critical pathways or other forms of case management. As health care moves toward capitated models of payment, the need to manage resources will be critical, and case management will be an effective mechanism for achieving this goal (Lumsdom, 1994). Case management can translate into significant cost savings for payers, providers, and consumers. However, although cost savings can represent positive outcomes in the short term, it will have long-term negative consequences if quality factors are not maintained.

Minimal data have been reported on improvement in health status or quality of life that is traceable to case management. The literature points to various indices that can be used to measure such outcomes (see Table 2). More rigorous research is needed to evaluate outcomes of case management, particularly in the realm of quality. These studies need to be longitudinal in order to ensure that short-term indicators of success do not lead to long-term negative consequences. For example, positive financial gains in the short term may disappear upon further evaluation of the patient's recovery process or ability to return to work in the future.

---

**Table 2.** *Quality of care outcomes of case management.*

| Improvement in health status | Improvement in quality of life |
|---|---|
| Activities of daily living | Social supports |
| Presence of symptoms | General well-being |
| Presence of co-morbid conditions | Patient satisfaction |
| Frequency of complications | Coping |
| Compliance | Stress |
| Presence of behavioral/psychological disabilities | |

---

Information management is critical to the monitoring and outcome function. Case management requires the identification and collation of an enormous amount of information. Paper systems for information management are not fast enough or extensive enough to manage a client's needs effectively. Computerized information systems are essential to the case management process.

Cummings and Abell (1993) suggested that the health care delivery system of the future will have a unified, computerized information system with a single point of entry for the entire health network. This type of system will integrate all information relevant to the patient's care, including medical, laboratory, administrative, financial, and psychosocial. The ability to tap into such an extensive information system will be an enormous asset for case managers in monitoring and coordinating patient care. If this system includes linkages to social services and other community-based programs, the advantages would improve exponentially.

The literature includes some discussion regarding the decision-supporting role of computers. Some professionals have been fascinated with the potential role of computer modeling to replicate clinical decision making (Falcone, 1979; Kane, 1992). Commonly referred to as artificial intelligence (AI), such technology represents both an opportunity and a challenge for practitioners. With a large, complex resource and delivery system, AI could facilitate timely identification of needs and available resources as well as help speed the learning curve (Taulbee, 1991). Case managers often must rely on years of experience when evaluating resources and alternatives to care. With AI, a new case manager would have the same level of knowledge at his or her fingertips on the first day of work. Some companies are entering the health care market with these types of programs, particularly in the area of community-resource availability. For example, software programs to locate appropriate and available nursing home beds and other types of community-based resources are becoming more prevalent in discharge-planning operations.

Artificial intelligence can also benefit the care process. Effective monitoring requires the case manager to be aware of important events and when they will occur. Follow-up to ensure that the client received care and knowledge of the outcome of care need to be continuously monitored to keep clients on track toward the achievement of their case management goals and/or to signal the need to modify a plan based on outcome data. Case managers often carry large case loads, and their ability to track the course and outcome of care can be compromised without high-quality information-management tools. Software programs are being developed to address this tracking function. Critical events in the care process can be entered into the system as triggers to alert the case manager to the need for follow up. Similarly, evaluation of outcome data can highlight trends that might call for modifications in the care plan.

However, for some practitioners, particularly professionally trained case managers, AI poses significant threats. Some practitioners fear that AI will replace clinical decision making and allow experienced practitioners to be replaced by less highly trained practitioners (Kane, 1992). Opponents of AI contend that case management and other clinical interventions are both science and art. Although the computer is a useful tool in the "science" component of the equation, it can never function as the "art" component. Although more research on the efficacy of computer decision making is needed, computer technology clearly is a powerful tool that case managers should consider incorporating into their practice.

The monitoring and evaluation function is a primary concern of health care providers. Anecdotal claims of decreased quality resulting from case management are rampant. Case management proponents, on the other hand, claim to influence care by promoting health through prevention programs, monitoring the appropriateness of treatment, and improving patients' adherence to treatment regimens (Henderson & Collard, 1992). For case management to assume a legitimate position within the armory of health care interventions, outcome data supporting these claims need to be documented.

# Challenges and Opportunities

Regardless of the outcome of the debate on the efficacy of case management in health care, it will likely be increasingly used because research data indicate that it is beneficial financially. What are the critical issues that need to be considered in the development and implementation of case management programs in the health care arena?

## ❏ Case Management Goals

Questions about the goals of case management permeate the literature on case management and have been discussed several times within this chapter. Although many authors point to the mutual importance of cost containment and quality of care, these two goals often do not co-exist peacefully. If the case management program overemphasizes cost containment, short-term decisions may lead to long-term negative consequences. In this scenario, the focus is on minimizing costs of hospitalization, tests and medical procedures, or preventive services. The overriding objection is to ration care rather than to rationalize it (Egdahl, 1986).

On the other hand, if one focuses exclusively on quality, the providers or the payers assume the costs for care. Quality can be an elusive issue. For example, patient satisfaction is often used as a measure of quality. A patient might be very satisfied with the plush environment of an expensive rehabilitation program, but does this warrant the cost? What one patient might consider necessary another might consider excessive.

It's safe to say that social workers would not have difficulty with quality of care as the primary health care goal. They would likely support a health care delivery system that focused on patient access and ensured that the patient's total health care needs were addressed. However, how should the social work profession respond to the goal of cost containment? If rationing care is the primary motive behind decision making, the social worker may be faced with implementing procedures that can have negative consequences for the patient. Social workers must understand these two goals as well as the potential ethical conflicts that can occur in realizing them. Although the ideal is to balance these two goals, it is likely that one will supersede the other, particularly if cost-containment measures are emphasized.

Social workers need to design services that do not work at cross purposes with these goals (Loomis, 1992; Merrill, 1985). For example, it does not do patients any good to be told that they "should be entitled" or they "should receive" certain services if the case management program will not pay for such care. The social worker needs to support the patient while understanding the limitations or restrictions inherent in the case management program and work with the patient and the case manager to identify and secure appropriate services. The social worker who chooses to resist the system risks being labeled as uncooperative and places his or her job in jeopardy. Although a social worker may choose to stand up for a principle by taking this risk, he or she nevertheless needs to understand that it is a choice and not blame the organization for the consequences of this choice.

Ideally, social workers need to find a way to integrate both goals. They need to make peace with the realities of cost containment and find ways to integrate it into their own service delivery. Cost containment will continue to be a major priority within health care delivery systems. The best strategy is to find creative ways to maximize service opportunities while holding down costs.

## ❏ Identifying the Client

Social workers in health care struggle with their commitments to clients versus their commitments to employers. As prospective payment and capitated systems of reimbursement replace cost-based models, patients may be discharged from hospitals or services before they or their family are ready. The time necessary to resolve reactions to illness is often not adequate within the period of hospitalization; pressures increase to move patients to lower levels of care as soon as possible (even if the patient is not emotionally ready for the transfer).

The issue of who is the client is accentuated by managed care and the subsequent rise in case management programs. Social workers are faced with increasing case loads. In addition to the patient and family, the worker must deal with (1) the physician, who is anxious to contain consumption of resources, particularly if he or she is paid through the capitation model; (2) the hospital, which wants to move the patient to a lower level of care in order to maximize its reimbursement; (3) the payer, who wants to be involved with or in control of the decision-making process; and (4) the professional discipline, which wants to retain control over practice, particularly those areas that historically have been part of its turf. Although this list may not be exhaustive, it illustrates the inherent conflicts when health care practitioners and/or case managers must address the competing interest and needs of multiple "clients."

## ❏ Organizational Placement

Another critical question that must be addressed is where the case management program is located in relation to the health care institution. It's hard to predict where the boundaries of the hospital will be drawn in the health care delivery system of the future. As health care organizations move to develop networks of care, the traditional boundaries of the hospital disappear. For example, most care maps/critical pathways are developed for inpatient episodes of care. Case management ends when the patient is discharged. A similar picture exists for outpatient care; case management ends when the patient is admitted to the hospital. In a health care delivery system characterized by care networks, the structure of case management will necessarily be changed if the health care system is responsible for patient care along the entire continuum.

Case management programs can be located within or outside the health care delivery system. Each location has advantages and disadvantages. If the program is external to the delivery system, the case manager can assume a more objective position in coordinating patient care. Because they exist outside the boundaries of one particular delivery system, these case managers are able to access a wide array of services and avoid pressures to use programs within a specific system of care. For example, if a patient requires rehabilitation, the delivery system may wish to transfer the patient to its own rehabilitation program even though an outside rehabilitation program offers a more cost-effective program. The external case manager has greater freedom to choose less costly alternatives.

A major disadvantage of external programs, however, is that the case manager often operates at a distance from the patient's health care team, which affects access to information and to team members. This separation can create problems in planning for the patient's care. Also, adversarial relationships more readily arise when case managers are outside the hospital, creating problems for the case manager, the health care team, and the patient and family.

A strategy sometimes used to reduce the negative consequences of external case managers is to incorporate them as members of the health care team. In this scenario, the external case manager learns from members of the health care team and participates in decision making.

Another alternative is to locate the case management program within the service-delivery system. In this model, the case manager is an employee of the same health care delivery system as is the patient's health care team. The case manager becomes a member of the health care team. The internal case manager understands how the delivery system works and has access to organizational decision makers if systemic changes are needed to improve the system. Depending on their power within the system, they may even be able to shape the behavior of other system providers. Their access to information throughout the system is unencumbered, which facilitates their ability to sequence and coordinate patient care.

The disadvantages of locating case management within the provider system parallel the advantages for an external program. Because the internal case manager is an employee of the delivery system, the resource alternatives are circumscribed. As care networks evolve, the case manager may be pressured to use resources within the system, even if these are not the most cost effective or of the best quality. Although the case manager is in a position to encourage system change, this task is not always easily or quickly accomplished.

Williams et al. (1993) studied a demonstration program in which six hospitals in Arizona and New Mexico established hospital-based case management programs. The researchers studied the question of organizational placement as a factor influencing the success of the program and found that "physical and organizational proximity to hospital functions facilitated program integration by promoting a focus on hospitalized patients, enhancing program visibility and encouraging relationships with hospital providers" (p. 65).

Regardless of geographic location, the case manager must be able to work effectively with the health care delivery system. This requires adequate access to information and involvement in decision making for the patient's care. The case manager must be viewed as a member of the health care team and have sufficient influence to improve system inefficiencies.

## ❏ Case Load

The size of the case manager's case load also affects the case management process. In some fields, particularly the medical-claims arena, case managers may carry case loads as high as 40,000 clients. Henderson and Collard (1992) report on a study that indicated that the ratio of case managers to eligible clients in HMO plans can range from 1 per 15,000 to 1 per 40,000. Clearly, not all of these clients need intensive case management services. Other experts indicate that a case manager can handle approximately 3 to 10 active intensive cases, which are defined as requiring attention by the case manager several times per week (Henderson & Collard, 1992). Obviously, case loads fluctuate, depending on various factors. The degree of risk and stability of the patient population will define the level of case management services required.

The goal of case management also influences the case-load size. If the primary goal is cost containment, activities might be more focused and/or limited and the case-load size might be larger. For example, if the case manager is responsible primarily for preauthorizations and utilization review, he or she may be able to accommodate case loads in the hundreds or thousands. If, however, the goal includes cost containment and improved quality of care, the case-load size will be smaller as a result of the increased intensity in the type and level of services incorporated into the patient's case management plan.

Case managers in health care should investigate other fields where the issue of case load has been examined more thoroughly. Intagliata (1982) reports that case-load size is inversely related to quality of intervention in the mental health field. As case-load size increases, the case manager becomes unable to initiate proactive interventions aimed at preventing problems and is able to respond to crisis situations only.

## ❏ Ethical Challenges: Confidentiality, Autonomy, and Justice

For social workers, some of the greatest challenges of case management in the health care field arise out of value dilemmas. As medical technology advances, health care surpasses science fiction in its ability to sustain life. The increasing importance of ethics in health care is reflected by the growing number and importance of ethics committees within hospitals and other health care institutions. Case management programs may not create new ethical dilemmas, but they often intensify existing issues or exacerbate old themes. Three key ethical dilemmas appear to arise within case management programs: Confidentiality, client autonomy, and justice. They are particularly relevant because they lie at the core of social work decision making.

Confidentiality requires the case manager to protect the client's right to privacy. Given the broad service networks mobilized by case management care plans and the increasing use of computerization, is it really possible to ensure confidentiality? Will the need to advocate on behalf of patients to gain access to needed services compromise confidentiality?

Confidentiality may be compromised when the case manager is external to the system. Social workers in health care struggle with this issue when working with external case managers because they are often responsible for coordinating discharge plans for the hospital. To what degree should the health care social worker share information with the case manager? If one uses the "need to know" yardstick, who defines what information is needed? Should external case managers be allowed to participate in case conferences? Should they have access to medical records? These questions have no easy answers.

Patient autonomy is another strongly held principle in social work practice. This value holds that social workers are obligated to help clients pursue goals that are personally meaningful to them and to involve them in decisions that affect their lives. How does one balance this value against declining resources and the expansion of managed care programs that limit individual choice? To control costs, case management programs often develop contractual arrangements with providers to reduce rates. What if the patient does not want to use the provider selected by the case management program? In the future, clients may have only one real choice—which managed care program to join. Social workers will need to reconcile their commitment to self-determination in an environment that curtails client choices.

Finally, social workers and health care practitioners must confront ethical dilemmas related to justice. Justice for whom? One might quickly answer that justice is defined according to the best interests of the client. But then we must return to the question of who the client is. It may seem "fair" to let a patient stay in the hospital for a few more days until he or she feels emotionally ready for transfer to a nursing home, but is it fair to the hospital that loses money during extended stays. Is it fair to the patient in the emergency room waiting on a stretcher because no beds are available? Finally, is it fair to citizens who must pay more for health coverage benefits?

Historically, issues of justice have been applied to the individual in terms of the question "What is in the best interest of the client?" As resources decrease, difficult decisions will need to be made regarding the best interests of the client versus the best interests of society.

## ❏ Authority

The authority of the case management program and/or the case manager will significantly influence the course and outcome of the case management process. It is important to begin with an understanding of what is meant by authority. Many interpret authority to be synonymous with power. This is partially correct. Power can be described as having two components—authority and influence (Berger, 1990). Authority represents the formal aspect of power and resides in one's position. If one case manager leaves and is replaced by another, the new case manager has the same authority as the previous one. Influence resides with the individual and reflects one individual's ability to change the behavior of another without using his or her authority. When the case manager's role is defined as having ultimate decision-making authority over the course of care and/or approval to fund services, this represents authority.

Ownership of the program is critical to the discussion of authority. Authorization for case management can come from private payers (e.g., insurance companies, employer), governments (e.g., federal, state, city), agencies (e.g., Area Agency on Aging), or organizational administration. The issue of ownership is significant for several reasons. First, the issue of ownership interacts with laws and regulations that govern health care services. Second, the authority of the case management program determines the degree to which services can be funded and provided. Third, the authority associated with ownership may determine where in the health care delivery system social services will be provided. For example, discharge planning has traditionally been a social work role within the hospital setting. However, external case managers may assume this role through the authority vested in the case management program (Loomis, 1992).

Authority over the funding of health care services may provide the case manager the strongest leverage to direct the patient's care. However, this type of power may evoke hostility from other members of the health care team. It's important to remember that authority may be potent, but it is not the strongest form of power (Berger, 1990). Individuals are able to undermine authority. For example, by restricting the case manager's access to information, the health care team can undermine the case manager's effectiveness.

When a case manager lacks authority, influence may be his or her only effective tool at hand to effect change. Without a formal locus of authority, many social workers might argue that they already perform many of the duties assigned to case managers (Loomis, 1992). Influence requires the case manager to establish excellent working relationships with members of the patient's health care team. The case manager uses his or her leadership skills to obtain support and compliance from others.

If case management's goal is cost containment, authority to fund services is critical. Without it, case managers may not have sufficient clout to alter the behavior of health care practitioners or guide patients to the most cost-effective providers available within the delivery system.

## ❏ Turf Battles and Organizational Politics

Nurses, social workers, and rehabilitation counselors often become caught in raging debates over which discipline is most appropriate for the role of case manager. Each profession points to the historical roots of case management within the profession (Miller, 1983).

Various factors contribute to the battles over who owns case management. First, as resources decline, struggles to control resources intensify. The decision-making environment becomes more politically volatile (Berger, 1993). The various interest groups in health care (physicians, nurses, social workers, rehabilitation counselors, physical therapists, etc.) compete over decreasing resources, and the game becomes defined as a "win–lose" venture. As ever more importance becomes attached to case management within the health care industry, disciplines jockey for control. Why is case management so coveted in health care settings? By assuring ownership of the case management function, a professional discipline can ensure that its services and/or role in the care process is not overlooked or its autonomy in decision making challenged.

The second factor contributing to the political maneuvering around case management is lack of clarity in goals (Berger, 1982). Case management means different things to different people. The lack of clarity in definition or goals creates ambiguity that allows competing interest groups to impose their definition of case management onto others. Then, on the basis of their own definition of the process and goals, they claim ownership. Many disciplines might describe their work with patients as parallel to the case management process. Nurses, social workers, utilization managers, and physicians can all point to their historic roles as informal case managers within the health care delivery system. Therefore, each discipline feels justified in claiming encroachment into their defined scope of care when formalized case management programs are proposed or developed.

Finally, this lack of clarity in definition and goals is exacerbated by the fact that case management does not fall within any specific educational domain. It is not a defined scope of practice governed by licensure, nor does any professional discipline offer a specific curriculum leading to case management as a practice subspecialty. Social work is correct that case management is consonant with social casework, but this applies only when one considers the models of social case management and medical–social case management. The lack of educational domain is reflected in the recent movement to provide case managers with credentials. The credentialing criteria do not limit certification to a particular discipline. In the absence of an educational domain, the question of ownership is open for debate.

One way to address the turf struggle is to abandon the "win–lose" mentality surrounding the debate. Perhaps the solution lies in creating case management teams. Some experts have found teams to be a more effective approach to the delivery of case management services. Koska (1990) reported on the use of case management teams with AIDS patients, whereby responsibility for the patient was distributed among several professionals. At the University of Washington Medical Center, researchers found that case management teams consisting of social workers and nurses were an effective intervention for improving pregnancy and birth outcomes among pregnant teenagers at risk for substance abuse (Berger, Gendler, Johnen, Blackman, Rosser, & Kirchoff, 1992). The Maternity Support Services Program at the University of Michigan Medical Center developed a similar case management model for working with at-risk pregnant women on Medicaid. A nurse, social worker, and dietitian work as a team to provide case management services, with one serving as the primary coordinator for the patient; the assignment is determined by the team and is based on determining which member is best able to meet the patient's most pressing needs. Case management teams may help resolve turf battles, but some believe that they do not represent cost-effective models for service delivery. Kane (1992) cautions against the use of teams as too top heavy and costly.

## ❏ Role Conflict

Role conflicts will continue to plague relationships between health care providers and case managers. Although this can be viewed as an extension of the turf debate, it also includes conflict emanating from other sources as well. First, one patient can potentially have multiple case managers. For example, the health care delivery system may assign an internal case manager. The insurance company may assign an external case manager. If the patient is connected to another social service agency, such as child protection services or programs related to developmental disabilities, yet another case manager may be involved with the patient. How can the efforts of these case managers be coordinated so that duplication of services and conflict do not negatively affect care delivery?

Role conflict over who has decision-making authority may also occur. Who will be ultimately responsible for determining the patient's care plan, particularly when conflict among providers and/or case managers occurs? The absence of a clear line of authority for clinical decision making increases the potential for role conflict. This issue needs to be addressed within each delivery system so that the patient does not get caught between warring providers. The case manager and health care providers need to determine how decisions will be made and how disagreements will be resolved.

Finally, the case manager is likely to struggle with role conflicts inherent within the case manager role. The issue of whether the case manager is also the service provider needs to be resolved. How and when the case manager intervenes needs to be clarified, or case managers may become caught in internal conflicts regarding their expected roles.

## ❏ Are Case Managers Also Service Providers?

Although the issue of case managers as services providers was discussed at length earlier in this chapter, it is revisited here to emphasize several key issues that social workers need to think about when deciding whether to serve as case managers. Although combining the roles has clear disadvantages, a strong case can also be made for integrating them (Kane, 1992; Loomis, 1992; Weil et al., 1985). A major complaint in many health care settings is that too many health care providers interact with patients on a daily basis, creating problems with effective communication, gaps and slippage in service delivery, and duplication of efforts. The patient may not know who is doing what. By combining the role of case manager and service provider, these problems can be reduced.

The major disadvantage in combining the roles is that it can create role conflict. What if the goals of clinical intervention and case management conflict? How can conflicts be effectively handled when one individual functions in both roles? The problem may be exacerbated if the case manager also has the authority to approve funding, thereby creating a conflict of interest. Careful planning and attention to funding mechanisms could ameliorate the disadvantages associated with combining these two roles. It's important that social workers clearly understand the implications of incorporating case management into their domain of service. The advantages and disadvantages need to be weighed and appropriate models developed.

## *Conclusion*

Case management means many things to different people. It is imperative that greater clarity in the definition of alternative models of case management replace the confusion that fuels ongoing debate and conflict among professionals. Regardless of the model, the goal of case management is to maximize the effective use of resources by ensuring that patients receive health and social services appropriate to their needs (Williams et al., 1993). Henderson and Collard (1992) identify three essential tasks:

- Locating the lowest-cost high-quality care
- Coordinating care among the patient, family, and providers
- Flexing benefit packages in order to optimize care for the patient

As social workers and other health care practitioners face a health care delivery system dominated by managed care, the case management role will grow in importance. What will this mean for providers, practitioners, and consumers of health care services?

Case management is not a new gimmick in health care that will disappear in a few years. Reports and preliminary research regarding its efficacy in containing costs and improving quality of care support its expansion throughout the industry. Therefore, health care practitioners need to increase their understanding of the goals and processes of case management, examine how to maximize its use within health care settings, and critically evaluate its strengths and weaknesses so that it becomes a tool for practice rather than a detriment.

Many social workers perceive case management as a threat, which leads to defensive behavior. Rather than focusing on how to fight case management, social workers need to accept it as a reality and focus their energies on shaping the process so that quality care is not sacrificed to cost containment. Greater attention needs to be focused on how case management is likely to evolve. Energy needs to be directed toward the adoption of the medical–social case management model, which offers the most comprehensive approach to patient care and recognizes the intrinsic importance of the relationship of social factors with illness. Finally, social workers need to explore developing partnerships with nurses to form case management teams. This model may offer the greatest potential to ensure that both the medical and social needs of the patient receive adequate attention, leading to improved quality of care and effective cost containment.

Social work has a choice. The profession can view case management from an adversarial stance and try to fight it or it can embrace case management as a model that may offer new opportunities for practice in health care and participate in shaping the process. The latter choice offers a more proactive stance that can ultimately benefit the patient, family, provider, and the social work profession.

## References

American Hospital Association. (1992). In S. Rose (Ed.), *Case management and social work* (pp. 149–159). New York: Longman.

Austin, C. D. (1983). Case management in long-term care: Options and opportunities. *Health and Social Work, 8*(1), 16–30.

Bartlett, H. M. (1940). *Some aspects of social casework in a medical setting.* Chicago: Banta Publishing.

Berger, C. S. (1982). *A political-economic analysis of hospital receptivity to social work.* Doctoral diss., School of Social Work, University of Southern California, Los Angeles.

Berger, C. S. (1990). Enhancing social work influence in the hospital: Identifying sources of power. *Social Work in Health Care, 15*(2), 77–93.

Berger, C. S. (1993). *Restructuring and resizing: Strategies for social work and human resource administrators in health care settings.* Chicago: Society for Social Work Administrators in Health Care.

Berger, C. S., Gendler, B., Johnen, J., Blackman, N., Rosser, H., & Kirchoff, S. (1992). *Final report of Project AFTER: Alternatives for teens through education and resources.* Demonstration grant #H86 DP 00472, Office of Substance Abuse Prevention, Alcohol, Drug Abuse and Mental Health Administration, Washington, DC.

Cannon, I. M. (1923). *Social work in hospitals: A contribution to progressive medicine.* New York: Russel Sage Foundation.

Cummings, K. C., & Abell, R. M. (1993). Losing sight of the shore: How a future integrated American health care organization might look. *Health Care Management Review, 18*(2), 39–50.

Egdahl, R. H. (1986). Managed care programs: The danger of undercare. *Hospitals, 60*(13), 136.

Falcone, A. R. (1979). *Development of a long-term care information system: Final report.* Lansing, MI: Michigan Office of Services to the Aging.

Germaine, C. (1984). *Social work practice in health care: An ecological perspective.* New York: Free Press.

Hammer, M., & Champy, J. (1993). *Reengineering the corporation: A manifesto for business revolution.* New York: Harper Collins.

Henderson, M. G., & Collard, A. (1992). Measuring quality in medical case management programs. In S. Rose (Ed.), *Case management and social work* (pp. 170–183). New York: Longman.

Henderson, M. G., & Wallack, S. (1987). Evaluating case management for catastrophic illness. *Business and Health, 4*(3), 7–11.

Itagliata, J. (1982). Improving the quality of community care for the chronically mentally disabled: The role of case management. *Schizophrenia Bulletin, 8,* 655–674.

Kane, R. A. (1984). *Case management in long-term care: Background analysis for hospital social work.* Chicago: American Hospital Association.

Kane, R. A. (1992). Case management in health care settings. In S. Rose (Ed.), *Case management and social work* (pp. 170–203). New York: Longman.

Koska, M. T. (1990, May 5). Case management: Doing the right thing for the wrong reasons. *Hospitals, 64,* 28–30.

Loomis, J. F. (1992). Case management in health care. In S. Rose (Ed.), *Case management and social work* (pp. 160–169). New York: Longman.

Lumsdom, K. (1994). Beyond four walls. *Hospitals and health Networks, 68*(5), 44–45.

Macnee, C. L., & Penchansky, R. (1994). Targeting ambulatory care cases for risk management and quality management. *Inquiry, 31,* 66–75.

Merrill, J. C. (1985). Defining case management. *Business and Health, 2*(8), 2–9.

Miller, G. (1983). Case management: The essential services. In C. J. Sanborn (Ed.), *Case management in mental health service* (pp. 3–16). New York: Hawthorn Press.

Miller, R. S., & Rehr, H. (1983). *Social work issues in health care.* Englewood Cliffs, NJ: Prentice-Hall.

Newald, J. (1986). Diversifying? Better think case management. *Hospitals, 60*(16), 84.

Omnibus Budget Reconciliation Act. (1981). *U.S. Code,* vol. 42.

Resnick, R. (1992). Case management evolves into a quality care program. *Business and Health, 10*(10), 51–52, 54, 56.

Rose, S. M. (1992). *Case management and social work.* New York: Longman.

Rosenberg, F., & Rehr, H. (1983). *Advancing social work practice in the health care field: Emerging issues and new perspectives.* New York: Haworth Press.

Rubin, A. (1992). Case management. In S. Rose (Ed.), *Case management and social work* (pp. 5–20). New York: Longman.

Rutstein, D. D., Berenber, W., Chalmers, T. C., Child, D. G., III, Fishman, A. P., & Perin, E. B. (1976). Measuring the quality of care: A clinical method. *New England Journal of Medicine, 294,* 582–588.

Schlesinger, E. G. (1985). *Health care social work practice: Concepts and strategies.* St. Louis: Times Mirror/Mosby College Publishing.

Shoor, R. (1993). Looking to manage care more closely. *Business and Health, 11*(10), 46–48, 50, 52–53.

Spitz, B., & Abramson, J. (1987). Competition, capitation, and case management: Barriers to strategic reform. *Milbank Quarterly, 65*(3), 348–370.

Taulbee, P. (1991). Case management: Solving the 70/10 Equation. *Business and Health, 9*(7), 54, 56, 58, 60, 64.

Weil, M. (1985). Key components of providing efficient and effective services. In M. Weil, J. M. Karls, & Associates (Eds.), *Case management in human service practice* (pp. 29–71). San Francisco: Jossey-Bass.

Weil, M., Karls, J. M., & Associates. (Eds.). (1985). *Case management in human service practice.* San Francisco: Jossey-Bass.

Williams, R. G., Warrick, L. H. Christianson, J. B., & Netting, F. E. (1993). Critical factors for successful hospital-based case management. *Health Care Management Review, 18*(1), 63–70.

Chapter 8

# Case Management in the Public Welfare System

*Sue Pearlmutter and Rae Johnson*

C ase management systems have appeared in welfare programs throughout the country in the past 10 years. Adopted as a means of ensuring the provision of social services as well as tangible resources and benefits to clients, case management systems vary from state to state. Employment requirements for welfare recipients are also relatively new, and it is important that we understand the role that case management can play in assisting clients to become economically self-sufficient. This chapter explores the historical developments that led to the establishment of case management, discusses its presence in current employment programs for welfare recipients, and suggests directions for the future of case management in a changing welfare arena.

## *History of Public Welfare*

### ❏ Welfare as a Federal Program

Federal support of welfare programs began in 1935 with the Social Security Act's federal relief and pension programs for persons who are elderly, unemployed, blind, and disabled as well as for dependent children without parental support (Trattner, 1994). Prior to 1935, states and localities had provided "mother's pensions" for widows raising children. In this realignment of responsibility for dependent children and others in need, the federal government mandated a system of federal aid to states in which persons and families in need would receive regular and recurring services and grant-in-aid (Trattner, 1994).

Aid for Dependent Children (ADC) was designed as a pension or entitlement, that is, permanent support for persons unable to work, not as relief or temporary aid for persons unable to work (Berkowitz, 1991). Federal and and state governments viewed welfare as a way to keep families together regardless of their income and as an economic necessity and moral obligation. In providing a pension to dependent children, ADC reflected the belief that women's place was in the home caring for children and men's place was in the labor force. Aid for Dependent Children also served as a mechanism for keeping white, middle-class widows out of the labor force. While these women stayed at home, women of color and lower-class women continued to work outside the home to support their families (Abramovitz, 1988; Brock, 1992; Miller, 1990). States had a lot of discretion administering federal grants. Many states set up restrictive regulations to deny funds to women based on their personal behavior. These restrictions effectively discriminated against low-income and nonwhite women and children, keeping the number of children receiving ADC relatively small. Until the Supreme Court overturned many of these restrictions, states successfully ensured that social workers dealt punitively with their clients and thus maintained social control over them. Thus, although social workers provided social services, they exercised significant control over resources and served only those whom they considered worthy or deserving of assistance (Abramovitz, 1988, Miller, 1990).

## ❏ A Changing System and Services

By the late 1950s, the demographic makeup of ADC recipients had shifted as a result of increases in divorce and separation rates and out-of-wedlock births from a population comprising primarily white widows with children to a more disenfranchised population of whom many were African American single mothers. Americans began to view the welfare system as a form of dependency rather than as an economic support for those in need. Recipients of ADC began to receive counseling to "overcome their personal shortcomings" as the notion of adding social services to ADC, including casework, gained support during these years (Trattner, 1994). The goal of casework was to rehabilitate recipients by evaluating their problems and strengths, counseling them, and assisting them to achieve economic self-sufficiency through training. The system attempted to contain costs by denying assistance and moving those who did receive assistance out of the system as quickly as possible. Because people believed that the increasing welfare rolls were related to the deterioration of the family, casework focused on keeping families together and preventing out-of-wedlock births.

In 1962, amendments to the SSA focused attention on individual aid and services through casework. Aid for Dependent Children was changed to Aid to Families with Dependent Children (AFDC) to reflect a 1950 amendment to the SSA extending the ADC grant to custodial parents and to reflect the shift of emphasis from economic assistance to children to social services for families. Caseworkers attempted to assess the ability of families to achieve economic self-sufficiency, to help families remove identified barriers, and to refer them to other social services that would assist them in achieving self-sufficiency. States had wide latitude and few specific guidelines to implement these amendments. Although the federal government offered to reimburse casework services at up to 75% of cost, few states initiated full programs (Brock, 1992). Caseworkers maintained large case loads and were able to see clients only once or twice, defeating the program's intent to provide intensive services to families and to help them achieve independence from the welfare system.

Legislation in 1964 updated the welfare regulations and allowed two-parent families with an unemployed parent to receive assistance. Advocacy efforts in communities in the early 1960s heightened awareness of welfare programs, and more people fought to establish their eligibility (Berkowitz, 1991). Casework and social services had not reduced the number of families on welfare, and the costs of the program continued to grow. Congress, frustrated with the system and failed attempts to rehabilitate recipients, introduced the Work Incentive Program (WIN) in 1967. Although the intent of the new legislation was to encourage self-support and strengthen the family, the emphasis for workers shifted from providing casework and other social services to determining eligibility for welfare programs.

Although a discretionary program at first, WIN attempted to offer recipients training, education, work experience, child care, housing, and eventual employment to help them obtain independence from the welfare system. The WIN program required unemployed fathers on AFDC and dependent youths aged 16 and older who were neither working nor in school to participate, but caseworkers seldom enforced sanctions for nonparticipation. In addition, most of the services were not directly job related. Amended in 1971 to require registration for all AFDC recipients, WIN was only marginally successful. Although the 1971 legislation emphasized employment-based training and tripled federal funding, resources were not sufficient to assure jobs for all participants (Brock, 1992; Gueron, 1987). Although WIN caseworkers assisted participants through the program's work-registration, job-training, and job-search activities, they maintained heavy case loads, often in excess of 200 clients. Social workers endured program instability, poor funding, and inconsistent program goals. They also experienced significant discomfort with requirements that women with children younger than 18 enter the labor force and were reluctant to enforce compliance with this regulation. Lack of enforcement and scarce resources resulted in WIN becoming a work-registration program rather than an employment and training program. Society's ambivalence toward welfare recipients was reflected by rules requiring women with children younger than 18 to enter the labor force.

## ❑ Discretionary State Efforts

Between 1972 and 1988, welfare programs focused increasingly on accurate determination of eligibility and compliance with policy. Workers became technical experts, consigned to constant awareness of regulations, eligibility certification, and reduction in the number of individuals who qualified for benefits. In 1981, the Omnibus Reconciliation Act created block grants to states that reduced reporting requirements, eliminated the need to target low-income populations, and cut funding for social services by 20% (Brock, 1992). These policies further restricted social workers' discretion in determining how to work with recipients and focused additional attention on determination of eligibility (Bane & Ellwood, 1994).

States designed their own welfare-to-work programs to meet local economic conditions and the specific needs of recipients. Many states developed WIN demonstration programs using flexible service arrangements. Others used combinations of services such as:

- Community work experience: Unpaid work assignments in public or nonprofit agencies whereby welfare recipients could "work off" their AFDC benefits

- Required job-search activities, including job clubs, work orientation, and job referrals

- Work supplementation/grant diversion: Using AFDC funds to develop and subsidize jobs for welfare recipients in the public and private sectors (American Public Welfare Association, 1992).

For the first time, caseworkers in these welfare-to-work programs functioned as case managers. They assessed participants' strengths and needs, developed an employability plan with them, and monitored compliance with the plan. They helped participants to access resources and provided support throughout the process.

## ❑ Emergence of Case Management

Recognizing the need for a more uniform approach to assisting poor families and a comprehensive review of the welfare system, Congress passed the Family Support Act in 1988. This legislation combined the expectation that parents become responsible for their families through payment of child support and participation in the labor force. The act also recognized that many families receiving welfare needed more than education and training to overcome the barriers preventing them from obtaining employment. Congress enacted under the Family Support Act a new welfare-employment program, the Job Opportunity and Basic Skills Training (JOBS) program, to serve as the primary vehicle through which participants could attain economic self-sufficiency. States were to provide various services, including basic education, job-skills training, job-readiness activities, job placement, and job development. States also had to provide at least two of four optional components: job search, on-the-job training, work supplementation, and community work experience. Policymakers recognized the value of case management services from individual state programs, WIN demonstration projects, and the advice of advocates and recommended case management as a service option for state JOBS programs (American Public Welfare Association, 1992, 1993; *Federal Register,* 1989; Hagen & Lurie, 1992).

## *Case Management Defined*

The American Public Welfare Association (1993) defines case management with welfare recipients as the "brokering and coordination of the multiple social, health, education, and employment services necessary to promote self-sufficiency and strengthen family life" (p. 6). This definition reflects the Family Support Act's purpose of helping families avoid long-term dependency. States have the ability to design and implement case management systems that meet the unique needs of both the participants and the state (Hagen & Lurie, 1994a). Although assessment, case planning, linkage to services, monitoring of service use and participant progress, and advocacy occur in all states, the extent and depth to which each function is carried out depends on how the delivery system is designed. The following sections summarize how these five functions are being implemented in the nation's JOBS programs, drawing extensively on a survey of JOBS case managers conducted by the American Public Welfare Association in 1991.

### ❏ Assessment

In all states included in the survey (American Public Welfare Association, 1992, 1993), assessment includes examining participants' educational background, work history, and child-care needs. Most states assess transportation needs, job interests and aptitudes, academic achievement, and personal characteristics such as health, history of substance abuse, and motivation to obtain employment. Many states also include a family assessment either in the formal assessment process or informally through the interaction between case managers and participants (American Public Welfare Association, 1992).

## ❏ Case Planning

In JOBS programs, planning focuses on developing an employability plan that includes an employment goal and the service components in which the participant will enroll and identifies barriers to participation and support services needed to overcome those barriers. Although intended to be a mutual process involving both the case manager and participant, case managers in some states may make these decisions unilaterally (American Public Welfare Association, 1992). Case managers are responsible for informing participants of their options and program requirements and helping them to develop a plan best suited to their needs.

## ❏ Service Linkage

Most programs view linkage to services as a joint effort between the case manager and participant, although some assign the task specifically to case managers or other staff. Only two of the surveyed states expect participants to find services themselves (American Public Welfare Association, 1992). The range of services includes basic education (literacy and high school equivalency), life-skills training, post-secondary education, job search and job club, community work experience, and immediate employment. Some states offer variations such as work supplementation, a service in which the state's welfare department agrees to subsidize jobs for participants, or on-the-job training, whereby participants receive training in specific skills for an agreed-upon period and employers receive a subsidy and pay wages to participants.

## ❏ Advocacy

State welfare agencies may encourage or discourage case managers' advocacy efforts on behalf of JOBS participants. Case managers may be able to advocate for and with participants with other agencies to obtain services or they may feel restricted when advocating for participants within their own agency or within external systems. Some programs emphasize this function and support case managers, giving them the authority to purchase services from other agencies. Some may contract directly with community agencies to perform specific components of the JOBS program, thus ensuring the availability of resources to participants. In other states, advocacy is virtually nonexistent due to lack of funding and administrative support (American Public Welfare Association, 1992, 1993; Hagen & Lurie, 1994a).

## ❏ Monitoring

This task includes case oversight and myriad activities for which case managers are responsible. Case managers track participation in program components to assure that the employability plan is being pursued. They must ensure that participants are properly using child care, transportation assistance, and special-need allowances. Case managers must see or speak with participants and complete forms or input data into an automated information system mandated by federal regulations (American Public Welfare Association, 1992, 1993; Hagen & Lurie, 1994a).

## *Models*

States use three case management models in implementing their JOBS programs. In addition, some states combine models to ensure effective coordination of services and efficient use of staff. The structure of case management depends a great deal on the view of the welfare agency with regard to the purpose of welfare and the needs of people targeted for case management services.

## ❏ Generalist Model

In more than 30 states, a single case manager works with a participant throughout his or her experience in the JOBS program. Case manager responsibilities include assessment, case planning, monitoring, and evaluation. Within these functions, the case manager provides supportive counseling and assists in obtaining resources that the participant and his or her family want and need. Although this model encourages continuity of service, it requires the case manager to have thorough knowledge of the program and the available service components (American Public Welfare Association, 1992; Hagen & Lurie, 1994a).

## ❏ Team Model

Seven states have adopted a team model, in which a case manager coordinates services for the participant and other specialists become involved with specific program activities. The team then works together to coordinate services. In some states, team members consist solely of staff within the JOBS program, whereas in other states the team may include staff from other agencies with whom the participant is involved. This approach is more comprehensive than the generalist model in its perspective of participant needs, but it is also more costly. Some states, for example, Maryland, which originally chose a team approach, have altered staffing patterns because of increased operational expenses. Other states, for example, Pennsylvania, use teams only with participants who require intensive services and limit the number of cases assigned to the team members (American Public Welfare Association 1992; Hagen & Lurie, 1994a).

## ❑ Specialist Model

In the specialist model, which is used in five states, different case managers assume responsibility for the case as the participant moves through the program. Although case managers are able to develop specific expertise, they may lose the more holistic approach of the generalist model. In addition, the approach may "perpetuate the fragmented service delivery system because it may not provide participants with the sense of continuity across programs envisioned as optimal case management" (American Public Welfare Association, 1992, p. 17).

## ❑ An Alternative Model

Another approach, used in Oklahoma, combines the tasks of income maintenance and social service workers. The worker assesses eligibility for services and performs case management functions. This may result in an emphasis on rules and regulations associated with determining eligibility and neglect the client-centered, individualized planning intended for case management, although it may be easier for the participant in that he or she has only one contact in the welfare agency (Hagen & Lurie, 1994a).

## *Funding*

Funding for case management services in public welfare generally comes from a combination of state and federal sources; that is, the federal government establishes a rate at which it will match state government expenditures. Funding for welfare employment programs prior to the passage of the Family Support Act came from combined federal and state dollars, state funds allocated for welfare assistance, private contributions from national and local foundations, and/or from demonstration-project funding provided by the U.S. Department of Health and

Human Services (Behn, 1991; Burghardt & Gordon, 1990; Friedlander, Riccio, & Freedman, 1993; Gueron, 1986; Herr & Halpern, 1991; Hershey & Patch, 1990; Kemple & Haimson, 1994; Okagaki, 1989; O'Neill, 1990). For the JOBS program, in which case management services are discretionary, the federal regulations indicated that each state with an approved JOBS plan would receive as its annual maximum payment the sum of the following two amounts:

- An amount that equals the state's WIN or WIN demonstration allocation of the fiscal year ended September 30, 1987.

- An amount granted from the remainder of the "national limitation on the basis of each state's relative average monthly number of adult [AFDC] recipients" (*Federal Register,* 1989, p. 42256).

Federal financial participation (the federal match to state funding) for case management services would then be available to each state in various ways:

- At a rate of 90% for those expenditures up to or equal to the state's WIN or WIN demonstration allocation for 1987. The state could match these federal dollars with cash expenditures or with in-kind services.

- Additional federal financial participation for case management and other direct services, up to the limit described above, would be provided to the state at an enhanced rate—the higher of the state's Medicaid reimbursement rate or 60%. Funds for child care were also available at the Medicaid reimbursement rate. However, federal financial participation was open-ended with no limit or cap. The states had to show actual cash expenditures to receive the match.

- The regulations specified a reduced rate of federal financial participation for states that failed to meet mandated participation rates for the program within the specified time lines.

- No federal financial participation was available to cover costs of participant education or training, whether initiated by the program or by the participant (*Federal Register,* 1989).

Federal funding for the JOBS program has risen from $800 million in 1990 to $1.3 billion in fiscal year 1995. Although some states have reached their federal cap, many have not. In fiscal year 1992, only 67% of the available federal match was used, and it was expected that in 1993 only 76% of the allocation would be accessed (Hagen

& Lurie, 1994b). Despite the failure of states to capture all of the federal dollars for JOBS, case management services suffer. They are subject to the JOBS cap described above, which limits overall spending in some states. In addition, states must appropriate the matching funds, and given the fiscal conditions in some states, full allocations for the JOBS program are not available. Finally, because JOBS emphasizes participation rates, case management services are not a priority.

Using Austin's (1990) delimiters of funding patterns, one would describe funding for this program as *pooled;* that is, the funding arrives at the state welfare agency from state general funds, federal matching funds, and private resources if these have been cultivated. Funding is *prospective:* The state legislature appropriates funding for the coming fiscal year, and welfare agency staff must work within the funding guidelines for the year. In addition, the funding is *capped* at the state level: The legislature authorizes only a specific amount to be used for the state's JOBS program, and when funds are no longer available, administrators trim services or income-maintenance workers fail to refer otherwise eligible clients.

## Legislative Mandate

Under the JOBS program, case management is an optional service. The regulations specify that

> the [state welfare] agency may assign a case manager to a participant and the participant's family. The decision to assign a case manager may be made on a case-by-case basis. The case manager must be responsible for assisting the family to obtain any services that may be needed to assure effective participation in the program (Federal Register, 1989, p. 42253).

States choosing case management are required to present a specific plan for the implementation of case management services in their design for operating the JOBS program.

Forty-nine states have opted to provide case management services to JOBS participants. Oklahoma, which for many years has used a single worker to determine eligibility for AFDC and provide social services to clients, has maintained this alternative model, viewing it as a mechanism for assuring oversight and management of its JOBS cases (Hagen & Lurie, 1994a). Within the states, legislation and regulations have established the individual JOBS programs, including specifications for the case management model to be used.

# *Cost*

In providing case management services, states have had to balance participant needs with available staff, financial, organizational, and community resources. Although federal expenditures for the JOBS program far outweigh those for previous welfare employment programs, costs at the state level continue to increase, often beyond the availability of state dollars needed to capture the federal match. In their attempt to contain costs, states have used several strategies. These strategies are discussed below, with attention to their impact on case management services.

*Case-load size.* Although the optimal case-load size for provision of case management services has not been specified, it is clear that "case loads must be small if they consist of high-risk populations [or those] with few personal or social resources" (Kanter, 1989, p. 367). In the JOBS program, in which "multiple needs must be met with multiple resources in order for clients to enhance their self-reliance" (American Public Welfare Association, 1993, p. 9), case-load sizes average more than 100 and range from 10 to 500 (American Public Welfare Association, 1993; Hagen & Lurie, 1994a). Case managers spend 30% to 40% of their time performing required data entry and information recording tasks, which leaves insufficient time for meeting the intensive needs of participants and their families. However, states' decisions to maintain high case-load sizes have held down personnel costs.

*Targeting the service population.* Federal regulations had specified that the target population for the JOBS program include all nonexempt AFDC recipients. Mothers with children older than three years of age are nonexempt as long as child care is available, and mothers younger than 20 years must participate, regardless of their child(ren')s age, if they do not have a high school diploma or its equivalent. In addition, at least one member of a two-parent AFDC family must participate. The regulations specified that by 1995, 20% of each state's nonexempt AFDC recipients should participate in the program. States were also required to spend 55% of the JOBS-related funds on specific target groups: (1) families that have received assistance for 36 of the past 60 months; (2) custodial parents younger than 24 years who have not completed high school, are not currently in school, and have worked little or not at all in the previous year; and (3) families in which the youngest child is within two years of becoming ineligible for welfare assistance (*Federal Register*, 1989). In an effort to contain costs and ensure the best use of available resources, states have sought federal waivers so that they can further target the program's intended audience to those who can best and most quickly benefit from the program's service components. Thus, the program's initial intent to serve those most vulnerable and those at risk for long-term welfare dependence is being thwarted by fiscal constraints. For case managers, the decision to control access to the program more tightly is a welcome relief. If waivers are approved, they will be working with participants who are, ideally, better prepared to use the scarce resources that are available and to move through the service components toward economic self-sufficiency.

*Use of existing community resources.* The regulations establishing the JOBS program require that states coordinate services and consult with "related services provided by other agencies" (*Federal Register,* 1989, p. 42247). State programs were to establish linkages with the Job Training Partnership Act entities and private industry councils available to them, the existing public education systems (for adult basic education), low-income housing resources, employment services, child-care resources, and programs within the welfare agency that would assist participants and their families. Although coordination of services and use of existing resources is significant in any model of case management, staff has often found that existing resources have not been adequate to meet participant needs and that some or all of the needed resources are not available to them (American Public Welfare Association, 1993; Hagen & Lurie, 1994a).

*Limited access to education and training.* Many states had at first permitted participants to access long-term training and four-year college education, recognizing that, for participants, maximum opportunity for achieving self-sufficiency lay with education and training. As program costs have risen, states have eliminated the flexibility of educational choices, partly because expenditures for such training cannot capture federal assistance. Case managers now have fewer resources available to them in assisting participants toward economic self-sufficiency.

*Limited availability of supportive resources.* States are required to ensure the availability of child care, transportation, and other supportive services for participants who are enrolled in and attending education, training, and job-search activities. Again, as program costs have increased, the availability of these resources has been reduced. Some states have restricted the number of hours of paid child care; others have reduced or restricted payments for transportation. Some states, which had provided allowances for special needs such as books, car repairs, or work clothing, have reduced or eliminated such allowances. Fewer resources means that case managers need significant creativity in finding and using the resources that are available.

*Time limitations.* The Family Support Act and the JOBS program are intended to "assure that needy families with children obtain the education, training, and employment that will help them avoid long-term welfare dependency" (*Federal Register,* 1989, p. 42245). Neither the legislation nor the regulations specified time limits for completion of training, education, or employment-search activities. As program costs have risen and state legislators have become increasingly invested in the rhetoric of welfare reform, many states have applied time limits to participation. Case managers, who recognize that these limits (in most cases two to three years) will decrease opportunities for their clients to become self-sufficient, must apply the time limits and assist participants in meeting them.

**Punitive measures.** Increasing costs of welfare programs and shrinking state budgets have led to stringent and punitive measures intended to move clients out of the welfare system. The regulations stipulated that sanctions be applied if a recipient failed to comply with an agreed-upon plan, refused work, or left work without good cause. Although sanctions withheld benefits from the individual who violated the rules, the children still received AFDC allotments. Sanctions were applied differentially for up to six months, depending upon the nature and extent of the violation of rules (*Federal Register,* 1989). Today, states are seeking to apply more extensive sanctions, including removal of the entire family from the welfare rolls, until compliance is assured. Case managers who have traditionally been helpers, acquirers of resources, and advocates are now assuming the role of "enforcer"—a role they neither anticipated nor desired.

**Competency of staff.** Although agreement is lacking regarding who should perform case management tasks, professionals generally agree that the person-in-environment frame of reference is the best complement to performing case management responsibilities (Austin, 1990; Hagen, 1992; Kanter, 1989; Moore, 1990; Moxley, 1989; O'Connor, 1988; Roberts-DeGennaro, 1987). States have various education and experience requirements for case managers. Some states require that part of the staff be composed of social workers and others of former income-maintenance workers and/or employment counselors. Few states have master's-level social workers among the ranks of JOBS case managers. In its survey of JOBS case managers, the American Public Welfare Association (1992, 1993) found that 22 states require a bachelor's degree and four an associate's degree. Seven states have no education requirement, and eight states require only a high school diploma. An additional two states accept a combination of education and work experience. Two states require that case management be licensed, and one state requires that case managers be bilingual. In part, the variance in educational backgrounds of case managers is related to the declassification of social work positions in public human service agencies. In the JOBS program, the lack of common experience and education has a significant bearing on differential approaches to the work. As a cost-containment strategy, this disregard for professional education has a direct impact on the quality of services to participants through salaries paid to case managers. In 45% of the states, case managers' starting salaries are less than $19,000 per year (American Public Welfare Association, 1992), resulting in low staff morale and high turnover.

## ❏ Participants' Responses

Cost-containment strategies present many dilemmas to program participants and potential clients. Participants state that they cannot contact their case managers and that their case managers often have little time available for them. Because of minimal state resources, participants are not able to secure adequate child care and cannot maintain reliable transportation. Participants fear that time limits and restrictions on participation will prevent them from achieving their educational goals or securing desired employment. They are concerned that the case manager, whom they have learned to trust and in whom they have confided, will leave and that they will have to begin again with a new person. Participants decry the intrusive nature of the welfare system and resent these new, more punitive measures that states are seeking to implement. Most important, participants place a high value on the emotional support and encouragement that case managers provide. For many recipients, case management is the first supportive service they have received within the welfare system. They need to move toward self-sufficiency (Glover, Gregoire, & Pearlmutter, 1993; Hagen & Davis, 1994a, 1994b, 1994c; Heimovics, 1994; Miller, 1990; Office of Inspector General, 1993; Quiroz & Tosca, 1990; Skricki, 1994).

## *Clinical Issues*

### ❏ Interventions

Case managers in JOBS programs intervene with individual participants, with other segments of the welfare agency, and with community resources. The purpose of their interventions is to help participants achieve economic self-sufficiency through completion of employability plans. At each level of intervention, case managers and participants face troubling dilemmas.

*Individual level.* Case management ideally should establish and maintain supportive, encouraging, and validating relationships with participants. For the most part, however, case management involves a series of clerical tasks (American Public Welfare Association, 1992; Hagen & Lurie, 1994a). Referrals to state JOBS programs come from income-maintenance workers when a family applies for and is determined eligible to receive cash assistance. In some states, referrals include only those who volunteer; in other states, workers may refer any recipient who fits within a target group. Case management tasks begin at the point of program orientation and assessment of participants. This process may occur in one day or during several days. Case managers engage the participant in discussions about education, skills, work experience, employment goals, wants and needs, and strengths and problems. During these initial meetings, the case manager and participant establish the relationship that will assist the participant to move through the program's service components.

After the initial assessment is completed, the participant and the case manager develop an employability or self-sufficiency plan. This formal plan states participant goals, activities to reach those goals, and supportive services to be provided (American Public Welfare Association, 1992). It usually requires the participant's signature and is considered a contractual agreement. Case managers must be prepared to apply sanctions if the participant does not fulfill the agreement and cannot show "good cause" for failing to meet the terms.

In many JOBS programs, service arrangements are also made jointly by the participant and case manager. Case managers help participants determine the appropriate service component and arrange for placement in that component. They may also assist in arranging child care, transportation, and other supportive services.

After arrangements are made, the participant is expected to implement the plan, and the case manager is responsible for monitoring and evaluating the participant's progress through in-person meetings or telephone calls and significant data collection. Monitoring progress is a cumbersome, intensive, and difficult process. Federal regulations require that participants engage in approved activities an average of at least 20 hours per week and attend at least 75% of scheduled program hours (*Federal Register,* 1989). In addition to monitoring attendance, case managers in many states must monitor expenditures for tuition, child care, transportation assistance, and use of special service payments.

***Institutional and systems level.*** Although the tasks and processes involved in individual interventions are well delineated, those involved in systems intervention and advocacy are not. Case managers clearly recognize that they must perform these tasks, assisting and modeling behavior for participants, but they also recognize that resources are scarce and that they lack the authority and the power to claim what participants want and need (American Public Welfare Association, 1992; Austin, 1990; Hagen & Lurie, 1994a; Moxley, 1989).

As case managers complete assessments, assist in arranging services, and monitor participant progress, they must coordinate services within their own agencies and among those in the community. They interact with educators, employers, child-care providers, mental health service providers, and others from whom they require services and information. Within the welfare agency, they must maintain contact with income-maintenance staff, child-protection staff, and others with whom participants might be working. If the state's program contracts for service with private agencies in the community, additional layers of coordination and information sharing are necessary. To acquire resources and obtain the information they need, case managers must be knowledgeable as well as creative.

## ❏ Settings

Welfare agencies are the primary setting for case management work. Participants come to the agency for orientation, assessment, and planning as well as for many of the service components. For many welfare recipients, the agency may be an inconvenient, sterile, and unwelcoming place that serves as a constant reminder that they are part of the welfare system. Case managers for JOBS attempt to bring warmth to the agency and to create a positive environment for the program:

- Case managers may station themselves in the agency lobby, personally welcoming participants as they arrive for orientation and assessment.

- Colorful brochures and posters advertise the opportunities that the program offers to participants.

- Bulletin boards highlight participant achievements, promoting those who have achieved high school equivalency and honors grades in postsecondary education and training, recognizing those who have completed training, and congratulating those who have become employed.

- To assure privacy and maintain confidentiality, case managers meet with participants in private meeting rooms or offices with doors rather than the standard cubicles or open work stations.

Some states or localities have adopted outreach mechanisms to ensure a positive image for the program and to increase participation. Case managers may be stationed in community agencies, public housing units, neighborhood organizations, schools, or health clinics. They may meet in participants' homes or in other settings mutually agreed upon by the participant and case manager. Training, education, and employment sites may provide additional opportunities for visits and monitoring of participant progress.

## ❏ Staffing

As discussed previously, JOBS case managers have various backgrounds. Many are experienced income-maintenance workers who have spent years determining client eligibilty for services in the welfare system. Others have significant education and experience in social services. In a study of JOBS programs in 10 states, Hagen and Lurie (1994a) found that case managers were "experienced human service workers [with an] average of 10 years' experience in human service work" (p. 13). They also found that their survey respondents had "extensive experience in their current agencies (averaging 6.9 years) and in their current positions (averaging 3.5 years)" (p. 13). In some states, JTPA workers, employment service workers, or workers in privately contracted agencies perform case management activities. In those states, workers may have human service experience but lack specific education or training for case management (American Public Welfare Association, 1992; Brock, 1992)

Case-load size is a major determinant of the frequency of case manager and participant contact and is a significant concern for case managers (American Public Welfare Association, 1992; Hagen & Lurie, 1994a). Although a few states have set case-load sizes small enough to permit intensive services, most have established case loads of 100 or more. Although case managers in these states recognize that participants have many needs and desires, they are unable to achieve the frequency or intensity of contact that participants require. In addition, administrative and paperwork requirements are often burdensome, adding to case managers' feelings of frustration.

Supervisory and administrative support are necessary components to the practice of case management in the JOBS program (American Public Welfare Association, 1993). Without such support, case managers

> can refer participants to activities and work with providers. But they do not have the authority to demand compliance or the resources to buy specialized services that participants may need. Even if their caseloads were more reasonable, it is not clear that they can be fully effective in linking together the various components of JOBS (Chisman & Woodworth, 1992, p. 80).

Recognizing this, administrators must create and maintain the community linkages and provide "energetic support throughout the agency in advocating for change within the community service network, as well as sufficient time to deal effectively with clients" (American Public Welfare Association, 1993, p. 75). Supervisors in the program can provide necessary feedback to case managers and administrators (Weil & Karls, 1985). They are in a "strategic position to: 1) clarify the service delivery structure to the case manager; and 2) interpret to JOBS administrators and other community leaders the client needs that have been identified through the case management process" (American Public Welfare Association, 1993, p. 75). When supervisors and administrators fail to recognize their essential roles in the operation of the program, participants are unable to access needed and wanted resources, case managers' authority and power are severely limited, and efforts to alter the welfare system are seriously hampered.

State JOBS programs have provided various training opportunities to case managers. However, few states offer training in areas in which case managers have great need: counseling with participants, understanding cultural diversity, problem-solving skills, relating to community agencies, building resource networks, dealing with substance-abuse problems, marketing and community relations, and monitoring and evaluation of case management activities (American Public Welfare Association, 1992; Hagen & Lurie, 1994a).

## Standards/Quality Assurance

Although the Family Support Act required that the U.S. Department of Health and Human Services develop a set of outcome-based performance standards by October 1993, no standards are in place to assure the quality of JOBS services in general or of case management services specifically. Standards would be particularly useful in this program, which considers participation as its primary outcome. An agreed-upon set of performance measures would

> ensure that case managers are exercising their discretionary authority in conformance with the agency's overall mission . . . that resources are being allocated in an effective manner and [would] assess changes in performance over time (American Public Welfare Association, 1993, pp. 66–67).

The American Public Welfare Association (1993, 1994) recommends that state JOBS programs first establish a set of tangible outcomes, such as the number of participants who will become employed full time at a specific wage, with benefits, or the number who will complete training. After the goals are set, program administrators can develop performance-based objectives related to the goals. They further recommend that welfare agencies examine both process and outcome measures to assure a complete analysis of the program.

*Process measures.* These standards would examine the ways in which participants move through the service components, assess the feasibility of participants' achievement of short- and long-term goals, determine if service referrals are used, explore the use of mechanisms to involve participants' families in assessment and care planning, and appraise participants' ratings of satisfaction with case management and the program service components.

*Outcome measures.* A set of standards focused on outcomes would determine whether skills are attained, training is completed, and well-paying permanent employment with benefits secured. These measures would determine whether teens and young adults in the program are meeting their basic educational goals and if receipt of child-support payments is increasing. They would assess the average placement wage and determine the average time that families in the program remain in the welfare system.

The etablishment of standards should involve administrators, supervisory staff, case managers, and participants. These groups are best prepared to articulate the strengths of the program as well as barriers to success and are most aware of the strategies for assisting participants to achieve desired outcomes.

## Evaluation

Because JOBS programs have been in operation in most states since only the early 1990s, national impact studies have not yet been published. However, exploratory studies in some states, qualitative studies, and results of programs upon which the design of the JOBS program was based have yielded some data.

### ❑ Studies of Pre-JOBS Employment Programs

Gueron and Pauly (1991) summarized the finding of nine broad-coverage welfare-to-work programs that offered services to targeted groups of mandated AFDC recipients and four programs that offered services to groups of voluntary participants. All of the studies included randomized assignment of clients to a program group and a control group. Case management was used as the primary mechanism to ensure participation and monitor activities in these programs. The studies examined two key impacts: (1) increases in income and (2) decreases in receipt of cash assistance. In seven of the nine broad-coverage programs, increases in average annual earnings for participants ranged "from $268 to $658 in the last year of follow-up. Depending on the program, these increases were 11 to 43% above the annual earnings for people in the control group" (Gueron & Pauly, 1991, p. 27). Participants in the voluntary programs increased their "annual average earnings by $591 to $1,121—14 to 34% above the control group's earnings" (p. 27). These outcomes were sustained for at least three years after enrollment in the program. Only 3 of the 13 programs showed at least moderate reductions in the number of people receiving welfare at the end of the follow-up period. Although case management activities occurred in these programs and had an impact on participants' progress, none of the studies examined case management's effectiveness. Gueron and Pauly (1991) conclude that the "substantial share of JOBS resources that will probably be devoted to these activities and the central role given this function in some state programs highlight the importance of further understanding the cost-effectiveness of different case management strategies" (p. 44).

## ❏ Studies of State JOBS Programs

Hagen and Davis (1994c), in their study of participants in 10 state JOBS programs, indicated that 280 of their 357 survey respondents (78.4%) considered encouragement and support as the most important service offered by their case managers. Almost 75% "rated their case managers as helpful or extremely helpful in assisting them to reach their goals" (p. 73). In a previous study, Hagen, Lurie, and Wang (1993) reported that case managers "identified their most commonly performed task as being the provision of on-going support and encouragement to clients" (p. 44). However, less than half of the case managers surveyed for this study of case management activities viewed those services as "successful in promoting and fostering on-going client participation in the JOBS program and in assisting clients to achieve their goals in the program" (p. 45). In a study of New Jersey's Realizing Economic Achievement Program, Hershey and Patch (1990) reported that program participants appreciated the efforts of their case managers but were often frustrated that case managers did not have time to attend to participants' needs or explore their personal or family situations. In addition, participants believed that case managers lacked information about program resources and felt pressured by program constraints. Other studies using participant focus groups and/or surveys (Glover et al., 1993; Heimovics, 1994; Office of Inspector General, 1993; Quiroz

& Tosca, 1990; Skricki, 1994) replicated these findings, citing as an additional concern that case managers at times treated participants with disrespect and condescension. Participants reported that

> The worker . . . was not supportive . . . made me feel inferior and treated me like I was stupid. The worker acted as though she did not want me to attend school (Office of Inspector General, 1993, p. 11).

> It would help if they listened to us more and told us the correct information about things, instead of just beating around the bush. They talk to you like you're just a welfare client, instead of being a person. . . . Sometimes, I get so frustrated, I think, let's just stop and trade places for a while so they could know what it's like for us (Glover et al., 1993, p. 15).

Despite these disturbing concerns, many JOBS case managers were seen as helpful, supportive, and a critical factor in participants' achieving their goals in the program.

> She really went to bat for me and helped me to get what I wanted from the JOBS contractor (Skricki, 1994, p. 36).

> She listened to me, she had enough time to talk and listen to me. . . . She gave me some advice like my girlfriend would talk to me. That gave me more self-confidence (Glover et al., 1993, p. 13).

## Issues for Research and Practice

*Case-load size.* In each study mentioned above, the size of the case load carried by case managers emerged as a factor deserving further research. Although case loads vary, they often exceed 100. Because case managers' responsibilities are varied and far ranging, involving interaction with individuals and systems, case-load size needs to be evaluated carefully.

*Case manager tasks.* Although some consensus exists across state programs regarding tasks that case managers perform, case managers do not perform one set of functions across all programs. Should one designated case manager perform one in-depth assessment, or are sequential assessments more productive? Should case managers be counseling participants, or should their primary role be that of monitoring an agreed-upon plan? What kinds of tasks should be included in monitoring activities? How much time should be devoted to required paperwork and data entry? How much time should be available for direct service with participants? These and other areas of case manager responsibility and boundaries require further examination.

*Skills, training, and experience.* Case management roles have been assigned to persons with varying education, experience, and skill levels.

Assisting participants to achieve their goals effectively and efficiently while providing support and encouragement requires staff who are able to recognize participant strengths as well as problems. It may also require specific education, training, and ongoing staff development. Research is necessary to ascertain the proper mix of skills, training, and experience necessary.

*Availability of resources.* Although anecdotal evidence regarding strategies that case managers use to access resources is available (American Public Welfare Association, 1992, 1993; Behn 1991; Heimovics, 1994; Kemple & Haimson, 1994), little is known about more effective ways to develop new resources in communities and states. In addition, coordination among disparate agencies has not always resulted in significantly greater access for participants. To ensure such access and to increase the available pool of resources, research and ongoing monitoring of case management practice are necessary.

*Overall quality of case management services.* Participants have clearly articulated their frustration and confusion about the responsibilities, behavior, and attitudes of their case managers. They want and need their case managers' respect. They wish to develop a plan with their case manager that reflects their individual desires and goals and to receive support and encouragement along the way.

*Cost-effectiveness of case management services.* Regardless of caseload size, staffing in the JOBS program is a significant expense. Previous research has not clearly demonstrated a relationship between the cost of services per participant and the impact of the program. Both program administrators and policymakers would benefit from knowing whether, in general, such a relationship exists and, more specifically, understanding the combination of services and procedures that most efficiently produce the desired effects.

*Human capital investment versus workplace attachment.* Welfare employment programs have vacillated between those targeting long-term strategies of education and training as a means to assist people to become economically self-sufficient and those focusing on immediate work for AFDC recipients. The JOBS program stresses long-term investment (although states may develop work-focused programs), and the case manager plays a crucial role. Despite more than 30 years of various employment programs, we do not know conclusively which strategy works better for participants and for welfare systems. Because case management is relatively new in these programs and is closely associated with long-term investment in people, we must critically examine its role and the strategy itself.

## Culturally Competent Practice

Case management practice in public welfare presents unique dilemmas for staff. For 50 years, the welfare system, reflecting society's values, has given conflicting messages to AFDC recipients. Single mothers were either moral in their behavior or they were seen as unfit, they cared for their children in "acceptable" ways or they were irresponsible, they were prepared and motivated for work or they were lazy and worthless. When most middle-class women stayed at home, women on welfare were expected to stay at home. When we began to see the value of women's low-wage labor in the work force and the proportion of women in the labor force began to grow, those on welfare were obliged to join them. Their obligation was both economic and moral: Poor women owed financial support to their families and to the welfare system that had supported them, albeit meagerly. Welfare workers, now case managers, hear and recount the stories: generations of African American single mothers with six or seven children fathered by different men are on welfare. Yet, at any given time, 48% of those receiving welfare are white, 42% have been married, and less than 4% have more than three children. Welfare is cyclic. Most women need welfare assistance periodically. Most families receive assistance for fewer than three years. However, for many families with various racial and ethnic backgrounds, participation in the welfare system can be lengthy. As Bane and Ellwood (1994) state,

> The welfare population is heterogeneous. The vast majority of people starting welfare at any point in time and the vast majority of people who ever have spells on welfare stay only a short time. Yet the majority of welfare recipients at a point in time are in the midst of a much longer spell, and most welfare funds are spent on them (p. 36).

### ❏ What Case Managers Can Do

Case managers respond to both the misconceptions and the realities of welfare. They must contend with the altered face of welfare—that persons from various backgrounds receive cash assistance and that the welfare system affects them deeply. To accord respect to participants and to develop relationships with them, case managers must

- Acknowledge their own cultural biases and recognize how these will affect participants

- Restrain from judgment of participants, their families, and their lives

- Respond honestly to cultural practices, traditions, and beliefs about which they have little or no understanding

- Recognize that a participant's culture can be a strength and find ways to use that strength in the work

- Respect and honor participants' traditions

## *Ethics*

### ❏ Individual Case Managers

Principles or values underlying case management practice in public welfare should reflect belief in the capacity of people to grow and change, recognition of their strengths and abilities, respect for their life experiences, and commitment to working *with* rather than *for* participants as they pursue their goals. Although it is not difficult to articulate these values, in practice individual case managers are beset with ethical dilemmas. For example,

- A participant uses excessively punitive measures when disciplining a child.

- A participant earns cash income and does not report it to welfare officials.

- A case manager, formerly an income-maintenance worker, had long experience and great difficulty with a participant recently assigned to her JOBS case load.

- A case manager and participant meet to establish an employability plan, but the participant is unsure about choosing a goal and doesn't understand what is involved in achieving goals.

- A participant is enrolled at a local community college but has not been attending classes regularly; if she does not maintain her grades, the program will not support her attendance.

All of these dilemmas arise either from competing values or from competing loyalties (Loewenberg & Dolgoff, 1988). Often workers are unsure about the identity of "the client" in their work. Is the client the participant, the family, the agency, the welfare system, the legislature, or the taxpayer? Confidentiality is highly valued but reporting of child abuse is not only valued—it is mandated. Program policies may not be just or equitable, and case managers must find ways to apply policy while remaining loyal to both the program and participants.

## ❏ The Welfare Agency

Organizational factors compound ethical questions faced by case managers. Staff must respond to state and federal administrators and legislators as well as work on behalf of participants. The agency must distribute few resources in an equitable manner, ensuring that participants receive services and entitlements and that staff are able to manage their responsibilities. It must ensure confidentiality and the primacy of participant rights while ensuring that programs operate according to policy and regulations. Thus conflicting obligations and expectations characterize the operation of JOBS programs. The state welfare agency must balance these obligations.

## *Future Directions*

### ❏ Proposed Legislation

Congress has been considering proposals to reform the public welfare system and fundamentally change the structure of services to cash-assistance recipients. If implemented, many of these plans would have severe consequences, including strict limitations on the duration of cash assistance availability, denial of services to unmarried teen mothers and their children and to families in which paternity has not been established, and elimination of the "entitlement" status of AFDC and other related programs. Under the current system, AFDC is an entitlement program and the federal government is obligated to allocate the funds to assist those who are eligible. Proposed legislation would make these programs "discretionary" and place them under a spending cap, creating a system of block grants to the states in place of combined federal and state funding for many individual programs. Each year Congress would determine how much money would be appropriated for the block grant programs, but "those who qualify under the program rules would have no *right* [emphasis added] to assistance" (CLASP, 1995, p. 1). States might not receive sufficient funds to help support poor families, and "a lifeline for poor families when a state runs out of money" may not be available (p. 1). If enacted, the legislation would effectively eliminate the federal government's role in ensuring assistance to poor families and would place no requirements on the states to continue their current efforts on behalf of those families.

### ❏ Case Management

Although the proposed legislation would give more power to states to plan and implement welfare employment progress, it is not clear how states would allocate the available dollars, how much funding would be available for employment programs, or how states would target recipients for participation in the programs. The impact of this proposed legislation on JOBS programs is also uncertain.

Case managers will continue to play a significant role in service delivery. Welfare agencies and case managers must adapt to a changing welfare system by changing the culture of welfare. Case managers must support participants through the system, while ensuring that the system itself remains viable. Corbett (1994–95) suggests several strategies that programs and staff should use:

- Deliver an unambiguous message. The main objective of the agency is to move individuals toward independence and self-sufficiency. Case managers should deliver this message unambiguously to employment-program participants. Workers must help participants understand that welfare assistance is transitional and that education, training, and employment provide the means to escape poverty.

- Involve clients in the employment program immediately. Participation in the program should begin as soon as possible after a client applies for and receives benefits. Case managers must have light case loads to ensure that they can attend to participant needs.

- Close monitoring is a must. Case managers are responsible for monitoring and tracking participant progress. They must have the flexibility to follow participants who are moving through the program.

- Provide ongoing support and problem resolution. Case managers must be available to assist participants through the program, helping them to meet challenges and overcome obstacles as well as to find and acquire needed resources.

- Focus on outcomes. The agency and all of the direct-service staff should consistently attend to the program's goal of assisting clients to achieve economic self-sufficiency. This focus requires that programs have sufficient resources to carry out the strategies presented above, that case managers have time and flexibility to work with participants, and that the agency have available jobs to meet the needs of clients.

Finally, as case managers assist participants to achieve their employment goals, they must recognize participants' strengths, capacities, and assets. Participants can overcome limitations, challenges, and barriers only when they see their own strengths and believe in their capacity to learn and grow. Case managers who know and understand their clients' strengths can best facilitate that belief.

## References

Abramovitz, M. (1988). *Regulating the lives of women.* Boston: South End Press.

American Public Welfare Association. (1992). *Status report on JOBS case management practices.* Washington, DC: Author.

American Public Welfare Association. (1993). *JOBS case management handbook.* Washington, DC: Author.

American Public Welfare Association. (1994). *Managing JOBS caseloads.* Washington, DC: Author.

Austin, C. D. (1990). Case management: Myths and realities. *Families in Society, 71,* 398–405.

Bane, M. J., & Ellwood, D. T. (1994). *Welfare realities: From rhetoric to reform.* Cambridge, MA: Harvard University Press.

Behn, R. D. (1991). *Leadership counts: Lessons for public managers.* Cambridge, MA: Harvard University Press.

Berkowitz, E. D. (1991). *American welfare state.* Baltimore, MD: Johns Hopkins University Press.

Brock, T. W. (1992). *The implementation of welfare reform: Policy and organizational effects on service delivery in Los Angeles County.* Doctoral diss., Department of Social Welfare, University of California at Los Angeles.

Burghardt, J., & Gordon, A. (1990). *More jobs and higher pay: How an integraded program compares with traditional programs.* New York: Rockefeller Foundation.

Chisman, F. P., & Woodworth, R. S. (1992). *The promise of JOBS: Policies, programs and possibilities.* Washington, DC: Southport Institute for Policy Analysis.

CLASP. (1995, January 20). House Republicans introduce the Personal Responsibility Act. *CLASP Update,* p. 1.

Corbett, T. (1994–95). Changing the culture of welfare. *Focus, 16*(2), 12–21.

*Federal Register.* (1989, October 13). 45 CFR, Part 205.

Friedlander, D., Riccio, J., & Freedman, S. (1993). *GAIN; Two-year impacts in six counties.* Washington, DC: Manpower Demonstration Research Corp.

Glover, B. M., Gregoire, C., & Pearlmutter, S. (1993, September). *A report of focus group discussions: Topeka area employment preparation services.* Lawrence, KS: School of Social Welfare, University of Kansas.

Gueron, J. M. (1986). Work for people on welfare. *Public Welfare, 44*(1), 7–12.

Gueron, J. M. (1987). *Reforming welfare with work.* New York: Ford Foundation.

Gueron, J. M., & Pauly, E. (1991). *From welfare to work.* New York: Russell Sage Foundation.

Hagen, J. L. (1992). Women, work and welfare: Is there a role for social work? *Social Work, 37,* 9–14.

Hagen, J. L., & Davis, L. V. (1994a). Women on welfare talk about reform. *Public Welfare, 52*(1), 30–40.

Hagen, J. L., & Davis, L. V. (1994b). *Another perspective on welfare reform: Conversations with mothers on welfare*. Albany, NY: Nelson A. Rockefeller Institute of Government.

Hagen, J. L., & Davis, L. V. (1994c). *Implementing JOBS: The participants' perspective*. Albany, NY: Nelson A. Rockefeller Institute of Government.

Hagen, J. L., & Lurie, I. (1992). *Implementing JOBS: Initial state choices*. Albany, NY: Nelson A. Rockefeller Institute of Government.

Hagen, J. L., & Lurie I. (1994a). *Implementing JOBS: Case management services*. Albany, NY: Nelson A. Rockefeller Institute of Government.

Hagen, J. L., & Lurie, I. (1994b). *Implementing JOBS: Progress and promise*. Albany, NY: Nelson A. Rockefeller Institute of Government.

Hagen, J. L., Lurie, I., & Wang, L. (1993). *Implementing JOBS: The perspective of front-line workers*. Albany, NY: Nelson A. Rockefeller Institute of Government.

Heimovics, C. (1994) *Process evaluation of Missouri's FUTURES program*. Kansas City, MO: Cookingham Institute of Public Affairs.

Herr, T., & Halpern, R. (1991). *Changing what counts. Re-thinking the journey out of welfare*. Evanston, IL: Center for Urban Affairs and Policy Research.

Hershey, A., & Patch, J. (1990). *Participants' views of the REACH program: Results of focus groups in four New Jersey counties*. Princeton, NJ: Mathematica Policy Research, Inc.

Kanter, J. (1989). Clinical case management: Definition, principles, components. *Hospital and Community Psychiatry, 40,* 361–368.

Kemple, J. J., & Haimson, J. (1994). *Florida project independence: Program implementation, participation patterns, and first-year impacts*. New York: Manpower Demonstration Research Corp.

Loewenberg, F., & Dolgoff, R. (1988). *Ethical decisions for social work practice*. Itasca, IL: F. E. Peacock.

Miller, D. (1990). *Women and social welfare: A feminist analysis*. New York: Praeger.

Moore, S. T. (1990). A social work practice model of case management: The case management grid. *Social Work, 35,* 444–448.

Moxley, D. P. (1989). *The practice of case management*. Newbury Park, CA: Sage Publications.

O'Connor, G. G. (1988). Case management: System and practice. *Social Casework, 69,* 97–106.

Office of Inspector General. (1993). *Participants rate the JOBS program*. Washington, DC: U.S. Government Printing office.

Okagaki, A. (1989). *Women and self-sufficiency: Programs that work, policy that might*. Washington DC.: Corporation for Enterprise Development.

O'Neill, J. (1990). *Work and welfare in Massachusetts: An evaluation of the ET program:* Boston: Pioneer Institute for Public Policy Research.

Quiroz, J. T., & Tosca, R. (1990). *On my own: Mexican American women, self-sufficiency, and the Family Support Act*. Washington, DC: National Council of La Raza.

Roberts-DeGennaro, M. (1987). Developing case management as a practice model. *Social Casework, 68,* 466–470.

Skricki, I. (1994). *Unheard voices: Participants evaluate the JOBS program*. Washington, DC: Coalition on Human Needs.

Trattner, W. I. (1994). *From poor law to welfare state*. New York: Free Press.

Weil, M., & Karls, J. M. (1985). Historical origins and recent developments. In M. Weil, J. M. Karls, & Associates (Eds.), *Case management in human service practice*. San Francisco: Jossey-Bass.

# Chapter 9

# Managed Care

*Robert W. McClelland*

---

To say that health care reform proposals calling for managed care have generated considerable controversy is a gross understatement. Managed care has been hailed by its supporters as the way to produce health care reform and pay for the extension of benefits to the millions of Americans currently uninsured. It has also been assailed by opponents as an infringement on consumer choice and as a threat to high-quality care. Managed care is said to give rise to unnecessary and costly bureaucracy. The concept was at the center of the debate over health care reform, a debate that may have generated more heat than light. As a result, the defining characteristics of managed care have become obscured.

Adding to the problem, significant confusion surrounds the differences between managed care and case management. Radol Raiff and Shore (1993) offer a way to distinguish between the two.

> *Managed care encompasses a series of strategies for assuring quality care while controlling the costs of service. . . . Individuals who make these important access decisions, monitor progress, suggest alternatives or recommend termination are called case managers (p. 146).*

This distinction is between the program (managed care) and individuals authorized to make care decisions within fiscal parameters (case managers). Case management is one strategy for controlling utilization found in managed-care programs. From a physician's perspective, managed care refers to the rules set by insurers that providers must follow in order to receive payment, whereas physicians utilize case management to practice cost-conscious medicine.

In most primary-care settings, case management is provided by physicians. In the insurance industry, case managers provide authorization for payment and are not responsible for the medical treatment of patients. Some health care settings have a designated case manager who helps mobilize and purchase services for consumers needing continuing care. Thus, it's no wonder that the public is confused about the nature of case management in health care. This confusion is compounded when case management is placed in the context of managed care.

Case management in managed health care differs from other forms of case management primarily in its emphasis on cost containment. In the managed-care context, case managers limit clients' choice of providers. Emphasis is on changing the patterns of service utilization through coordinating services in the delivery system. Perhaps the most distinguishing feature is that providers/case managers assume financial risks that are normally assigned to insurance carriers. Primary care physicians serve as both patient advocates and utilization gatekeepers. In the managed-care environment, responsibility for implementing structural change and addressing cost-containment goals falls on the primary-care provider. Cost containment is a shared responsibility among the consumer, the provider, and the insurer. The managers in managed-care systems create policies (rules and procedures) that influence the organization and financing of health care in order to produce a more efficient and effective delivery system (Feldman, 1992; Giles, 1993).

Although case management has been incorporated into publicly administered programs, in the managed-care setting case management evolved primarily in the context of private health insurance. It has been shaped by traditional insurance concepts such as pooling risk, provider risk, adverse selection, and consumer copayment. For the purposes of this chapter, case management provided within managed health and mental health care is only *one* strategy for addressing the fiscal, organizational, structural, and policy issues related to the provision of efficient and effective services. Managed care is a much broader approach than is case management.

Both managed care and case management emerged in response to the fragmentation, distortions, and perverse incentives in the health and mental health delivery systems. These inefficiencies result in the misallocation of both human and financial resources. Distortions in the health care system are frustrating to say the least, resulting in frequent efforts to regulate or restructure key components of the system. The history of efforts to influence the dynamics of health care is worth examining because it has greatly influenced what we now call *managed care*. The history of case management in managed mental health care will be discussed later in this chapter.

## *Historical Roots of Managed Health Care*

Whereas many countries have introduced government control over the financing and sometimes the delivery of health services, the United States has followed its own unique service-delivery path based on private health insurance. The historical antecedents are important in understanding the reasons for and nature of managed care in the United States today.

Early efforts to restructure and reform medical care focused on reducing the uncertainty of consumers' payment to health care providers through the provision of private health insurance plans. Before health insurance coverage was available, the out-of-pocket fee-for-service system of reimbursement made access to care difficult for everyone except the affluent. Between 1936 and 1945 Blue Cross and Blue Shield insurance plans were introduced. These plans made physician and hospital care affordable and predictable through prepaid health insurance. A community-rating system spread the risk of costly medical care broadly enough to make health insurance affordable to a large portion of the public. Private insurance plans also supplied a reliable source of funding that stimulated growth in the health care sector. Third-party payers accepted a cost-based pricing structure that virtually guaranteed upward spiraling costs. Frequently, services provided in hospitals were covered by insurance but the same procedure delivered on an outpatient basis was not. Such rules provided strong incentives to hospitalize people unnecessarily.

During the same period—1936 to 1945—prepaid group-practice models also emerged. The Group Health Association in Washington, D.C., and the Kaiser Permanente model in California are good examples of consumer- and employer-organized and -sponsored prepaid group practice. These early efforts to organize health care attended to the relationship between the financing and delivery of health services, providing the foundation for managed health care in the United States today.

In time, other indemnity-oriented insurance companies entered the field and competition forced Blue Cross/Blue Shield to abandon the community-rating system. Experience rating, a system in which groups were charged according to their projected use of health services, became the norm. Insurance companies tried to attract groups with low-utilization rates and/or markets consisting of large groups with predictable usage. The goal was to spread the risk of providing care for high-cost enrollees across a larger group in order to create a risk pool. Providers were reimbursed for "usual and customary fees," and insurance intermediaries passed on rising costs through higher premiums. Employer-paid health benefits became the mark of a good employer.

The tax exemption for employer-paid health benefits, which was introduced during World War II, provided further stimulus for growth of private insurance mechanisms of all kinds. It also created circumstances whereby the consumer was no longer aware of the cost of medical care.

In 1948, the Hill-Burton legislation provided funds for hospital construction, which helped thrust acute care to prominence and introduced the era in which high-tech specialized service was considered synonymous with quality care. Health insurance for the elderly (Medicare) and the poor (Medicaid) via the Social Security Amendments of 1965 passed through Congress with initial assurances that the normal and customary practice of medicine would not be disturbed. The infusion of tax-supported funding for the poor and elderly further escalated the cost of health care.

In the early 1970s, as health care costs climbed, efforts were made to control hospital expansion and acquisition of expensive new technologies. State-sponsored certificate-of-need requirements along with federal legislation in 1974 provided health-planning agencies with greater regulatory authority over the approval of capital expenditures for hospitals. These efforts proved unsuccessful, however, in controlling increases in hospital costs. In retrospect, too much was expected of a strategy that required no shifts in hospital reimbursement methods or changes in patient usage and provider behaviors (Feldstein, 1993).

As costs spiraled upward, federal and state governments began to entertain mechanisms to contain costs by using their purchasing power. The prospective-pricing system, called diagnosis related groups, was initiated by the federal government in 1983 in an attempt to control costs for hospital stays through Medicaid. Both physicians and hospitals believed they were being treated unfairly, but felt that some payment was better than nothing at all. Although both federal and state efforts to control costs had some effect on costs, these efforts also demonstrated that regulation of costs was not enough. More fundamental structural changes were needed.

As the health care sector grew, analysts expressed concern that the industry was not responding to traditional market mechanisms and was both fragmented and inefficient. Costs were escalating at an alarming rate, and attempts to regulate growth proved ineffective. Nevertheless, prepaid group practices were fairly successful in their efforts to address the lack of competitive market forces. They utilized various administrative and structural mechanisms to shift incentives toward cost containment.

Prepaid group practices recognized the value of applying a comprehensive strategy for managing consumer usage, provider behavior, and fiscal incentives. They demonstrated the capacity within their organizations to cut costs without reducing quality of care, which allowed them to offer more competitive premium and benefit packages than offered by most insurance intermediaries. Nevertheless, this approach was *not* universally embraced by providers.

Many physicians viewed prepaid group practice as an example of corporate medicine that would lead to the loss of practitioner autonomy and overemphasis on cutting costs at the expense of quality. In many states, legal barriers to the formation of such organizations were sponsored by medical societies. Physicians who considered joining these groups were ostracized. Many consumers also avoided such organizations because they valued free choice of physician more than they did the cost savings or added benefits offered by these plans.

In the past 50 years, health care legislation has attempted to (1) increase access to needed health care for specific populations and (2) contain rising costs (Friedman, 1986). It has proven to be easier to expand the delivery system than to contain costs.

Faced with escalation of health care costs, the federal government introduced the Health Maintenance Organization Act of 1973 to promote competition in the health care industry. This act sought to stimulate development of prepaid group practices, renaming them health maintenance organizations (HMOs). The earlier successes of prepaid group practices in cost containment provided a compelling rationale for passage of this act. The legislation overrode restrictive state legislation under particular conditions, which stimulated growth of HMOs across the country. Physicians, hospitals, insurers, employers, and consumers endorsed HMOs. Both not-for-profit and proprietary HMO models emerged, and various approaches to managed health care emerged from the HMOs. These variations infused different cost-containment incentives into the delivery system, which served to balance concerns about access to providers and quality of care with potential savings.

## Managed Care Today

Today, more than 20 years after the Health Maintenance Organization Act of 1973 passed through Congress, managed health care is preferred by many consumers, providers, and insurers but is not universally embraced. Insurance companies have also adopted utilization-review and risk-management strategies, increasingly asking consumers to share the cost of their health care. The basic elements of managed care today are summarized in the following insurance-based concepts:

- Financial risk sharing between providers and consumers through capitation and copayment mechanisms

- An administrative structure vested with the authority to allocate resources within the system

- Gatekeeping and coordinating responsibilities assumed by designated case management staff to assure the delivery of services by the least expensive yet qualified staff

- Emphasis on ambulatory and outpatient care in place of services delivered in hospitals

- Cost savings through economies of scale from combined purchasing of supplies and services

- Efforts to promote healthy behaviors such as smoking cessation and prevention and seat-belt use

- Emphasis on preventive services such as prenatal care and immunization to avoid more serious needs

The first three elements—financial risk sharing among stakeholders, an administrative structure that manages resources, and gatekeeping to control utilization—are key aspects of managed care.

## ❏ Financial Risk Sharing

Financial risk sharing has been a major factor in controlling costs in HMOs. Instead of being reimbursed on a fee-for-service basis, providers in a staff-model HMO either (1) accept a capitated payment for each member enrolled or (2) are paid by salary. The providers agree to deliver all benefits and consumers agree to seek care only from their designated physician group. Costs of physician-initiated referrals outside the plan are covered by the provider group. This shift in financial risk makes the primary-care physician aware that referrals for more expensive specialist and hospital services will reduce their profits. Unnecessary referrals are minimized, and consumers are not covered by insurance if they seek services outside the group without a referral. This reduces self-referral to outside providers. Physicians are the primary gatekeepers in these delivery systems.

Because staff-model HMOs are self-contained, they are generally considered the "gold standard" of managed health care plans (Federa & Camp, 1994). In staff-model HMOs, physicians are employees. They are in the best position to reshape the organizational context and financial incentives that shape both provider and consumer behaviors. Despite these advantages, many consumers prefer other managed-care models that offer more freedom of choice in providers.

The exclusive provider organization functions like an HMO with prepaid comprehensive coverage and a primary-care physician as a gatekeeper, but it allows members to opt out of the plan if they are willing to assume a higher deductible and copayments. Physicians typically participate in a fee-for-service reimbursement system that rewards cost containment but does not go as far as capitation.

The least restrictive variation on this theme is the preferred provider organization, which offers a discounted fee-for-service indemnity plan in which enrollees are encouraged to select from participating providers but allowed to self-refer to outside providers. In return, consumers pay more out of pocket when they choose nonparticipating providers. Individual practice associations can contract with the HMO but remain autonomous businesses. According to InterStudy, a research institute devoted to studying managed health care, more than 60% of all HMOs and 82% of recently formed HMOs (less than six years old) rely upon the independent provider association approach (cited in Federa & Camp, 1994).

In managed care, the goal is to strike a delicate balance between freedom to choose one's provider and efficiency. Physicians in closed-panel HMOs, acting as gatekeepers, must find ways to conserve resources while providing quality care for their patients. If costs are not contained, they lose money. If services are of poor quality, consumers will change plans.

Enrollees agree to certain restrictions as well. In closed-panel HMOs, consumers can use services delivered only by the contracting group. If they use outside services, they must bear the costs. Incentives to enhance cost containment can be substantial in self-contained HMOs; however, consumers generally select less restrictive managed-care options.

## ❏ Management Control over Resource Allocation

Management authority to control resource allocation within the managed-care system has also contributed to efficiency. Rather than relying solely on the cost incentives and sanctions for physicians and consumers, managers actively monitor utilization. Managed-care programs incorporate well-developed information systems and planning capacity to monitor utilization and prescribing patterns. These activities support greater efficiency within the plan. They would, for example, evaluate the efficacy of using various providers to deliver a specific service. If a nurse practitioner can provide initial screening and thus allow primary-care physicians to be used more efficiently, management would be expected to hire more nurse practitioners. Likewise, if it costs less but is just as safe to provide outpatient surgery rather than inpatient care, management would be expected to encourage the use of outpatient services and facilities. Finally, as large purchasers of pharmaceuticals and other medical supplies, HMOs can produce economies of scale by negotiating discounts with suppliers.

## ❏ Gatekeeping and Coordinating Responsibilities

Gatekeeping and coordinating responsibilities are usually the responsibility of primary physicians or nurse practitioners. Gatekeepers guide consumers to qualified providers who deliver care at the least cost. They control access to high-cost services.

Applebaum and Austin (1990) identify authorization power and purchase capacity as essential aspects of gatekeeping. Case managers distinguish between care management and managed care. The difference between care management and managed care has to do with the gatekeeper function. In care management, the case manager functions as a service coordinator and consumer advocate, helping to arrange and access needed services. In managed care, the case manager is also expected to function as a gatekeeper, authorizing access to or purchase of cost-effective services. Physicians frequently assume this role, but other professionals such as nurses and social workers are increasingly assigned these responsibilities.

Where accessing nonmedical community-based services is the primary goal, the case management role may be delegated to nurses or social workers who have varying degrees of authority to commit the resources of the organization on behalf of the consumer through gatekeeping. Case managers who are not physicians usually provide care management but frequently they are *not* given authority to manage care through gatekeeping. When examining the role of case management in a managed-care system, it is important to determine where the gatekeeping authority resides because this decision has a fundamental influence on the gatekeeping role.

When financial risk sharing, management authority to allocate resources better, and gatekeeping are combined, managed systems such as HMOs are able to correct some of the structural disincentives to efficient health care delivery that plague the current system.

## Publicly Managed Health Care

Skyrocketing Medicaid spending has become a fiscal crisis for both state and federal governments. Virtually every state has considered managed care as a vehicle to control the cost of providing health care to high-risk, low-income populations. Petersen's analysis of Health Care Financing Administration data indicates that approximately 12% of Medicaid enrollees nationally were covered by managed-care plans in 1992 (cited in Witek & Hostage, 1994). The arrangement has been difficult to establish.

Established HMOs that did not need to increase their membership were frequently unwilling to enroll Medicaid beneficiaries because they feared adverse selection and were concerned about low capitation rates. The Medicaid population consists of children, single parents, the disabled, and the elderly. A Kaiser Family Foundation (1992) study noted increased poor health in the Medicaid population as a result of HIV and AIDS, substance-dependent infants, violence-related trauma, and an increased population of elderly with long-term care needs. The Medicaid population was perceived as less healthy and less compliant, reflecting various psychosocial concerns and access problems (Witek & Hostage, 1994).

The General Accounting Office has expressed concern that the combination of low reimbursement rates and a high-risk population in a managed-care environment with an inadequate enrollee population will adversely affect quality of care (cited in Witek & Hostage, 1994).

Clearly, it has been difficult to get HMOs to assume the risk of providing care via a capitated payment for vulnerable, high-risk populations. However, the potential for cost containment keeps policymakers exploring these options. Witek and Hostage (1994) conclude, "Although volumes have been written on the experience of Medicaid managed care providers, the verdict is still unclear on managed care performance measured in cost, access and quality, and financial viability" (p. 65).

Nevertheless, high-cost, high-risk populations, particularly the elderly, have been well served by managed-care plans. These plans assign case managers to members with chronic illnesses and disabilities. Members with complex needs work with case managers to develop care plans, including home, community-based, and institutional services. Case management is the cornerstone of most managed programs for high-risk consumers, particularly the elderly.

The social health maintenance organization (S/HMO) is a managed delivery system serving the elderly in which case management is a prominent service. The S/HMO provides acute, ambulatory, community-based, and long-term health care services to a representative group of elderly consumers, including the well and the frail. Funding is provided via a pool of consumer premiums and both Medicare and Medicaid payments, which cover a prepaid service package. The S/HMO is designed to keep consumers out of nursing homes as long as possible by providing community-based services that address quality-of-life preferences of consumers and cost-containment objectives of government payers. The S/HMO uses case management to (1) assess needs, (2) develop care plans, (3) mobilize community-based services for persons certified for nursing-home care, (4) coordinate service delivery, and (5) monitor client functioning and care-plan effectiveness. Case managers are fiscally accountable and responsible for targeting, gatekeeping, care planning, and monitoring client functioning.

On Lok is another example of a managed-care program serving the high-risk, frail elderly. On Lok is a community-based nonprofit agency in the Chinatown, North Beach, and Polk Gulch areas of San Francisco (Shen & Iversen, 1992). The agency focuses solely on frail elderly who are assessed as requiring nursing-home level of care. On Lok incorporates three basic managed-care concepts:

- A comprehensive package of services, from acute to long-term care
- Vigorous case management of all care by a multidisciplinary team of health care providers
- Financing through capitation rather than fee-for-service payments, with the provider at financial risk

On Lok data indicate that fewer than 6% of enrollees are actually placed in nursing homes and that hospital care has been effectively controlled. A comparison group study found that On Lok's hospitalization rate was five times lower than that of the comparison group and that nursing-home utilization was 1.4 times lower (Shen & Iversen, 1992). Like the closed-panel HMO, On Lok sets a standard that is difficult to achieve by health care systems that rely on a brokerage model in which case managers are not part of a unified delivery system.

Stakeholders in managed programs need to recognize and respond to the realities of serving high-risk, high-cost populations rather than bemoaning the fact that Medicaid patients do not behave like middle-class folks. Adverse selection is a fact of life in plans serving the frail elderly. Programs like On Lok, however, have learned how to successfully serve vulnerable, frail elders. Other managed-care providers would do well to learn what On Lok and the S/HMO have to teach rather than trying to avoid enrolling elderly because they are high risk and use too many services. Likewise, government policymakers will need to recognize that there is no free lunch. It costs more to provide services to people with complex needs.

## *Managed Mental Health*

Since the mid-1960s, mental health services have grown as a proportion of national health care expenditures. In 1992 more than 10% of health care dollars was spent on privately insured mental health and substance abuse services (Goran, 1992). Fiscal intermediaries have turned to various forms of managed care to control costs. Three cost-containment approaches are commonly found in these insured mental health benefit packages:

- Utilization review, prior authorization, and preadmission screening
- Use of case management
- Reliance on specialized provider networks

### ❏ Utilization Review, Prior Authorization, and Preadmission Screening

Utilization review, prior authorization, and preadmission screening have been used extensively in managed-care indemnity insurance plans and HMO-style delivery systems. Criteria are developed to screen the need for costly services such as inpatient care. Other than for emergency situations, physicians must request prior authorization from reviewers to refer patients to inpatient mental health services. If prior authorization is not received, physicians run the risk of having their claim rejected for reimbursement. Physician consultants employed by the fiscal intermediary have the final authority to approve, deny, or suggest an alternative treatment plan for those cases that require additional professional judgment. In the provision of mental health services, disagreements frequently focus on either the need for inpatient care or the length of treatment.

### ❏ Use of Case Management

In many mental health benefit packages, case management is handled by a primary-care physician who functions as a gatekeeper and controls access to other services in the system. Consumers must obtain referrals to specialists; they cannot self-refer. Primary-care physicians are expected to treat many of the conditions that would have previously been referred to more expensive specialists.

Some HMOs have assigned the initial assessment to designated and specifically trained intake staff such as nurses or social workers. In these plans the basic principle in case management is to direct consumers to the least costly, yet appropriate, provider.

Many consumers seeking mental health services may not be comfortable with needing to see a physician or case manager prior to visiting someone who can treat them. As gatekeepers, primary-care physicians have greater credibility as medical diagnosticians than as counselors. Consequently, some managed plans have opted for "carving out" mental health and alcohol-abuse services. These services are provided through specialized mental health provider networks.

## ❏ Reliance on Specialized Provider Networks

Specialized provider networks offer an alternative to prescreening members. Mental health and substance-abuse services are often delivered through a specialized network of providers who agree to deliver the mental health benefits under specific conditions. Generally, insurers will contract with mental health providers who are willing to address cost-containment goals by stressing brief therapy lasting for a prescribed number of sessions and outpatient services in place of more costly inpatient treatment.

Goran (1992) identified common policies and procedures that guide the provision of services in managed mental health plans. These policies cover the following concerns:

- Whom the client should call when services are desired

- Who is responsible for the initial patient evaluation

- Whether clinicians who do the initial patient evaluations should be allowed also to treat the patient

- The use of cost-effective treatment such as brief outpatient psychotherapy and alternatives to inpatient care

- The role of nonmedical mental health professionals in the diagnosis and treatment of patients

- The role of group, family, and other therapies

- The use of psychoactive medications

- Diagnosis and treatment of the seriously mentally ill

- Selection of and contracting with practitioners and facilities
- Treatment options for substance abuse and dual diagnosis
- Adolescent and child diagnosis and treatment options
- The relationship of the managed mental health program to the general medical plan
- Utilization and quality management
- Levels and methods of compensation for providers
- The degree and type of fiscal incentives or risk sharing

## *Public Sector Managed Mental Health*

Managed mental health care in the public sector preceded managed care in the private sector. As the provider of last resort, the public system, through psychiatric hospitals, was responsible for the inpatient and outpatient mental health services for many chronically mentally ill citizens. Deinstitutionalization shifted the delivery of care from psychiatric hospitals to community mental health centers responsible for coordinating a range of mental health services for individuals living in a specified catchment area (Hadley, Schinnar, & Rothbard, 1992). Despite early plans and efforts to improve coordination, the public system has not developed adequate levels of coordination and integration in the provision of mental health services.

Recently, with continued growth of Medicaid expenditures, some states have begun seriously to consider negotiating prepaid contracts for mental health services with managed-care systems. Demonstration projects have been conducted in Minnesota, South Carolina, Pennsylvania, New York, and Rhode Island (Hadley et al., 1992) Funded by the Robert Wood Johnson Foundation, these demonstrations include several common features: a central authority that combines fiscal, administrative, and clinical responsibility for care; emphasis on continuity of care; a full range of services; a housing plan; and new sources of financing. These demonstrations represent a comprehensive approach to managed-care services for the chronically mentally ill.

Public mental health providers and HMOs under contract with public entities have approached managed mental health care cautiously. The HMOs are concerned that the service demands for this population are unpredictable. Public providers worry that the capitated payment system will produce incentives to underserve a vulnerable population.

Case management is a key strategy used by managed mental health systems to control costs for high service users. It is particularly valuable when the targeted population has a history of seeking help through hospital emergency rooms, which increases the likelihood that the patient will use more expensive inpatient services.

## Balancing Quality and Cost

When cost containment assumes a prominent position in the delivery of services, inevitable questions concerning quality assurance arise. This is particularly true given the fact that so many cost-containment methods have been incorporated into health and mental health programs. The variety of cost-containment methods is striking: preadmission screening or prior authorization for admission, authorization of specific procedures and number of units of service, second opinions, ongoing utilization review, cost sharing by consumers, and restrictions on the selection of providers. Individually or in combination these methods are designed to control overall utilization or reduce the price of specified units of service. Humphreys and colleagues observed that the emphasis on cost containment "has added to the growth of the case management concept by making the case manager an integral part of the financial planning process and [permiting] the manager a great deal of latitude in the allocation of services" (cited in Radol Raiff & Shore, 1993, p. 149).

Although the underlying concept of managed care is linked to the goal of cost containment, it can be judged effective only if it addresses quality-assurance criteria as well. Efficiency at the cost of effectiveness produces the illusion of success. Treatment must meet professional standards as well as cost targets or the arrangement will inevitably lead to poor-quality service and consumer complaints.

Managed care can be seen as a further step to refine utilization-management strategies such as preadmission screening and approval. It must be applied within an ethical framework of professional ethics that advocates for the consumer's right to quality care. Supporters of managed care argue that the quality of patient care need not be diminished and that managed care has proven to be at least equal to or better than unmanaged care such as in fee-for-service arrangements (Blum, 1992).

Health maintenance organizations have had to respond to charges that consumer interests may be subordinated to the organization's fiscal concerns. Consumers demand both quality and economy. To achieve these standards, providers and consumers will need to recognize that familiar utilization patterns must be changed. In particular, managed care directs (and sometimes limits) the selection of health personnel and services for both consumers and providers (Interstudy, 1991, 1993). This is not necessarily indicative of lesser quality.

Quality-assurance efforts in the managed-care environment must recognize the potential conflicts of interest in the delivery system. Assessments should evaluate both over- and underutilization by answering various questions. Were the consumers correctly diagnosed and did they receive appropriate services? Was a treatment plan developed and followed? Did consumers have adequate choice of mental health providers? If screening mechanisms were used, were they appropriately applied? Did case management decisions satisfy the consumer? Were follow-through and follow-up procedures initiated (Spierer, Sims, Micklitsch, & Lewis, 1994)?

To answer these questions, stakeholders must develop a consensus on the indicators used to evaluate the standards. These indicators are manifest as information routinely collected and reviewed by peers. Both internal and external quality-assurance audits are needed for credibility (Berlant, 1992). Indicators of efficacy as well as of adverse outcomes go beyond the typical ethical standards promulgated by professional associations. Such issues can be difficult and politically sensitive.

In pursuing these two goals of quality care and cost containment, weaknesses in managed-care systems are bound to emerge and to become targets of quality-assurance programs. For example, experience has shown that attention should be focused on thee key concerns: (1) barriers in communication between client and clinician as a result of the involvement of anonymous staff responsible for service authorization, (2) intrusiveness of periodic utilization reviews to the treatment process, and (3) maintenance of client confidentiality.

## Conclusion

Case management in the managed-care environment represents a departure from the traditional case management practice. The role conflict is stark: Can the case manager simultaneously be a client advocate and a system agent who controls costs? Some case managers are not at ease with case management in the managed-care environment because it represents a departure from traditional emphasis on service coordination and advocacy. The introduction of fiscal accountability and responsibility for the financial aspects of care planning represents a fundamental change in the case manager's role.

Some case managers working in managed-care systems may no longer view their role as that of client advocate and may view their priorities in the delivery system as reflecting corporate interests rather than client need. Radol Raiff and Shore (1993) emphasize the importance of the fiscal component in the case management function, stating that "the financial control elements . . . are essential components of advanced practice without which the service's potential is irretrievably diluted" (p. 149). Client advocacy and cost containment are not mutually exclusive. Contemporary paradigms in professional education for the human services would do well to reflect the relationship between client advocacy and fiscal control. New knowledge and skills are required for case managers to provide effective, client-centered services in managed-care systems. The link should be made between the case managers' authority to allocate resources and the potential for advocacy through system change.

## References

Berlant, J. L. (1992). Quality assurance in managed care. In S. Feldman (Ed.), *Managed mental health services* (pp. 201–221). Springfield, IL: Charles C Thomas.

Blum, S. R. (1992). Ethical issues in managed mental health. In S. Feldman (Ed.), *Managed mental health services* (pp. 245–265). Springfield, IL: Charles C Thomas.

Federa, R. D., & Camp, T. L. (1994). The changing managed care market. *Journal of Ambulatory Care Management, 17,* 1–7.

Feldman, S. (Ed.). (1992). *Managed mental health services.* Springfield, IL: Charles C Thomas.

Feldstein, P. J. (1993). *Health care economics* (4th ed.). Albany, NY: Delmar Publishers.

Friedman, E. (1986, May). Fifty years of U.S. health care policy. *Hospitals, 51,* 95–104.

Giles, T. R. (1993). *Managed mental health care.* Boston: Allyn and Bacon.

Goran, M. J. (1992). Managed mental health and group health insurance. In S. Feldman (Ed.), *Managed mental health services* (pp. 27–43). Springfield, IL: Charles C Thomas.

Hadley, T. R., Schinnar, A., & Rothbard, A. (1992). Managed mental health in the public sector. In S. Feldman (Ed.), *Managed mental health services* (pp. 45–59). Springfield, IL: Charles C Thomas.

InterStudy. (1991). *The InterStudy edge, managed care: A decade in review, 1980–1990* (special ed.). Excelsior, MN: Author.

InterStudy. (1993). *The InterStudy competitive edge (databook): Biannual report of the managed health care industry* (Vol. 2, No. 2). Excelsior, MN: Author.

Kaiser Family Foundation. (1992, December 2). *The Medicaid cost explosion: Causes and consequences.* Baltimore, MD: Author.

Radol Raiff, N., & Shore, B. (1993). *Advanced case management.* Newbury Park, CA: Sage Publications.

Shen, J., & Iversen, A. (1992). PACE: A capitated model towards long-term care. *Henry Ford Medical Journal, 40*(1–2), 41–44.

Spierer, M., Sims, H. W., Micklitsch, C. N., & Lewis, B. E. (1994). Assessment of patient satisfaction as part of a physician performance evaluation: The Fallon clinic experience. *Journal of Ambulatory Care Management, 17*(3), 1–7.

Witek, E. J., & Hostage, J. L. (1994). Medicaid managed care: Problems and promise. *Journal of Ambulatory Care Management, 17,* 61–69.

# Chapter 10

# Comprehensive Case Management With HIV Clients

*James Brennan*

The reemergence of case management as a method of practice coincided with the emergence of the AIDS epidemic in the United States. In early 1981, rare forms of pneumonia and cancer began appearing among gay men in Los Angeles, San Francisco, and New York. By the end of the year, cases of the new disease syndrome, known as gay-related immune deficiency, were diagnosed among intravenous-drug users. Within a year, the initial handful of cases multiplied to more than 100 and the syndrome was evident in an increasingly diverse population including infants, hemophiliacs, and people who had received blood transfusions. The disease was renamed acquired immune deficiency syndrome (AIDS), and the public health community began to combat the human immunodeficiency virus (HIV), the infectious virus that tears down the immune system of infected individuals, resulting in AIDS (Shilts, 1987).

Even before AIDS was given a name, social workers were providing services to persons with related illnesses. In 1981, social worker Diego Lopez worked to develop support services for gay men diagnosed with Kaposi's sarcoma, services that expanded to become the Gay Men's Health Crisis, a multiservice agency in New York City that remains at the forefront of service provision for persons affected by HIV/AIDS (Getzel, 1992). As the impact of the epidemic has become clear, so too has the need for a broad range of medical, social, and psychological services.

By the end of 1994, more than 440,000 individuals in the United States were diagnosed with full-spectrum AIDS (infection with HIV and diagnosis with at least one of approximately 30 related illnesses). Of those, 270,000 have died (Centers for Disease Control, 1994). The Centers for Disease Control and Prevention (CDC) estimate that at least one million additional Americans are infected with HIV and that most are unaware of their infection. Worldwide, it is estimated that more than 18 million adults and 1.5 million children have been infected with HIV. The World Health Organization estimates that by the year 2000, more than eight million people will have died from HIV-related causes (World Health Organization, 1995).

HIV infection is behaviorally transmitted. The only documented means of transmission are through (1) either heterosexual or homosexual intercourse; (2) exchange of blood from an infected individual to a previously uninfected person, such as through sharing drug-injection equipment, blood transfusions, or blood products; and (3) perinatal transmission during pregnancy, during birthing, or during breast feeding (Centers for Disease Control, 1994). In the United States, significant social aspects surround HIV infection and AIDS. The preponderance of cases of AIDS have been among gay or bisexual men and intravenous-drug users, traditionally socially disenfranchised groups. Women represent the fastest growing diagnosis group. Of those diagnosed with AIDS, 47% are racial and ethnic minorities; among women, 75% of those diagnosed are from minority groups, as are 80% of children (Centers for Disease Control, 1994). The fact that the majority of individuals with AIDS are either uninsured or receive Medicaid indicates that a significant proportion are poor and dependent on the public system of care (Brennan, 1994; Isbell, 1993). This diversity among persons infected with HIV and the accompanying societal biases associated with race, gender, and sexual orientation have created significant problems in our attempts to address the epidemic.

HIV cannot be viewed or treated in isolation. A growing proportion of individuals with HIV have been infected either directly or indirectly through substance abuse. Individuals with cognitive impairments or chronic mental illness may have difficulty integrating and acting upon prevention information and thus are at increased risk of infection. Poverty limits access to health services at all phases of disease and prevention. Homosexual behavior remains highly stigmatized in our society and may result in alienation from family and prejudice in service delivery. Thus, by its very nature, prevention and treatment of HIV requires interactions with a wide spectrum of individuals and service structures.

## Medical Aspects of HIV Disease

HIV disease can be categorized into three general phases. The primary phase occurs among individuals whose HIV antibody status is unknown (in general, HIV infection is determined through blood tests). Obviously, the vast majority of the U.S. population falls into this category, though for purposes of targeted education and intervention the population is narrowed to persons who have participated in risk behaviors since 1980 and those who currently or may in the future participate in such behaviors. The most significant risk behaviors are (1) injection-drug use during which paraphernalia is shared by multiple users; (2) sexual activity with more than one mutually monogamous partner, with risk increasing exponentially according to the number of partners and type of sexual activity; and (3) receipt of blood transfusions or blood products, especially prior to 1986 when universal blood testing procedures for donated blood were implemented. Risk can be mediated by prophylactic measures such as condom use in oral, anal, and vaginal intercourse or thorough sterilization of shared drug-injection equipment. The primary interventions for this phase of HIV disease are education and testing for antibodies. Whereas an individual who tests positive for antibodies would become classified at the secondary level, those who test negative remain at the primary level, possibly requiring direct interventions such as substance-abuse treatment or counseling supports to avoid future infection.

The second phase of HIV disease encompasses those individuals who have tested positive for HIV antibodies and who are free of overt symptoms of disease or who display a range of symptoms or infections but without secondary infections that qualify for an AIDS diagnosis. Symptoms displayed during this phase range from mildly irritating to debilitating. Medical interventions during this phase often focus on attempts to slow or halt the replication of HIV within the individual and to prevent the onset of AIDS-defining illnesses. In this phase, clients often need extensive information related to treatment options and assistance in accessing appropriate treatments. Mental health interventions are often needed, and social service needs tend to increase. HIV-infected parents must begin the process of planning for their children's well-being. Moreover, many HIV-infected children at this stage of illness experience the loss of their parents, whose illness has preceded their own.

During the tertiary phase, the infected individual is diagnosed with at least one AIDS-defining illness. This phase is generally marked by a steady decline in health status, repeated hospitalizations, and increasing needs for social, financial, and emotional support as the infected persons' capacities for employment, self-care, and caregiving decline. The individual may need assistance with activities of daily living (ADLs), housing, long-term care, transportation, finalization of plans for the future care of dependents, or advocacy and assistance in attaining his or her desired quality of life (see Figure 1).

**Figure 1.** The Spectrum of HIV Infection

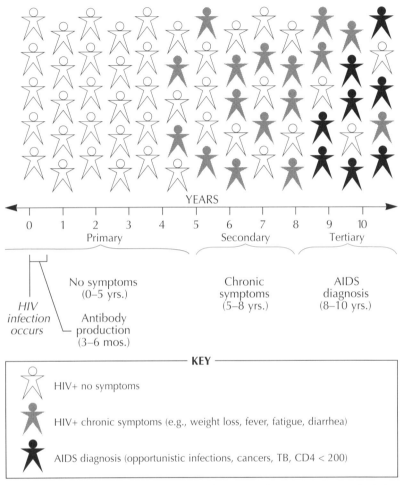

Adapted from Fischer, G., & Stein, J. (1994). *HIV/AIDS at Work: A training program for Federal employees: Participant's manual.* Arlington, VA: Center for HIV/Substance Abuse Training.

An insidious aspect of HIV disease is its impact on the central nervous system. Ninety percent of persons who die of AIDS show neuropathologic abnormalities; up to two-thirds of patients demonstrate neuropsychological abnormalities during the advanced stages of disease; nearly half show evidence of clinical dementia by the time of death (Buckingham & Van Gorp, 1994). This biologically based deterioration in cognitive functioning can significantly impair infected individuals' capacity for self-care and decision making and may present as delirium, psychosis, depression, or mania. Cognitive impairment may not be readily apparent or sensitive to brief tests of gross mental status. Clearly, comprehensive mental health assessment and services should be available to all persons with HIV.

## Service Aspects of HIV

Unlike terminal illnesses such as most forms of cancer, an AIDS diagnosis carries tremendous social stigma. AIDS is generally associated with promiscuity and illicit drug use. Unlike many terminal illnesses, AIDS is infectious, leading many people to avoid persons who are infected. In addition to being affected by a family member's AIDS diagnosis, family members may be infected with HIV. Because of the multiple needs of persons with HIV, health and social service professionals may feel overwhelmed (Roberts, Severinsen, Kuehn, Straker, & Fritz, 1992).

The span from time of infection to the onset of symptoms may be as long as 10 years, and duration of life with full-blown AIDS is often longer than three years. Thus people with HIV/AIDS have various service needs: health care, financial assistance, emotional and mental health support, assistance with daily activities, drug treatment, housing, and/or family services. Table 1 itemizes a range of likely service needs and acuity levels across the spectrum of HIV disease.

Many women and ethnic minorities infected with HIV are diagnosed later in the course of illness and thus have significantly shorter life expectancies from the point of diagnosis. This variance may be attributable to poverty and the lack of access to health services. Although the period during which services are delivered may be shorter, the service needs of these individuals may in fact be acute.

Among respondents to a survey conducted by Piette, Thompson, Fleishman, and Mor (1993), more than 80% of people with AIDS reported needing assistance in at least one of six areas—home care, mental health, drug treatment, housing entitlements, or transportation—during the previous three months, and one-third needed three or more services. More than half of all respondents reported that they needed mental health services. The majority of those reporting a need for housing or transportation stated that their needs were unmet. A significant proportion of those with one unmet need also had other needs that remained unresolved. Men, whites, and those living with others reported the fewest needs, indicating that women, people of color, and persons who live alone should generally be identified as at risk or potentially needing psychosocial services.

As physical and mental impairments such as impaired mobility or dementia increase during the course of the illness, client needs across the biopsychosocial spectrum increase. An individual with adequate financial resources during early phases of illness may become impoverished if forced out of the workplace as a result of increasing disability or by "spending down" or using up cash resources in order to qualify for income-based insurance or service programs. Social supports available

**Table 1.** *Service Needs and Acuity Levels across the Spectrum of HIV Disease*

| Type of Service | Case Management Services | | |
| --- | --- | --- | --- |
| | Primary | Secondary | Tertiary |
| Education regarding prevention | ● | ◐ | ◐ |
| HIV testing and counseling | ● | ◐ | ○ |
| Emotional support | ○ | ◐ | ● |
| Substance-abuse treatment | ● | ● | ◐ |
| Mental health services | ◐ | ● | ● |
| Assistance with entitlement benefits | ○ | ◐ | ● |
| Assistance with insurance benefits | ○ | ◐ | ● |
| Housing | ○ | ◐ | ● |
| Transportation | | ◐ | ● |
| Assistance with child welfare/ permanency planning for surviving children | ○ | ● | ● |
| Assistance with child welfare for infected children | ◐ | ● | ● |
| Home health/homemaker services | | ◐ | ● |
| Assistance with ADL | | ○ | ● |
| Advocacy/assistance in treatment access | ○ | ● | ● |
| Hospitalization | | ◐ | ● |
| Outpatient medical care | ◐ | ● | ● |
| Health status monitoring | ○ | ● | ● |
| Advocacy/education with related systems such as schools, workplace, etc. | ◐ | ● | ◐ |
| Education of service providers | ● | ● | ● |
| Legal services | ○ | ◐ | ◐ |

○ = low level of need; ◐ = moderate level; ● = high level.

to individuals will likely change during the course of illness as other family members may become overwhelmed by the presenting care needs or their own deteriorating health status. Thus, no psychosocial aspect of the client remains static, and reassessment must be ongoing.

## Case Management and HIV

Because of the complex and concurrent medical, psychological, and social-service needs of persons with HIV disease, comprehensive case management services are clearly an essential aspect of patient care. Rather than debating the worthiness of case management, experts in the HIV community have argued about where case management services should be based and who should be the case manager.

Because HIV affects every area of human functioning—physical health and ability, mental health, economic stability, family functioning and stress, child welfare, and social interactions—virtually any model of case management can be applied in coordinating services for persons with HIV. Intervention at the "direct" or "individual" level is needed because of the catastrophic effect of the illness on individuals with HIV and families. The fact that most health care delivery systems and social services are designed primarily to serve the young or old rather than middle-aged and young adults—the primary population affected by HIV diseases—means that interventions must also be directed at the "indirect" or "systems" level. Rather than adopting specific models of case management services, many HIV case management programs have developed from the core functions of case management.

Despite the ongoing turf battles among professions, nurses and social workers provide strikingly similar definitions of the case manager's role and function. The National Association of Social Workers (1992) defines social work case management as a method of providing services whereby a professional social worker assesses the needs of the client and, under appropriate circumstances, the client's family. Based on that assessment, the social work case manager then arranges, coordinates, monitors, evaluates, and advocates for multiple services to meet the client's complex needs. Client-level interventions include (1) outreach, referral, identification, and engagement; (2) biopsychosocial assessment; (3) development of a service plan; (4) plan implementation; (5) coordination and monitoring of service delivery; (6) advocacy on behalf of clients, including creating, obtaining, or brokering resources; (7) re-assessment; and (8) termination of the case when services are no longer warranted.

Similarly, the American Nurses Association (1992) defines the core functions of nursing case management as (1) interaction with clients, families, and service providers; (2) assessment; (3) plan development; (4) implementation; and (5) evaluation. Both professions recognize the potential role of the case manager as provider of direct services as well as care coordination. The primary difference between disciplines is the explicit expectation that social workers will also participate in system-level interventions, including resource development and social action, agency policy review and modification, and data collection and information management (Brennan & Kaplan, 1993; National Association of Social Workers, 1992).

These professional definitions are reflected in actual program definitions. In a 1992 evaluation of the Robert Wood Johnson Foundation (RWJF) AIDS case management programs, five basic functions of case managers were identified, regardless of discipline or training level: (1) intake, (2) assessment, (3) planning and implementation, (4) monitoring, and (5) advocacy (Piette et al., 1993). Reports on other programs (Indyk, Belville, Lachapelle, Gordon, & Dewart, 1993; Piette, Fleishman, Mar, & Thompson, 1992; Sonsel, Paradise, & Stroup, 1988) provide similar definitions.

The core functions of case management are identified in both community-based and hospital-based case management programs, but the training of case managers often appears to vary widely between these settings. Within the RWJF evaluation, 65% of hospital-based case managers held a degree in social work and 15% had degrees in nursing. This contrasts significantly with community-based programs in which 68% of case managers held no degree in either social work or nursing. Whereas 96% of hospital-based case managers held either a bachelor's or master's degree, 20% of community-organization-based case managers reported having as associate's degree or less as their highest level of training (Piette et al., 1993).

Not surprisingly, hospital-based case management programs are often more reliant on medical models (American Health Consultants, 1994b; Indyk et al., 1993; Piette et al., 1992, 1993). Piette et al. (1993) found that clients entering case management in hospital settings were more likely to be assessed as having problems requiring urgent or immediate attention and were more likely to be identified as needing residential placement and/or some form of long-term care. Hospital case managers also reported having more clients who needed individual psychological counseling compared with clients in community-based settings, who were more likely to need legal services, emotional support from volunteers, and assistance with financial entitlements.

The same survey found that hospital-based case managers had less difficulty obtaining financial services and entitlements, residential drug treatment placements, and home health and homemaker services compared with community-based case managers. It is likely that the differences in both assessment and outcome can be accounted for by the difference in provider training as much as by the setting.

Thus, one of the primary issues to be addressed in developing case management services for persons with HIV is the development of a continuum of care within case management itself. While community-based case managers are in a position to identify and intervene with help covering a full range of problems, many of these problems remain unidentified until they reach an acute level or the client becomes hospitalized. This phenomenon may be the result of lack of training in the community or the failure of hospital-based case managers to inform their community-based colleagues of current medical conditions and symptoms or needs to monitor. Services and benefits based on the acuity of illness of the person with HIV may be easier to access either because eligibility criteria favor those who are hospitalized or because the hospital is likely to have longstanding relationships with a range of provider groups, whereas a community-based HIV service agency is likely to be comparatively young and have fewer relationships. A key to successful HIV case management is creating a bridge between community- and hospital-based programs.

## Effectiveness of HIV Case Management

Unlike many settings, HIV case management has shown documented successes in both reducing the costs of HIV treatment and improving quality of life for clients (American Health Consultants, 1993, 1994b). An internal study by the community-based AIDS Atlanta, which places trained case managers in hospitals throughout the city, found that the mean hospital costs of patients who received case management was $11,143, compared with $20,523 for patients who did not receive such services. Additionally, the case-managed group had an average of 533 days between diagnosis and death and a mean 337 days between first hospital admission and death. Those who did not receive case management services had an average of 321 days between diagnosis and death and a mean of 262 days between first hospitalization and death (American Health Consultants, 1994b; Sowell, Gueldner, Killeen, Lowenstein, Fuszard, & Swansburg, 1992).

Similarly, analysis of long-term AIDS survivors (i.e., persons who live with AIDS longer than three years after diagnosis) in New York City showed that patients receiving supportive counseling and advocacy services were more likely to identify with "life-sustaining" factors such as the maintenance of hope and quality of life than were short-term survivors. Disorders such as clinical depression were reported more often among clients who received fewer supportive services (Dilley, Helquist, & Marks, 1991; Stein & Hodge, 1993).

Various other evaluation programs of HIV case management are currently being conducted. The most significant of these are the evaluations of programs funded by the Ryan White CARE Act. Through this funding mechanism, the Health Resources and Services Administration has supported case management programs in virtually all of the HIV epicenters in the United States as well as sponsored several demonstration projects utilizing case management services.

As a result of the demonstrated effectiveness of HIV case management, the Agency for Health Care Policy and Research published federal clinical guidelines for early intervention and case management in HIV. Although the guidelines represent various aspects of successful case management programs, some professional organizations and expert providers have cited significant failures in the areas of prevention of secondary infections and key psychosocial aspects of care (American Health Consultants, 1994a). The National Association of Social Workers joined several other national organizations in refusing to endorse the guidelines because of their failure to address basic psychosocial aspects of care (American Health Consultants, 1994a; National Association of Social Workers, 1993).

## Comprehensive Model for HIV Case Management

Case management models include medical, family-centered, clinical, and systems case management among others. Many of these models emphasize one aspect of the biopsychosocial needs of the client over other needs. Because of the complex nature of HIV disease, successful case management with this population requires the ability to shift emphasis of care according to the nature and level of illness and client's needs.

HIV disease can be categorized into the areas of primary, secondary, and tertiary in the same way as case management can be categorized into these three areas. Using a case management model that reflects these three levels of health services allows for fluidity, adaptability, and continuity of care and services across the span of HIV disease and client needs. Whereas the core functions of case management remain intact across these three levels, the tasks undertaken and the required level of provider skill will vary. Table 2 illustrates the way service emphasis shifts toward comprehensiveness and, in many cases, clinical services as the client advances through the stages of disease. During the secondary phase of both the disease and case management, a nurse case manager may serve as the primary medical manager for the patient, though this function will likely step down to medical monitoring and coordinating in the tertiary stage, during which the physician's role is predominant. As the mental health needs of clients increase, a social work or advance-practice nurse case manager may provide psychological counseling to both the client and his or her family. Ongoing comprehensive assessment is important.

With differentiation among levels of case management, it is also possible to triage clients to various levels of intervention on the basis of predetermined criteria. For example, active substance users or sexually active clients may require extensive services because of their high-risk behaviors even if they are currently HIV negative. However, in general, most clients at a particular level of diagnosis will require the services of the corresponding level of case management (see Table 3).

According to the level of case management, various skills and training are needed. Whereas a peer-outreach will be successful at building trust and engaging clients to participate in services or prevention activities, she or he will likely not possess the necessary skills to identify or treat serious medical or mental health problems. Similarly, a nurse case manager is best prepared to deal with complex physical-treatment issues, whereas a social work case manager is trained to access psychosocial services. Nevertheless, each of these providers offers significant contribu-

*Table 2. Key Case Management Functions*

| Primary | Secondary | Tertiary |
|---|---|---|
| Outreach | Engagement | Engagement |
| Referral | Basic assessment | Comprehensive |
| Identification | Plan development | assessment |
| Engagement | Periodic monitoring | Plan development |
| Monitoring | Advocacy | Implementation |
| Advocacy | Reassessment | Ongoing monitoring |
| | | Advocacy |
| | | Reassessment |
| Other Tasks | | |
| Emotional support | Medical management | Medical monitoring |
| | Mental health services | Mental health services |
| | Emotional support | Family interventions |
| | | Emotional support |

tions at each level of case management. The peer provider can offer emotional support, advocacy within an agency, and ongoing monitoring in the tertiary stages, and a highly trained social worker can provide assessment and counseling services for primary-level clients with multiple risk factors. Ideally, a team that includes peer provider, nurse, and social worker will follow clients throughout the course of their illness. Table 4 describes the various roles that each level of provider may play across the spectrum of case management.

This model of case management coordination offers flexibility and continuity. As with any case management model, a primary case manager who can coordinate service across multiple agencies and providers should be identified. Dialogue and service flow must be established between community-based and hospital-based case management activities. The client should be given the opportunity to offer his or her input regarding the designation of the primary case manager. In too many

**Table 3.** *Level of HIV Case Management Services by Client Status and Risk Factor*

|  | Primary | Secondary | Tertiary |
|---|---|---|---|
| At-risk for HIV | Bulk of clients fall in this area<br><br>*Key service needs: education, emotional support, information, and referral* | Substance users in recovery, other infected/diagnosed family members | Active substance users, chronically mentally ill, sex workers |
| HIV+ non/low symptomatic | Clients with no symptoms | Bulk of clients fall in this area<br><br>*Key service needs: education, information and referral for treatment and/or clinical trials, empowerment* | Debilitating symptoms, uninsured, multiple diagnosis, unmet basic needs |
| AIDS diagnosed HIV+ highly symptomatic | Family members/ caregivers for for identified primary client | Clients with extensive family and financial resources | Bulk of clients fall in this area<br><br>*Key service needs: emotional support, assistance with benefits and entitlements, prophylactic treatments, caregiver support* |

cases, persons with HIV are forced to spend valuable time managing their various case managers.

The case manager must be continually aware of the differences among clients and be willing to adjust services appropriately. For example, a woman with young children may have difficulty attending appointments if child care is not available. This is not an indication of noncompliance, but rather is a reflection of the realities of her life. Other caregiving responsibilities may similarly affect clients' accessing of services. Client views of medical treatment based on cultural factors or personal beliefs may influence decisions regarding treatment and services. Case managers may have to bridge the gap between traditional medical and social services and nontraditional or alternative treatments and services that the client may wish to pursue. The most effective means of bridging this gap is to facilitate communication between the client and other direct-service providers to develop strategies whereby various treatment and service alternatives may coexist. Simultaneously, the case manager must maintain awareness of other psychological factors such as depression or dementia that may influence the client toward inappropriate or harmful choices.

**Table 4.** *Key Tasks at Each Level of Case Management by Level of Practitioner*

|  | Primary | Secondary | Tertiary |
|---|---|---|---|
| Peer provider | Outreach, identification, education | Outreach, identification, engagement, monitoring, advocacy | Emotional support, task assistance, monitoring, advocacy |
| BSW/RN | Education, referral | Engagement, basic assessment, service plan, referral, periodic monitoring, advocacy, reassessment, assessment for appropriateness | Implementation of service plan, referral, ongoing monitoring, advocacy, assessing treatment appropriateness/qualification, family support |
| MSW/advanced-practice nurse | Comprehensive assessment for clients with multiple risks, consultation | Engagement, comprehensive assessment, plan development, consultation | Engagement, comprehensive assessment, plan development, referral, monitoring, mental health services, family treatment |

## *Quality Assurance*

Quality assurance and improvement are key pieces of the monitoring function of case management and an essential aspect of systems-level practice (National Association of Social Workers, 1992). In addition to monitoring the quality of case management for individual clients, it is imperative that practitioners and agencies look at the quality and effect of services across their client population. In the face of overwhelming case loads, this can seem a daunting task.

The current emphasis in health and human service organizations on continuous-quality-improvement (CQI) and total-quality-management (TQM) models is transferrable to HIV service programs. The CQI and TQM models emphasize ongoing improvement in quality of services, which is generally measured by assessing process, outcomes, and client satisfaction.

Various tools have been developed to assist in monitoring and improving quality in both process and outcomes (Collard, Bergman, & Henderson, 1990), the most applicable of which are clinical indicators. Although clinical indicators are not direct measures of clinical performance, they may serve as "flags" that signal the need for problem analysis or peer review. Although few specific indicator models for case management have been developed, model indicators for medical practice settings developed by NASW can easily be imported and modified for use in case management programs (National Association of Social Workers, 1990a, 1990b, 1995).

Figure 2 provides an example of a process indicator that assesses whether case managers in an agency have followed guidelines for comprehensiveness in psychosocial assessments. Other process measures might include assessing whether the intervention was initiated in a timely manner. Did the practitioner gather all relevant information? Were the appropriate care providers consulted? Were referrals made? This type of information is essential in examining the components as opposed to the whole of intervention.

Figure 3 provides an example of an outcome indicator measuring the effectiveness of an agency in ameliorating a designated problem experienced by clients. Rather than examining the method of intervention, outcome measures evaluate the results of intervention. In this example, the agency could identify any given problem experienced by a client, such as impending eviction, the need for entry into substance-abuse treatment, or the need to establish long-term custody arrangements for surviving children. Selecting one specific problem at a time (e.g., entry into substance-abuse treatment) and covering a specific period (e.g., the first half of the agency's fiscal year), the charts for clients identified with a specific problem would be reviewed to determine the effectiveness of intervention. The outcome could be stated in various ways. In this example, the reviewer could use a simple checklist with the following categories: *resolved* (client admitted to and enters a treatment program), *partially resolved* (client placed on waiting list at two or more facilities), *unresolved* (client not in treatment or on waiting list, though action was taken), *problem unaddressed* (client not cooperative, client died during intervention). If many clients fall into categories other than *resolved,* the agency will need to examine the factors that influence this outcome, such as lack of available treatment programs or inappropriate clinical assessments. Such information will then be used to help

**Figure 2.** Process Indicator

| | |
|---|---|
| Indicator: | Comprehensive psychosocial assessment |
| Important aspect of care: | Assessment, evaluation, treatment planning, collaborative input/awareness. |
| Rationale: | To guide planning and decision making adequately, the comprehensive psychosocial assessment addresses both strengths and problems in the patient and his or her situation and spells out the implications of this information for treatment planning and delivery of care. |
| Operational definition: | The percentage of reviewed psychosocial assessments that address the problems and strengths of the client, including physical, environmental, behavioral, emotional, economic, and social factors, and their implications for treatment. Areas to be evaluated by the social worker include mental health status; preexisting health or mental health problems; an appraisal of the client's needs and the resources of the client's informal support system; social role functioning; environmental issues including economic situation, employment status, and other basic needs; substance-abuse history; relevant cultural and religious factors; and an intervention plan based on the findings of the assessment and mutually agreed-upon goals. |
| Threshold: | 95% |
| Data elements: | The number of reviewed charts that meet the criterion for comprehensiveness divided by the total number of charts reviewed, on a sample basis if necessary. |
| Other influencing factors: | Patient leaves treatment prior to completion of period needed for timely assessment. |

**Figure 3.** Outcome Indicator

| | |
|---|---|
| Indicator: | Psychosocial problem resolution; patients' psychosocial problems related to HIV and treatment are ameliorated. |
| Important aspect of care: | Psychosocial intervention. |
| Rationale: | The intent of social work intervention is to improve or resolve the patient's psychosocial problems related to his or her medical condition and treatment. Problem improvement or resolution is an indicator of whether the intervention has achieved its goal. |
| Operational definition: | Percentage of problems ameliorated within 90 days of problem identification. |
| Threshold: | To be determined on basis of problem being tracked. |
| Data elements: | Number of patients experiencing problem X with ameliorated as the outcome divided by the number of social work patients experiencing problem X as identified within a 30-day period. |
| Other influencing factors: | Problem identified within seven days of end of review period. |

the organization develop treatment alternatives or staff development and training programs.

Agencies need to assess the appropriateness of the case management process in relation to intervention outcomes. Agencies should also compare outcomes within client groups, such as gay versus nongay persons; potential differences by race, ethnicity, or gender; or source of payment for services. One such area might be the relevance of the assessment or treatment plan to the interventions made or services delivered. For example, an agency might review the assessments of all clients participating in mental health services to determine whether mental health problems or needs were identified in the assessment. Similarly, the treatment plans for all women with children might be reviewed to determine whether activities related to permanency planning were included in the objectives and then further assessed to see if those activities were conducted.

Client satisfaction is another key aspect of quality assurance. The HIV case manager serves various clients: the person with HIV, the family of that person, medical and mental health providers, agencies that deliver direct services, and service funders. Simple measures of client satisfaction, for example, surveys, for each of these populations can provide illuminating information to the agency and individual case managers. Different instruments should be used for each identified group, and the method of gathering information (such as oral or written) should recognize the needs and abilities of the client.

Quality-assurance activities also provide agencies with the opportunity to assess their services in light of cultural and other factors. Assessment of process and outcomes as they relate to specific client groups, for example, African American women, gay men, or Latino drug users, should also be conducted. Using some of the same instruments while focusing on specific subgroups allows the agency to examine the effects of culture on services and outcomes and to compare the effectiveness of interventions among different groups. Such methods facilitate assessment of the agency's cultural competence.

By gathering data related to processes, outcomes, and client and provider satisfaction, agencies position themselves to defend funding requests and justify expanded services. Such data can also guide the redirection of existing resources and staffing issues. The atmosphere of crisis surrounding HIV and resulting services appears to be diminishing, thus changing the criteria for service development. Access to these types of quality data become vital to the survival of agencies.

## Cultural Factors in Service Delivery

The fact that epidemiological data related to HIV can be discussed in terms of affected cultural groups and subgroups indicates the need for cultural competence among service providers. The behaviors to which most cases of HIV infection to date are attributed—same-sex sexual activity, drug use, and medical treatments involving blood products—separate most individuals with HIV from the mainstream society. If culture is viewed as the accumulation of a shared pattern of values, attitudes, roles, assumptions, and behaviors (Ka'opua, 1994), such behaviors can be tied clearly to particular cultural groups.

The cultural aspects of HIV are compounded by the disproportionate impact of HIV disease on communities of color. Even as the disease affects more non–drug-using, previously healthy heterosexuals, its greater effect is on ethnic and cultural groups with little influence on the content and design of health and social services. If services are to be effective, useful, and desired by target populations, providers must recognize and adapt to cultural considerations (Morales & Bok, 1992).

According to Ka'opua (1994), the provider moves from cultural sensitivity to cultural competence when she or he actively listens for, elicits, and uses cultural information. This involves eliciting information about differences, acknowledging differences, and negotiating a plan of care. Without such actions, services are likely to be underutilized or terminated early, or clients may not follow through with the care plan.

The methods for gathering relevant information differ among various client groups. One core method is for the case manager to become comfortable discussing issues of sexual orientation and activity, drug use, and issues of death and dying. These core content areas are applicable to all HIV-related practice, and service providers must be able to demonstrate their own comfort with these subject areas in order to build the comfort and trust of clients. Among clients of some cultural groups, these subject areas may be acceptable for discussion only indirectly.

Case managers should also ask clients to describe and define their support system or family system. If the client states that someone other than a spouse or immediate blood relative is a primary care provider or potential surrogate decision maker, the case manager should assist in documenting that role and possibly include referrals to establish legal power of attorney and advance health care directives or a simple confidentiality release form for that individual. Taken early in the course of illness, these steps can prevent later conflicts among family members and others involved in the care of the client.

The case manager must also consider the individual client within a cultural context. Applying a label of "gay man" or "African American woman" provides only a sketchy outline of the individual. A comprehensive biopsychosocial assessment should address the strengths and weaknesses of the client within the context of physical, environmental, behavioral, psychological, economic, and social factors to obtain the information necessary to provide appropriate services (National Association of Social Workers, 1992).

## Caring for Professional Caregivers

Regardless of the professional discipline or level of training of the case manager working with persons affected by HIV, the case manager will experience significant personal and professional stress. The realities of the HIV epidemic are harrowing: Most people infected with HIV will die within a few years of a full-blown AIDS diagnosis; many of the "natural caregivers" (partners, spouses, parents, friends) will experience the loss of multiple loved ones as a result of the disease and/or may be infected themselves. The number of infected persons continues to grow, especially among adolescents and young adults.

The realities of the epidemic in turn create new realities for case managers: constantly growing case loads, loss of clients with whom relationships may have been nurtured for years, observing the rapidly declining health status and abilities of previously healthy individuals, and confronting death of persons in age groups in which death is not considered a "normal" occurrence. Professional training often fails to prepare providers to cope with these significant challenges, leaving them to rely on their own experience, the experience of peers, or inappropriate models of grief and loss. These realities, in turn, often result in burnout.

The stages of death and dying as modeled by Kübler-Ross (1969) were developed in relation to the individual dying, not his or her caregiver. It is essential that case managers distinguish between their work with people who are dying and issues surrounding their own eventual death. Recognizing the emotional stress that results from work with people who are dying, Harper (1977, 1994) proposed a developmental construct that considers the emotional stages of professional caregivers.

- **Stage I:** Intellectualization—knowledge and anxiety
- **Stage II:** Emotional survival—trauma
- **Stage III:** Depression—pain, mourning, and grieving
- **Stage IV:** Emotional arrival—moderation, mitigation, accommodation
- **Stage V:** Deep compassion—self-realization, self-awareness, self-actualization
- **Stage VI:** The doer—inner knowledge and wisdom, inner power, strength

The characteristics implicit in each stage significantly influence the provider's ability to engage with clients as well as influence transference and countertransference issues. Thus, case managers and their supervisors must recognize their own emotional needs and develop strategies to progress through these developmental stages.

Supervision for case managers working with HIV-infected clients must include both functional and emotional strategies in the supervisory process. Functional supervision should include information sharing, review of resources and tasks, and quality assurance. Emotional support for case managers must also be available to case managers through the supervisor, peers, and consultants so that case managers have an outlet for their anger, hostility, frustration, guilt, depression, and grief. Although these emotions are often experienced within the context of the case manager's relationship with a particular client, the case manager should be encouraged to examine these emotions within the context of his or her own life and death issues. The direct supervisor and peers can provide direction, encouragement, acceptance, and assistance (Harper, 1994). Outside consultants or employee-assistance professionals with expertise in death and dying issues should be made available to provide counseling and assistance to case managers.

## Conclusion

The complex nature of HIV disease; the health care needs it creates, from prevention to hospice care; the declining ability of the individual to care and advocate for him- or herself as the disease progresses; changes in mental status; and the social disenfranchisement of those who are infected and most at risk for infection make comprehensive case management an essential component of care. However, case management cannot be seen only in the context of interventions during the tertiary phase of illness. To be fully effective, varying levels of case management services must be available at each phase of prevention and infection. The level of case management should be based on the needs and risk factors of individual clients and adapted according to changing needs. Case management professionals come from various backgrounds and should be assigned tasks that relate to their training and client needs. Ongoing quality-improvement activities should focus on both the process and outcomes of case management services, with client satisfaction a key criterion.

A comprehensive case management model provides the flexibility needed to address both individual and service-system needs. As the epidemic continues to spread, case management and concrete services will be in great demand by diverse client populations.

## References

American Health Consultants. (1993). CM program decreased costs, length of stay for AIDS patients. *Case Management Advisor, 4*(5), 57–58.

American Health Consultants. (1994a). New guidelines can help CMs better plan AIDS clients' care. *Case Management Advisor, 5*(4), 51–53.

American Health Consultants. (1994b). Community coordination closes the gaps in HIV management. *Case Management Advisor, 5*(5), 66–72.

American Nurses Association. (1992). *Case management by nurses.* Washington, DC: Author.

Brennan, J. (1994). HIV/AIDS: Implications for health care reform. *Families in Society, 75,* 385–392.

Brennan, J., & Kaplan, C. (1993). Setting new standards for social work case management. *Hospital and Community Psychiatry, 44,* 219–222.

Buckingham, S., & Van Gorp, W. (1994). HIV-associated dementia: A clinician's guide to early detection, diagnosis, and intervention. *Families in Society, 75,* 333–345.

Centers for Disease Control and Prevention. (1994). *HIV/AIDS Surveillance Report, 6*(2).

Collard, A., Bergman, A., & Henderson, M. (1990). Two approaches to measuring quality in medical case management programs. *Quality Review Bulletin, 16*(1), 3–8.

Dilley, J., Helquist, M., & Marks, R. (1991). Report from the International Conference: Hope and apprehension. *Focus, 6*(10), 2.

Getzel, G. (1992). AIDS and social work: A decade later. *Social Work in Health Care, 17*(2), 1–9.

Harper, B. (1977). *Death: The coping mechanism of the health professional.* Greenville, SC: Southeastern University Press.

Harper, B. (1994). *Death: The coping mechanism of the health professional* (rev.). Greenville, SC: Swiger Associates.

Indyk, D., Belville, R., Lachapelle, S., Gordon, G., & Dewart, T. (1993). A community-based approach to HIV case management: Systematizing the unmanageable. *Social Work, 38,* 380–387.

Isbell, M. (1993). *Health care reform: Lessons from the HIV epidemic.* New York: Lambda Legal Defense and Education Fund.

Ka'opua, L. (1994). Cultural competency in the HIV epidemic. In 1994 *National HIV Frontline Forum Multimedia Self-Study Kit.* New York: NCM Publishers.

Kübler-Ross, E. (1969). *On death and dying.* New York: Macmillan.

Morales, J., & Bok, M. (1992). Multicultural human services for AIDS treatment and prevention: Policy, perspectives and planning. *Journal of Multicultural Social Work, 2*(special issue), 1–119.

National Association of Social Workers. (1990a). *NASW clinical indicators for social work and psychosocial services in the acute care medical hospital.* Washington DC: Author.

National Association of Social Workers. (1990b). *NASW clinical indicators for social work and psychosocial services in the acute psychiatric hospital.* Washington, DC: Author.

National Association of Social Workers. (1992). *NASW standards for social work case management.* Washington, DC: Author.

National Association of Social Workers. (1993). *NASW clinical indicators for social work and psychosocial services in nursing homes.* Washington, DC: Author.

National Association of Social Workers. (1995). *NASW/NFK clinical indicators for social work and psychosocial services in nephrology settings.* Washington, DC: Author.

Piette, J., Fleishman, J., Mor, V., & Thompson, B. (1992). The structure and process of AIDS case management. *Health and Social Work, 17*(1), 47–56.

Piette, J., Thompson, B., Fleishman, B., & Mor, V. (1993). The organization and delivery of AIDS case management. In V. Lynch, G. Lloyd, & M. Fimbres (Eds.), *The changing face of AIDS: Implications for social work practice.* Westport, CT: Auburn House.

Roberts, C., Severinsen, C., Kuehn, C., Straker, D., & Fritz, C. (1992). Obstacles to effective case management with AIDS patients: The clinician's perspective. *Social Work in Health Care, 17*(2), 27–40.

Shilts, R. (1987). *And the band played on: Politics, people, and the AIDS epidemic.* New

York: St. Martins Press.

Sonsel, G., Paradise, F., & Stroup, S. (1988). Case management practice in an AIDS service organization. *Social Casework, 69,* 388–392.

Sowell, R., Gueldner, S., Killeen, M., Lowenstein, A., Fuszard, B., & Swansburg, R. (1992). Impact of case management on hospital charges of PWAs in Georgia. *Journal of the Association of Nurses in AIDS Care, 3*(2), 24–31.

Stein, J., & Hodge, R. (1993) Substance abuse and HIV disease: A multidimensional challenge to caregivers. In V. Lynch, G. Lloyd, & M. Fimbres (Eds.), *The changing face of AIDS: Implications for social work practice.* Westport, CT: Auburn House.

World Health Organization. (1995, February). *WHO recorded statistics on AIDS.* Geneva, Switzerland: Author.

# Chapter 11

# Cultural Competency of Case Managers

*David Este*

C ase management is a major service technology in the human service field. It is also a rich and dynamic field for scholars and practitioners committed to improving the circumstances of clients and the
service-delivery system. With both the federal and state governments in
the United States preoccupied with deficits and debts, it is imperative
that organizations utilizing case managers provide tangible evidence
that case management indeed is an efficient and effective modality in
dealing with the array of client problems and issues.

Case managers, like all other human service professionals, are
under increasing pressure to become more comfortable, knowledgeable, and skillful in their work with racially, ethnically, sexually, and
religiously diverse populations as well as in their work with persons
with disabilities. Social service and health care organizations are
being challenged to develop and provide services that reflect the
diversity that exists in their communities. For example, in one city,
organizations that receive funding from the local United Way are
engaged in a multicultural organizational change process, whereby
participating agencies are developing action plans designed to
enhance the accessibility and utilization of services provided by members of diverse groups. The change process also focuses on creating
organizational environments within agencies to accept, promote, and
value diversity.

## *The Need for Culturally Competent Case Managers*

Changing demographics in the United States make it highly likely that case managers will interact and work with clients from different
cultural backgrounds and experiences. As Table 1 indicates, in 1990
approximately 25% of the American population consisted of visible
minorities. Thomas (1992) states,

> Workforce 2000 has projected that from [the years] 1985 to 2000
> minorities, women, and immigrants will compose 85 percent of the
> growth in the work force. Workforce 2000 projects the highest rate of
> increase for Asian Americans and Hispanics (p. 5).

Three primary factors contribute to population diversity in the
United States:

- Immigration has exceeded 700,00 per year, not including illegal
  immigrants, since 1990.

- Compared with the non-Hispanic white population, immigrants
  tend to have more children.

- Today, minorities are in the majority in approximately 6% of
  U.S. counties. By the year 2060, minorities may claim a majority for the entire United States (Moore, 1994).

**Table 1.** U.S. population by race and ethnicity–1990

|  | Number (in 000s) | % of total population |
|---|---|---|
| White, non-Hispanic | 187,137 | 75.2 |
| Black* | 29,986 | 12.1 |
| Native American, Eskimo, Aleut* | 1,959 | .08 |
| Asian or Pacific islander | 7,274 | 2.9 |
| Hispanic (of any race) | 22,354 | 9.0 |
| Total | 248,710 | 100.00 |

*Includes a small number of Hispanics
Source: U.S. Bureau of the Census

Changing demographics require case managers to practice in a culturally competent manner. Case managers cannot assume that their formal
training provides them with the knowledge and skills required to work
in a pluralistic society.

Other factors contribute to the need for case managers to provide
services in a culturally sensitive manner. Green (1982) maintains that
ethnic and minority groups are entitled to receive competent professional services. Case managers must take into consideration the values,
beliefs, and norms of the client system receiving services. In stronger
language, Casimir and Morrison (1993) contend that "anything other
than full commitment to cultural competence in the delivery of mental
health services must be viewed as a violation of consumers' civil rights"
(p. 558).

Increasingly, diverse populations demand that service providers be more sensitive and responsive to the issues and needs of particular groups. These diverse populations are also demanding that they be given the opportunity to become involved in the planning and delivery of services. For example, aboriginal communities in the United States are asking for greater involvement or complete control of the human service infrastructure in their communities.

The multicultural perspective is growing throughout the social sciences, which represents another factor prompting the need for professionals to become culturally competent (Pedersen, Fukuyama, & Health, 1989). Chau (1990) describes the impact of the multicultural perspective on social work education:

> The rapid growth and increasing visibility of ethnic and racial groups constitutes an important force that revives and reshapes the ever-growing interest in educating for social work practice in cross-cultural contexts (p. 124).

Furthermore, mental health professionals are developing treatment models and services that are responsive to ethnic, racial, and religious identities as well as addressing gender, age, disability, and sexual orientation issues (Giordano, 1994).

Given this diversity, case managers need to recognize how the backgrounds and experiences of individuals and groups affect utilization of services (Pedersen et al., 1989). Moreover, case managers must be aware of how their cultural values, norms, and experiences influence their work with clients with different cultural backgrounds, values, and experiences.

## Defining Cultural Competence

In the literature, various terms are used to describe cultural competence, for example, cross-cultural practice, ethnic competency, and multicultural practice. In discussing cultural competence, it is necessary to define the following concepts: culture, competence, and cultural competence.

Defining "culture" is critical in any discussion of cultural competence. Culture refers to the concepts, habits, skills, art, instruments, and institutions of a given people in a given period. Similarly, Olandi (1992) defines culture as "the shared values, norms, traditions, customs, arts, history, folklore, and institutions of a given people (p. vi). According to Kavanaugh and Kennedy (1992), culture applies to all aggregates or categories of people whose "life patterns discernibly influence individual communication behaviors" (pp. 12–13). In the context of cross-cultural relationships, culture can be thought of as

> *those elements of a people's history, tradition, values, and social orga-*
> *nization that become explicitly meaningful to the participants during an*
> *encounter. [Culture] assumes that some of the things that characterize*
> *the background and experience of each individual are, at least at the*
> *moment of communication, more important than other things (Green,*
> *1982, p. 7).*

In their classic work, Cross, Bazron, Dennis, and Isaacs (1989) discuss culture in terms of integrated patterns of human behavior reflecting the thoughts, communications, actions, customs, beliefs, values, and institutions of racial, ethnic, religious, or social groups. In other words, culture determines one's world view, that is, "the way in which people perceive their relationship to nature, other people, and objects [and determines] how people behave, think, and define events" (English, as quoted in Schiele, 1994, p. 22). As a case in point, Afrocentrism is a "world view identifying those elements in the African-American life and culture which are distinctively African" (Jeff, 1994, p. 103). Knowledge about the world views of particular groups is critically important for case managers.

Competence, the second critical concept, suggests the ability or capacity to function effectively. Case managers need to be competent in assessment, planning, linking, monitoring, and advocacy in their work with clients.

In defining cultural competence as a developmental process, Cross et al. (1989) points out that cultural competence recognizes the importance of culture and of assessing cross-cultural relations. Practitioners must be aware of the dynamics resulting from cultural differences as well as expand their cultural knowledge and adapt services to meet culturally specific needs. Olandi (1992) defines outreach cultural competence as

> *a set of academic and interpersonal skills that allow individuals to*
> *increase their understanding and appreciation of cultural differences*
> *and similarities within, among, and between groups. This requires a*
> *willingness and ability to draw on community-based values, traditions*
> *and customs and to work with knowledgeable persons of and from the*
> *community in developing focused interventions, communications, and*
> *other supports (p. vi).*

This definition is relevant to case management practice. Case managers need to be knowledgeable about different cultural groups (gay and lesbian, mentally ill, senior citizens, religious, ethnic, and racial) as well as develop an appreciation for differences in values, beliefs, and customs among groups. In so doing, case managers are able to link clients with individuals and agencies in the community that can provide needed services.

Cultural competence is multidimensional in nature and involves various aspects of knowledge, attitude, and skill development. These vary along a continuum from high to low. The Cultural Sophistication Framework depicted in Table 2 illustrates the developmental process whereby case managers become culturally competent.

**Table 2.** The cultural sophistication framework

|  | Incompetent | Sensitive | Competent |
|---|---|---|---|
| Cognitive dimension | Oblivious | Aware | Knowledgeable |
| Affective dimension | Apathetic | Sympathetic | Committed to change |
| Skills dimension | Unskilled | Lacking some skills | Highly skilled |
| Overall effect | Destructive | Neutral | Constructive |

In the initial stage, the culturally incompetent case manager is not aware of the need to be and/or may not possess the desire to become culturally competent. In practice, such an individual does not consider how cultural factors may affect his or her work with clients. This approach can be very destructive to the client–case manager relationship and may prohibit clients from obtaining the services they need.

In the second stage, the culturally sensitive case manager is aware of the nuances of his or her own culture and other cultures. Case managers at this stage possess a measure of cultural competence and are likely to be receptive to increasing their knowledge of different cultures.

In the final stage, the culturally competent case manager is very knowledgeable about the values, norms, and customs of diverse communities and has acquired the skills needed to practice in a culturally competent manner.

## Case Example

Cultural competence and incompetence in case management practice are illustrated in the following case example:

*An elderly Vietnamese man was admitted to the hospital with congestive heart failure. Several family members remained at his bedside day and night. A 35-year-old daughter was in constant conflict with the staff, making numerous demands, frequently asking that the doctor be called, and wanting a nurse present in her father's room at all times. She exhibited considerable anger and anxiety.*

*The nurses reported that they made every effort to meet the needs of the patient but that they were unable to satisfy the daughter. A member of the staff reminded the daughter that her father wasn't the only patient on the unit. The staff also began to enforce visitors' hours and went out of their way to avoid the daughter.*

*Finally, the staff met to discuss the family's needs, to verbalize their feelings, and to set limits in order to prevent manipulation of the staff and to promote respect for the staff. The unit staff decided that they needed to be consistent and to work with the family to resolve conflicts. The head nurse met with the family to inform members of the care that was being provided. Despite these efforts, the behavior of the family did not change (case adapted from Kavanaugh & Kennedy, 1992, p. 88).*

## ❑ Culturally Incompetent Case Management

The following behaviors highlight culturally incompetent case management in this case situation. An incompetent case manager would

- Fail to acknowledge the concerns of the family.

- Lack knowledge about Vietnamese language, customs, beliefs, family organization, and family processes, such as caregiving responsibilities and roles, decision making, and problem solving.

- Not attempt to obtain information in the areas listed above but instead utilize the same approach with all families without consideration of cultural factors that influence behavior.

- Not attempt to get the family and staff to discuss the situation. (The case manager would probably side with the hospital staff, for example, by agreeing with the staff's enforcement of visitors' hours.)

- Not seek out culturally appropriate services and supports in the community.

Such behaviors would likely increase the discord between the family and the hospital and intensify frustration and hopelessness among family members, especially the older daughter. Family members would likely feel that the case manager did not understand and was not interested in their situation.

## ❑ Culturally Competent Case Management

The culturally competent case manager, on the other hand, would likely do the following:

- Complete a thorough assessment of the situation, including an evaluation of the patient's medical condition.

- Become knowledgeable about Vietnamese language, customs, beliefs, family organization, and family process (caregiving roles and responsibilities, decision making, and problem-solving skills) by seeking out individuals in the community who possess this information.

- Meet with the family to listen to and try to understand members' fears, concerns, and expectations of care.

- Bring the staff and family together to discuss the situation and find solutions to the conflict.

- Begin to identify supports and services the family might utilize after the patient was discharged from the hospital by networking with both formal and informal services such as churches and community associations.

Such behaviors would be a clear indication to the family that the case manager understood their concerns and wished to work with the family. By understanding and involving the family, the culturally competent case manager recognizes that the family possesses culturally specific strengths that can be used to resolve conflicts.

## Knowledge Competencies

Case managers need to be knowledgeable about the characteristics of cultural groups such as gays and lesbians; understand phenomena such as racism, sexism, ageism, and discrimination; and be familiar with concepts such as assimilation, melting pot, social class, and ethnic conflict (Aponte, 1995). Perhaps the first step toward cultural competency is admitting one's lack of knowledge about other cultures and committing oneself to learn about them (Ronnau, 1994).

Lum's description of the knowledge base required of professionals working with minority populations is relevant to case managers' understanding the life situations of minority populations: "It involves history, cognitive–affective behavioral characteristics, and of the societal dilemmas of people of color" (quoted in Manoleas, 1994, p. 47). The types of knowledge identified by Lum in work with people of color are applicable to case managers' work with clients from diverse populations such as the disabled, gays and lesbians, mentally ill, and persons with AIDS. Each of these communities has distinct values, beliefs, norms, and histories.

Case managers who aspire to become culturally competent must begin by becoming aware of their own culture. Culturally sensitive individuals are cognizant of how their own cultural background affects their interactions with clients from other backgrounds. They understand that cultural background affects their thoughts and actions. Obviously, such awareness requires a measure of introspection and sensitivity to one's own biases, stereotypes, and values (Neukrug, 1994; Ronnau, 1994).

Acquiring knowledge to become culturally competent is an ongoing process. Case managers cannot be expected to have comprehensive knowledge of all of the various cultures of clients with whom they work. However, the ability to identify gaps in knowledge and resources for information is a desirable and realistic goal. Case managers can identify gaps in cultural knowledge through their interactions with clients and practitioners who work with diverse groups. It is important that case managers become knowledgeable about the world views of clients and attempt to understand these views without making negative judgments (Jeff, 1994; Moore, 1994).

The culturally sensitive professional understands the negative and sometimes devastating effect of racism, sexism, homophobia, and ageism. Commenting on racism, Edwards (1994) states,

> Racism victimizes the dominant culture by obliterating any distinction or glory to its heritage, in an effort to define difference as negative and undesirable and its own ways as standard. Consequently the pride of identifying with a culture of one's own is lost (p. 5).

As a part of the knowledge-development process, case managers need to acknowledge the existence of differences among cultural groups. Edwards (1994) states that case managers' willingness to acknowledge and address valid cultural differences between themselves and clients is the most difficult stage in becoming culturally competent.

Moore (1994) believes that case managers should have knowledge of family structures, hierarchies, sex roles, and kinship networks of various cultural groups. In addition, case managers must be knowledgeable about caregiving roles among diverse populations (Manoleas, 1994).

Case managers must also be knowledgeable about the community structures of diverse populations, for example, demographic data, employment status and income, housing, educational facilities, transportation systems, and prevailing social problems in the community. Case managers need to be informed about the health and social services available to gays and lesbians, the physical and mentally challenged, and individuals with AIDS. Professionals need such knowledge to link clients to community resources. Case managers must be able to identify barriers that limit both access and utilization of services by diverse populations. Although advocacy is a typical case management activity, case managers who work with disadvantaged and marginal populations may need to engage extensively in advocacy activities to ensure that clients receive the services they need and to overcome biases, prejudices, and discriminatory practices within the community.

In sum, the acquisition of knowledge to become a culturally competent case manager is an ongoing process. By interacting with their clients in their daily practice, case managers gain on-the-job training from individuals from diverse backgrounds.

However, case managers need more than knowledge. Their greater challenge is learning to apply such knowledge in ways that will benefit their clients. Case managers must be creative not only in their assessments but in the types of interventions they employ.

## *Skills*

Case managers require specific skills in their work with clients from diverse backgrounds. As Lum (1986) states, the skill base for culturally competent practice focuses on "developing a helping relationship with an individual, family, group, and/or community whose distinctive physical/cultural characteristics and discriminatory experiences require approaches that are sensitive to ethnic and cultural environments" (p. 3).

Empathy is critical in the development of a trusting relationship with clients. In cross-racial helping relationships, clients are concerned about whether helping professionals understand their social realities. Case managers need to be able to understand the point of view of others, accept differences, and communicate this acceptance (Neukrug, 1994).

Case managers must be able to conduct thorough assessments that consider the ways in which cultural factors may influence clients' behaviors and circumstances. As part of the assessment process, case managers should evaluate a client's world view and his or her level of acculturation, especially if the client is an immigrant. Edwards (1994) suggests that the following questions be posed:

- When and how did you or your families migrate to your present community?
- Why did you move?
- Did you seek to escape oppression?
- Did you wish to escape war in your homeland?

- How did you effect your escape?

- How have you adjusted to your new life? What was most easy and what has been most difficult in your adjustment?

Case managers must be skilled with various helping styles and approaches in their daily practice. An important skill is facility with a second language. For example, in certain parts of the United States it is essential that case managers speak Spanish. Case managers who do not have second-language skills must have access to translation and interpreting services. Language skills not only assist in the communication process, they indicate to clients that the case manager has cultural knowledge and thus is likely to understand their needs.

In conducting interviews, case managers must be cognizant of the culturally appropriate level of intrusiveness and directness that should be used, including social distance to be maintained and the level of formality with which clients should be addressed. Manoleas (1994) states,

> *Effectiveness of direct or indirect practice is closely related to the worker's ability to communicate and form positive relationships. The communication of respect is especially important for clients who have experienced oppression at the hands of the system, for immigrants not used to the casualness of [the United States], and for others who may be inherently skeptical about social agencies (p. 50).*

Case managers must be aware of and sensitive to both the verbal and nonverbal communications of their clients. The ability to interpret nonverbal communications of particular cultures, as reflected in gestures and facial expressions, enhances a case manager's ability to understand and thus communicate with clients.

In the interviewing process, case managers need to be able to recognize and manage defensiveness and resistance on the part of clients. Kavanagh and Kennedy (1992) state,

> *At times communication is associated with risk, such as when there is uncertainty about how exposure of reactions will be received, especially if the others have power or are in some way potentially threatening. When involved in a situation that is uneasy, defensiveness, anger, or hurt may occur. . . . Defensiveness occurs when personal security is perceived to be threatened (p. 56).*

Case managers can use various techniques to minimize defensiveness. First, however, they must understand that defensiveness may be revealed through the client's expression, affect, manner, and tone of voice. The case manager should attempt to understand what the client's behavior means from his or her own perspective. Humor, particularly self-directed humor, can be a powerful tool in reducing defensiveness and in building rapport. By disclosing selected, culturally appropriate personal information, the case manager can reduce defensiveness by sharing and promoting acceptance. Nonjudgmental behavior is critical to establishing an atmosphere that facilitates open communication across cultural boundaries. Furthermore, defensiveness can be better managed when clients' autonomy is respected and used in a culturally appropriate manner.

> Resistance involves barriers to trust or opposition to the goal of mutual communication. Providers may find themselves resisting the use of a client's perspectives in problem definition and resolution. Clients, on the other hand, may resist professional views of the problem, strategies, or goals (Kavanaugh & Kennedy, 1992, p. 58).

Culturally competent case managers can employ several strategies to deal with client resistance. First, it is important to demonstrate acceptance and understanding by clearly identifying the client's concerns. Cultural awareness helps the case manager understand that the way the client describes his or her situation may differ substantially from how the worker would describe it. The case manager must assess culturally specific coping patterns and responses to stressful situations. This kind of focused assessment helps the case manager to understand and anticipate potentially resistant behaviors.

Questions must be asked in a way that is consistent with the client's cultural and linguistic expectations. For members of some groups, only open questions are socially acceptable. For others, closed questions are preferred. Still others, including some American Indian groups, prefer indirect inquiries whereby questions are posed in a story-like scenario (e.g., "Some people find that when such and such happens it is best to . . .").

Accurate reflection, clarification, interpretation, and reframing of the client's behavior, beliefs, and ideas communicate recognition and understanding of the client's perspective. It is critical that the case manager understand that informal or natural helping systems are powerful social structures in many cultures. Culturally specific knowledge and awareness makes it possible for case managers to address and minimize client resistance in a productive manner. It should be noted, however, that resistance on the part of clients may be positive. For example, resistance may be a manifestation of assertiveness and may reflect the client's desire to be independent and protect core cultural beliefs and values.

In forming relationships with individuals, communities, and organizations, case managers must work to establish and maintain contacts and networks that can provide culturally specific information and services. Consulting with traditional healers and spiritual leaders as well as with practitioners who have experience working with culturally diverse clients can be very helpful.

## *Values*

A culturally appropriate value base is also an important aspect of becoming culturally competent (Manoleas, 1994). Case managers must value cultural diversity and respect its worth. Ronnau (1994) maintains that being a culturally competent professional is, to a large degree, an attitude.

In discussing the value base that human service workers, including case managers, need in order to become culturally competent, Manoleas (1994) states that professionals must acknowledge and accept the existence of cultural differences and their impact on service delivery and utilization. The lack of acknowledgment regarding cultural differences may limit the effectiveness of a case manager in his or her work with clients from different cultural backgrounds.

Diversity with cultural groups is as important as diversity among groups. Professionals who fail to recognize differences within groups run the risk of developing stereotypical attitudes. For example, not all immigrants from the West Indies share the same cultural values, norms, and beliefs. The West Indies comprise several different nations, each with its own distinctive cultures. Waxler-Morrison, Anderson, and Richardson (1990) state:

> while there are usually shared beliefs, values, and experiences among people from a given ethnic group, quite often there is a widespread intra-ethnic diversity. Factors such as social class, religion, level of education, and area of origin in the home country (rural or urban) make for major differences (p. 246).

Thus, it is important that case managers view and respect clients as unique individuals within their cultural groups.

Effective case managers have a culturally relativistic view of the world. Cultural relativism asserts that people view and interpret phenomena differently but that no particular world view is superior, better, or more correct than another. This value is extremely important for case managers. In understanding and accepting the concept of cultural relativism, case managers are open to learning about other world views and are creative in their work with clients from diverse backgrounds.

Holding the values specified above does not ensure that a case manager is or will become culturally competent. Possessing relevant knowledge and acquistion of required skills are essential. In addition, administrators of agencies that employ case managers must ensure that their organizations value and support cultural competence as a core organizational commitment. This support can take various forms. For example, the agency can provide case managers with training opportunities in culturally competent practice. It is important to ensure that the organizational climate supports diversity. Agency administrators can provide opportunities for case managers to participate in agencies' plans to improve cultural competence. These initiatives will ensure that cultural competence is viewed as individual and organizational processes requiring ongoing commitment and support.

## *Culturally Competent Case Management Practice*

Primary case management functions include intake, assessment, case planning, linking, monitoring, and reassessment.

### ❑ Intake

This function involves the case manager obtaining client information regarding (1) public information such as name, address, date of birth, and gender; (2) private data, including education and employment status, marital status, race, ethnic background, religion, languages, immigration status, and citizenship status; and (3) understanding the clients' or the referring agents' explanation of the problem. This preliminary information assists the case manager in completing the next critical function—assessment. Eligibility decisions are frequently made at intake.

### ❑ Assessment

Thorough assessments are key to the outcome of case managers' work. Assessment is a challenging task for case managers working across cultures. In this phase, case managers continue to obtain information from the client as well as begin to make sense of the client's cultural reality. The types of data case managers should attempt to obtain include information on the client's current and past situation, social information (culture, values, issues of prejudice and descrimination, access, availability of resources, attitudes toward services and service providers, and language and custom differences from those of the larger community), nature of interpersonal relationships (marital and family, peer group, social support, and work relationships), and assessing the client's physical environment (housing, transportation, and neighborhood). Assessment provides the basis for the care-planning function.

## ❏ Care Planning

At this stage, the case manager develops a culturally appropriate care plan in consultation with the client. This decision-making process usually involves family members and significant others as well as other professionals if they are needed. One of the primary tasks of the case manager is to ensure that the individuals involved understand the care plan and their respective roles in its implementation. Many care plans rely on the active participation of extended families and social networks of various cultures. Translators may need to be involved at this point. Planning is not enough. Case managers also must develop a feasible plan that can be implemented. Implementation requires cultural awareness and insight.

## ❏ Linking

Linking requires case managers to be knowledgeable about resources both within and outside the ethnic/racial community and how to make referrals and advocate for services. Cross-cultural practice requires case managers to have comprehensive knowledge and contacts in both mainstream and culturally specific delivery systems. To facilitate the linking process, a culturally competent case manager may require the assistance of an interpreter/translator to make sure that the client understands the rationale behind the care plan and knows what to expect when services begin. As part of this process, experienced case managers take advantage of contacts and relationships with culturally appropriate and diverse individuals, programs, and agencies.

## ❏ Monitoring

The culturally competent case manager follows up in an appropriate and sensitive fashion in order to determine the effectiveness of the care plan. This requires contacting and involving the client, family, significant others, and service providers regarding the client's status and whether changes need to be made in the care plan. Such changes should be explained and negotiated in a culturally appropriate fashion to facilitate continuity of care for the client.

## *Training Culturally Competent Case Managers*

Who should provide training to develop culturally competent case managers? Because case managers come from various professional backgrounds, such as nursing, psychology, occupational therapy, and social work, these professional disciplines should provide both the knowledge and opportunities for skill development in the area of cultural competence. The social work profession has made considerable progress implementing a multicultural perspective, and models showing how to infuse cross-cultural content within the curricula of professional disciplines are available (Chau, 1990; Devore & Schlesinger, 1991). Pedersen et al. (1989) contend that training programs should include the following components: consciousness raising, cognitive development, affective awareness, and skill development.

One or two courses do not ensure that prospective case managers will be culturally competent. Cultural competence is a long-term process. Case managers must continue to develop their knowledge of and skills in work with clients from diverse cultural backgrounds. It would be inaccurate to assume that even the most skillful and knowledgeable culturally competent case manager can deal with the myriad situations that clients from diverse groups may experience. For example, culturally defined sex roles may limit a case manager's involvement or intervention. In such cases, case managers need to understand the limits of his or her effectiveness and seek alternative strategies. It is possible to argue that a case manager who recognizes his or her limitations in relation to culturally competent practice is indeed working in a culturally competent manner. To provide quality services, educators, administrators of human service agencies, case managers, and clients share responsibility in contributing to the cultural competence of case managers.

## References

Aponte, C. (1995). Cultural diversity course model: Cultural competence for content and process. *Arete, 20*(1), 46–55.

Casimir, G., & Morrison, B. (1993). Rethinking work with multicultural populations. *Community Mental Health Journal, 29,* 547–559.

Chau, K. (1990). A model for teaching cross-cultural practice in social work. *Journal of Social Work Education, 26*(1), 124–133.

Cross, T., Bazron, B., Dennis, K., & Isaacs, M. (1989). *Towards a culturally competent system of care.* Washington, DC: CASSP Technical Assistance Center.

Devore, W., & Schlesinger, E. (1991). *Ethnic-sensitive social work practice* (3rd ed.). Toronto: Collier Macmillan.

Edwards, V. (1994). Understanding culture as a process. In R. Surber (Ed.), *Clinical case management: A guide to comprehensive treatment of serious mental illness.* Newbury Park, CA: Sage Publications.

Giordano, J. (1994). Mental health and the melting pot: An introduction. *American*

*Journal of Orthopsychiatry, 64,* 342–345.

Green, J. (1982). *Cultural awareness in the human services,* Englewood Cliffs, NJ: Prentice-Hall.

Jeff, M. (1994). Afrocentrism and Afro-American male youths. In R. Mincy (Ed.), *Nurturing young black males* (pp. 99–118). Washington, DC: Urban Institute Press.

Kavanaugh, K., & Kennedy, P. (1992). *Promoting cultural diversity: Strategies for health care professionals.* Newbury Park, CA: Sage Publications.

Lum, D. (1986). *Social work practice and people of color: A process-stage approach.* Pacific Grove, CA: Brooks/Cole.

Manoleas, P. (1994). An outcome approach to assessing the cultural competence of MSW students. *Journal of Multicultural Social Work, 3*(1), 43–57.

Moore, Q. (1994). A whole new world of diversity. *Journal of Intergroup Relations, 20*(4), 28–40.

Neukrug, E. (1994). Understanding diversity in a pluralistic world. *Journal of Intergroup Relations, 22*(2), 3–12.

Olandi, M. (1992). Defining cultural competence: An organizing framework. In M. Olandi (Ed.), *Cultural competence for evaluators: A guide for alcohol and other drug abuse prevention practitioners working with ethnic/racial communities.* Rockville, MD: U.S. Department of Health and Human Services.

Pedersen, P., Fukuyama, M., & Health, A. (1989). Client, counsellor, and contextual variables in multicultural counselling. In P. Pedersen (Ed.), *Counseling across cultures.* Honolulu, HI: University of Hawaii Press.

Ronnau, J. (1994). Teaching cultural competence: Practical ideas for social work educators. *Journal of Multicultural Social Work, 3*(1), 29–42.

Schiele, J. (1994). Afrocentricity as an alternative world view for equality. *Journal of Progressive Human Services, 5*(1), 5–25.

Thomas, R. (1992). *Beyond race and gender: Unleashing the power of your total work force by managing diversity.* New York: American Management Association.

Waxler-Morrison, N., Anderson, J., & Richardson, E. (1990). *Cross-cultural caring: A handbook for health professionals.* Vancouver, BC: University of British Columbia Press.

Chapter **12**

# Practice Dilemmas and Policy Implications In Case Management

*Robert W. McClelland, Carol D. Austin, and Dean Schneck*

C ase management has taken on a larger-than-life presence in the
human services. It seems to be everywhere. Although it has its
critics, case management in general has been widely accepted. Beneath
this veneer of consensus, however, lie conflicts, dilemmas, contradic-
tions, and uncertainties. These controversies are often obscured by the
daily demands of providing service to clients. Nevertheless, they are
present and have an influence on both direct delivery of services and
policy development. The extensive review of case management practice in this volume illustrates the policy and practice complexities
underlying this popular service.

## *Practice Dilemmas*

### ❏ Professional Turf

Rapp and Kisthardt (chapter 2) note that "case management is not
a profession. It is a methodology. People who deliver the case management services have diverse educational training." Persons trained in
social work, psychology, counseling, education, theology, nursing, and
various other disciplines are frequently employed as case managers.
The most notable professions laying claim to case management are
nursing and social work. This chapter discusses case management primarily in the context of social work practice.

Principles and policy objectives such as a holistic approach, community-based care, strengths-based perspective, family-based practice,
and cultural relevance are part and parcel of the expanding definition
of case management. This is understandable for several reasons: (1)
despite protests to the contrary, case management bears a striking
resemblance to casework practice and process; (2) case management
has become the favorite technology of powerful providers and payers
in their attempts to contain costs; (3) many social workers lean toward

functional or methodological identifications such as psychotherapist, social planner, group worker, and so forth rather than the more generic social worker identification. But is case management really good old-fashioned social work updated in the form of generalist practice?

Social, health, and mental health services need to be competently delivered, coordinated, and monitored. Issues of fragmentation, access, timing, and system complexity all demand the services of a coordinating mechanism—case management. When case managers skillfully assess problem situations, provide direct services, secure and coordinate both formal and informal resources, evaluate interventions, and assure follow-up, they are performing core generalist social work practice tasks.

The roles and skills represented in case management clearly represent the *in vivo* application of many long-standing conceptualizations of social work practice: the person-in-environment perspective, the social-interactionist orientation, the systems basis of generalist practice, and the social ecological framework. Case management also serves the basic mission of social work through its focus on ameliorating psychosocial stress, providing supports to individuals and families during times of crisis, and providing "social prosthetics" to enable people to meet their daily needs and perform their social roles. Though frequently driven by cost containment and resource-utilization factors in the current environment, the access and quality-of-care objectives are much closer to core social work values and therefore ought to be more compelling for social work practitioners. It is ironic that many social workers are currently engaged in a turf struggle with other professions to recapture or retain the functions that some practitioners viewed as being of little professional interest in the recent past.

Although case management is pivotal to the delivery and coordination of services, it should not be elevated to a quasi discipline or serve as a proxy for social work practice in general. Rather, it should be seen as a unifying method to be employed in conjunction with other classic social work methods that contribute to the profession's leadership in social welfare policy, program development, and practice innovations that serve diverse client populations. In addition to its obvious benefits to direct client care, case management provides an approach that incorporates varying strategies for change at the micro, mezzo, and macro levels (Kirst-Ashman & Hull, 1993). These include practice concepts such as problem solving, advocacy, systems change, the ecological model, the interactional approach, and functional work on behalf of clients and the broader community (Compton & Galaway, 1994; Germain & Gitterman, 1986; Hepworth & Larsen, 1993; Miley, O'Melia, & DuBois, 1995; Sheafor, Horejsi, & Horejsi, 1994; Shulman, 1992; Wood & Middleman,

1989; Zastrow, 1995). In theory, case managers have a powerful opportunity to influence and shape the political economy of social resources on behalf of some of the most vulnerable members of society.

Is case management a professional role? This question has been raised from various perspectives. One concern is the extent to which all tasks included under the umbrella of case management require professional expertise. Do assessment and care planning require the same knowledge and skills as does monitoring? The quality of case managers' assessment skills are reflected in how well care plans are individualized in relation to program costs. Skillful assessment includes valid and reliable use of instruments as well as highly developed interviewing skills. In the assessment phase, case managers utilize their knowledge of the etiology, course, interventions, and potential outcomes associated with the target group being served. In contrast, the screening and monitoring functions may not require professional staff. Screening involves the application of specific criteria, and monitoring is designed to identify changes in a client's situation. Screening and monitoring do not require the same level of skills and knowledge as do assessment and care planning. The division of labor in case management tasks along these lines has implications for recruitment, staffing, supervision, and costs.

Case-load size is another indicator of professional case management practice. Some case loads can be so large as to preclude face-to-face contact between client and case manager. Professional case management requires face-to-face assessment and collaborative care planning. Case management services provided by telephone are more accurately labeled data collection, verification, authorization, and approval. These tasks may not even require a background in the human services. It would hardly be surprising if case-load sizes increased in many settings. If case loads grow beyond the point where it is feasible for case managers to work with clients in person, case management as we have come to know it will no longer exist.

## ❏ Advocacy and Social Control

Case managers have an excellent opportunity to advocate not only on behalf of their individual client, patient, or family, but also for the larger community. An effective advocate defines and promotes the well-being of the client and the client population, underscoring humane treatment and service as well as the consequences of abrogation or omission of needed care. In the context of cost containment and program cuts, advocacy can be lost in the rhetoric and reality of the current attack on health and social welfare programs, particularly programs targeted toward the poor. So much attention is focused on the costs of care that society loses sight of the cost of not caring.

What does advocacy mean in this environment? The primary role conflict inherent in case management emerges here. How can case managers be advocates in the program in which they are employed given the current punitive atmosphere? Case managers are responsible for implementing the ever increasing restrictions and limits on services and benefits. In situations in which case managers identify more with their program than with their clients, social control is emphasized and client-based advocacy discouraged. A public policy environment based on a "meaner and leaner" philosophy promotes resource control, self-reliance, time limits on how long clients can receive service, close monitoring, restricted service choices, and high levels of family involvement. Proponents of this ideology clearly believe that human service programs address an extremely residual social function, that clients should be able to do more with less, and that clients are not now and may never be full participants in society.

This ideology certainly does not promote a conducive setting for case managers whose training, values, and philosophy assume an expanding resource base. Many of the authors in this volume point out how preventive interventions and flexibility in services will often obviate far more costly care over time. Thus, what is good for the individual client may also be the less expensive option for society. However, society cannot "cost contain" or case manage its way around or out of a central value and social policy dilemma. That is, social, health, and mental health services in this country have been and are continuing to be underfunded at all levels. Concerns about the adequacy of social provision are no longer in fashion. Given the current political context, advocacy may very well be met with hostility. Thus case managers who take their system-change goals seriously now have an opportunity to embrace advocacy as critical to their practice and to work toward change at macro and mezzo levels.

## ❏ Fiscal Accountability

Do case managers know the costs of the care plans they develop? Some case managers are required to know these costs because their care planning is constrained by cost caps, time limitations, and approvals for exceptions. Fiscal accountability has become one of the watchwords of contemporary human services. In each of the settings examined in this volume, fiscal accountability along with care coordination drive program development. Cost savings, reduced costs, and cost containment are key terms in program rhetoric. Each program seeks to become more cost effective and efficient. What are the implications of this heavy emphasis on costs?

> *Case managers, when seen as brokers of services and monitors of compliance, become extensions of the service delivery system and all of its problems. . . . Client outcomes remain fixed: reducing costs of care through improved (rationed and rationalized) consumption" (Rose, 1992a, p.1).*

The focus is on utilization patterns, consumption, and expenditures. In such an environment, case managers can become confused about who is the client and may identify the goals and needs of the provider or the funder.

Substantial goal displacement occurs in case management practice; in the absence of sufficient client focus, case managers can lose sight of the need for quality in service-delivery outcomes. Rose (1992b) identifies three models of case management: client driven, funding-stream driven, and provider driven. In the provider-driven model, the case management relationship is characterized as brokering services and monitoring compliance. Case managers working in a funding-driven setting emphasize obligations and commitments to the funder. In contrast, the client-oriented case manager focuses on the collaborative development of a care plan. In provider- or funder-driven settings, clients become marginal reactive participants whose opportunity to exercise their self-determination is reduced or removed.

Balance is necessary. It is possible to pursue more than one goal at a time. The Standards for Social Work Case Management promulgated by the National Association of Social Workers (1992) stress the need for commitment to client-centered services as well as fiscal budgetary responsibility, even though it may prove difficult to reconcile the two:

> *Expanded fiscal accountability may create ethical dilemmas. . . . Social work case management practice requires the professional to put the client's needs first, as well as to justify how resources are spent on behalf of the client. Attainment of these goals requires that the social work case manager develop and maintain fiscal management skills (p. 19).*

### ❏ Supporting Caregivers—Balancing Formal and Informal Care

Contemporary public policy is based on the assumption that the family is the most appropriate location for providing care to dependent or disabled persons. A further assumption is that caregivers are present, willing, and able to provide services. The family provides shelter and refuge from the public world. As McDaniel (1993) states, "Family policies have been built on the myth of the caring, large and extended family; a myth that works to instill a sense of responsibility to fulfill family caregiving obligations" (pp. 126–127). Families are supposed to be homogeneous in their caregiving capacity and remain a warm, safe, and private place of refuge. Social policies, such as are reflected in community care, reflect and reinforce this belief, assuming that the family, particularly women, can provide the support that is needed to allow vulnerable members to live in the community. This notion of the primacy of families supports the nonintervention policies of government, at least until families become so overwhelmed that the state has to intervene.

What is the ideal relationship between family caregiving and formal services? How tenuous must the family situation become before formal services are introduced? How much can or should be expected from overburdened and overwhelmed families? These questions are critical for case managers as they collect assessment data and develop care plans with their clients. Families' capacities to provide the necessary amounts and intensity of care must be thoroughly evaluated by case managers during the assessment process.

Without adequate support some caregivers experience deterioration in their own health, which diminishes their ability to provide care. In the absence of adequate assistance, caregivers themselves can become vulnerable and require services. Case managers need to advocate for caregivers who are at risk by exploring how program procedures can be utilized to provide support. If informal caregivers are the backbone of community care, their well-being must not be taken for granted. Case managers must weigh program requirements against families' assessed capacities to continue caregiving. From both policy and practice perspectives, the availability and quality of informal caregiving is critical for client/caregiver well-being and program success. Case managers need to advocate for caregivers within the programmatic context. Such advocacy includes supporting vulnerable caregivers who cannot meet program expectations for participation. In daily practice, case managers will determine the relationship between family caregiving and the expectations of public programs.

## ❏ Policy, Program, and Practice Innovation

Case managers function in a real-life laboratory in the design and delivery of social, health, and mental health services. By virtue of their coordination and networking functions, as well as their collaboration with other professional disciplines, case managers obtain extensive information from diverse sources. Case managers are in a position to synthesize such information and shape a foundation for progressive policy goals and subsequent program development. They are in a position to implement important practice principles, particularly those relating to client self-determination, cultural diversity, and least-restrictive interventions.

Innovation can take the form of revitalization of community helping networks, design of alternative treatment methods and techniques, configuration of alternative structures, and coordination of diverse organizations and new programs to fill unmet needs. Clearly the service network must not be static, particularly in light of extensive changes in social structures, life-style, family constellations, and community systems. It is necessary to respond to these changes with creative and effective innovations. Recent innovations have drawn heavily from community-organization methodology, with an emphasis on nontraditional or alternative resources and the mobilization of community assets.

Thus, case management is not only an important service in itself but is linked to systems change through creative efforts to connect community resources and professional helping systems. When viewed in this light, case management enriches and expands the mission of the human service professions. Unfortunately, the dominance of conservative politics means that opportunities to increase services are few and far between. In the current political context, what may at first appear to be opportunities to secure new resources may turn out to be covert attempts to extend social control under the guise of cost containment. If we believe that quality care is both good business and good practice, the case manager is thrust squarely into the marketplace where better ideas and programs, not simply less expensive ones, must be compelling and competitive.

Case management can produce a salutary benefit in the critical area of staff morale. Job distress and staff morale are closely linked to autonomy, recognition, and accomplishment. Many human service professionals feel entrapped and controlled by external forces as well as unrecognized and unappreciated. To the extent that staff feel dominated or controlled by others, their morale declines and frustration mounts. High turnover rates among mental health case managers is evident. Job demands, minimal recognition of their working with challenging client populations, and low salaries create considerable stress for case managers, many of whom choose to leave their job as a result (see chapter 2). Power and influence legitimately earned through efforts to institute a new program, secure a grant, or generate new resources yield enhanced esteem and recognition for case management practice while benefiting the most vulnerable members of society. Innovations are nurtured only in environments where such efforts are stimulated, recognized, and rewarded. Opportunities for innovation, whether at the policy, program, or practice level, are significantly reduced when fiscal austerity dominates. This does not mean that case managers should abandon ways to develop and improve practice. Rather, it means that such opportunities should not be overlooked or missed in underfunded programs.

## ❏ Quality Assurance

Quality-assurance programs focus specifically on whether case management activities are implemented according to plan and whether case management services comply with program standards. Quality assurance is not about program outcomes alone. Before measuring outcomes, it is necessary to determine whether the program has been delivered as was intended. If the program deviates substantially from its intended objectives and no effort is made to determine the presence and extent of these deviations, outcome findings are meaningless (Kane & Kane, 1987; Quinn, 1993).

Quality-assurance programs are designed to describe how well various program elements have been implemented. How well were program eligibility and targeting criteria implemented; that is, how do clients enter the program? Are client assessments and care plans completed in a timely fashion? Timeliness is an indicator of efficiency. Timeliness of response is particularly important in programs serving vulnerable and unstable clients. To what extent do care plans meet clients' assessed needs? That is, are the care plans adequate? To what degree are care plans developed with costs in mind? Have service plans been implemented as intended? Have providers delivered quality services? Are clients satisfied with their services? It is challenging to separate satisfaction with provider services from satisfaction with case management (Applebaum & Austin, 1990).

Quality assurance is an important facet of professional accountability. Too often, in our rush to get to outcomes, we overlook quality-assurance concerns. Without such process information, the quality of outcome evaluation will suffer. In the quality-assurance approach, focus originates from the individual client perspective, which is consistent with case managers' emphasis on client-level services. Information generated through quality-assurance activities reflect the daily realities of case management practice. This valuable feedback should be used by case managers to refine and improve their work with clients.

Making the case for quality care and social services on humanitarian grounds or altruism is a necessary but no longer sufficient rationale in today's environment. Case managers must be able to demonstrate the salutary benefits to society in terms of economic savings, productivity gains, and reduction of costs associated with dependency and marginality.

## ❏ Education and Training

Currently, degree-granting programs focus little attention on case management. Case management has been viewed as a set of specific skills laid on top of a foundation of generalist professional practice. For the most part, case managers are trained to function within the programs in which they work. Such instruction is program specific, focusing, for example, on the assessment instrument or rules governing care planning. Recently, professional associations of case managers have emerged in the health care field. Organizations such as the Case Management Society of America offer their members training opportunities that lead to recognition for specific levels of achievement. National conferences of major professional organizations usually include sessions on case management. In this context, most presentations are didactic, with little if any opportunity for skill development.

Consensus is lacking on the most appropriate location for educating and training case managers or on what level such opportunities should be offered. This debate will continue. Case managers can be trained at community colleges, in undergraduate social work programs, in graduate social work programs, in certificate programs, in specialized workshops, and on the job. With the development of practice standards, the appropriateness of certificate programs for case managers who already hold a degree will likely be considered. Practice standards will also be useful in the development of case management content within human service professional degree programs (Case Management Association of America, 1995; Connecticut Community Care, 1994).

Regardless of the location of training, practicum experience is a critical portion of a case management training program. Hands-on experience with clinical and service-delivery challenges provide students with opportunities to encounter daily practice situations. Practica should be carefully structured to ensure that students will experience the breadth and complexity of the case management role. Interdisciplinary practicum programs should be developed when routine approaches to practice involve several disciplines. If case managers work with colleagues from several disciplines after completing training, it stands to reason that they should experience interdisciplinary practice in the practicum setting. Little knowledge of the language, customs, and hierarchy of other disciplines will inhibit effective practice, and clients will not receive the quality of care they deserve.

Case manager training and education are both generic and specific. Generic skills and knowledge can be applied to work with a range of client groups, whereas specific content focuses on the target population served in a given program. A comprehensive curriculum might contain clinical-practice theory, cultural competence and ethnicity, life-span development, intervention skills to empower clients, health and social service programs (for relevant populations), financing and reimbursement, case management models, intervention techniques, communication theory, group process, community analysis, program development, ethics, quality assurance, public policy and lobbying, program evaluation, and research (Applebaum & Wilson, 1988; Haw, 1995). Much of this content should focus on the specific client population served in the case managed program. Because course work covering all aspects of this comprehensive curriculum may not exist, new classroom and practicum courses may be required.

Case managers work in a multicultural world. Yet the practice literature does not report on how case management might be molded to serve specific ethnic, racial, or cultural groups effectively. "Specific knowledge, values, and skills that are culturally relevant, ethnically sensitive and antidiscriminatory must be included as core content in the education and training of case managers" (Rogers, 1995, p. 60). Case managers must become aware of their own blinders and biases before they can work appropriately with clients from diverse backgrounds. The concept of culture incorporates racial and ethnic groups as well as minority groups living alternative life-styles. For example, working with HIV-positive or AIDS clients in the gay community requires the same sensitivity and awareness as does working with members of ethnic- and racial-minority groups.

Education and training programs should provide avenues and opportunities for case managers to develop and maintain self-awareness, sensitivity, and insight. Case managers must develop effective cross-cultural communication skills and devote sufficient time to developing relationships with culturally diverse clients. Regardless of their cultural background, clients are entitled to carefully developed and individualized services. To engage culturally diverse clients, case managers must be self-aware and understand the issues and situations that their clients face.

## Policy Implications

Case management has been enshrined in federal legislation. It has been incorporated into the Health Maintenance Organization Act of

1973, Community Support Act of 1978, Child and Adolescent Service System Act of 1984, Comprehensive Omnibus Budget Reconciliation Acts of 1981–85, Omnibus Budget Reconciliation Act of 1987, and the Family Support Act of 1988. Case management makes up part of legislation governing child welfare, health care, managed care, community-based long-term care, public welfare as well as programs for the chronically mentally ill and severely disturbed children and adolescents. Thus, case management has been legitimized and embraced by the human services establishment.

Just what are we trying to accomplish with case management? What functions does it serve for policy purposes and in the delivery of services? Access, quality, and costs are three overriding issues in contemporary human service programs (Kane & Kane, 1987). At-risk individuals should have access to appropriate quality services at reasonable costs. To a certain extent, case management addresses these problems, although it clearly is not the only way to deal with these three fundamental service-delivery challenges. It is commonly observed that the provision of case management services varies greatly. Different models are designed to address the needs of specific client groups and to reflect the nature of the program (Radol Raiff & Shore, 1993). Despite the extensive variation in case management practice described in the previous chapters, several themes can be identified.

## ❏ Coordination

Coordination is the strategy most widely employed in efforts to alter service delivery, particularly in the development of community-based programs (Aiken & Hage, 1975; Gilbert & Specht, 1974). It is consistently identified as a core policy goal and case management task. At the policy level, its importance is obvious. It is a service-delivery virtue. Coordination is viewed as positive and as something that can always be improved. Rhetorical commitment to service coordination is commonplace. Who on Earth could be against coordination? It is motherhood and apple pie.

Improving service coordination is an ongoing challenge because the potential to coordinate services is constrained by dysfunctional and highly fragmented delivery (Applebaum & Austin, 1990; Rose, 1992b). Form follows funding; that is, splintered funding produces disconnected and discontinuous service delivery. Nevertheless, agencies can coordinate by sharing information, budgets, programs, and clients. Coordination in any one of these areas does not imply coordination of any of the other areas. Agencies sharing information about their clients is different from coordination of their programs and budgets. Sharing information about clients is necessary to maximize coordination of services on their behalf. But fiscal information is not freely shared. Because agencies are most comfortable with sharing information at the client level, opportunities to improve coordination at the program and system levels are often missed (Benson, 1975).

In many programs, case management at the client level is the primary coordination method. Case managers are expected to overcome barriers to service coordination in serving their clients. Although agencies make commitments to service coordination, case managers encounter obstacles and roadblocks in their efforts to serve clients. The need to protect agency autonomy on the one hand and to coordinate services to clients on the other creates tension. A commitment to coordinated service delivery is expected from provider agencies; yet this commitment often creates conflict, revealing the agency's fundamental ambivalence toward the realities imposed by service coordination (Austin, 1983). As long as coordination is restricted to sharing client-related information, delivery-system fragmentation will be reinforced. Coordinating information at the client level does not alter organizational relationships within the delivery system. From a pragmatic perspective, if the goal is to increase coordination, more substantial organizational relationships must be established and maintained. At the policy level, however, improving coordination appears to be the more attainable goal. Substantial differences exist, however, between the role case management plays in coordinated compared with integrated delivery systems.

The terms coordination and integration are often used interchangeably and both terms are frequently cited as policy goals (Aldrich, 1978; Fleischman, 1990; Galaskiewicz, 1985; Scott & Black 1986). If coordination has proven to be a difficult goal to accomplish, integration presents an even greater challenge. Coordination efforts involve strengthening and facilitating interorganizational exchanges, without formally changing the relationships and the budgets of the participating organizations. On the other hand, integration involves the creation of new, formal, administrative procedures and structures. Integrated systems involve strengthening, rationalizing, and centralizing administrative authority and fiscal relationships. The strength of an integrated delivery system derives from its integrated budgeting and planning. Integration and coordination are different. Integration involves administrative consolidation, linking organizations together into a cohesive network. Coordination is designed to facilitate the flow of resources between independent entities through coordinating mechanisms. Integration produces a blurring of boundaries between agencies, whereas coordination maintains them. Integration is a structural change in the delivery system; coordination maintains the *status quo* (Fleischman, 1990; Gilbert & Specht, 1974).

McClelland's analysis of managed care provides a clear example of integration (see chapter 9). He notes that several characteristics of managed care systems involve integration and centralization of key system components. Fiscal relationships require risk sharing and a centralized administrative structure with authority to allocate resources within the system. Economies of scale are derived from combined purchasing of services and supplies. Rapp and Kisthardt's (chapter 2) comparison of case management models in programs for the chronically mentally ill focuses primarily on coordination. The underlying focus of the various case management models are identified as linkage, mentorship, advocacy, improved living skills, and the reduction and management of symptoms. In these programs, the case manager's autonomy often includes authority to allocate discretionary funding to help clients in emergency situations. However, this does not suggest system integration involving the creation of new administrative structures or fiscal relationships.

## ❏ System Change

For some service system analysts, case management is the primary vehicle for promoting system change. Kingsley (1991) adopted this perspective, stating that "case management can and should become an institutionally authorized force for system change; to foster comprehensive and coordinated service delivery while identifying and correcting system weaknesses" (p. 3). These goals cannot be attained with an *ad hoc* approach to case management.

> It is more typical for ad hoc brokering strategies to come up short. Case managers are usually held accountable for helping clients obtain services they need, yet lack authority to assure that other organizations will cooperate (p. 2).

Policymakers interested in creating significant system change do not rely on case management alone to accomplish this goal. Policy is imperfect; it can be poorly conceptualized, badly implemented, or both. Case managers deal with unanticipated consequences and unexpected outcomes. In this respect, case management serves as a system-maintenance function (Grisham, White, & Miller, 1983; Weil & Karls, 1985).

Case managers are rarely equipped to produce system change unless they have sufficient fiscal and administrative leverage to modify incentives and behaviors in the delivery system. Case managers generally are not in this position. Most case managers function as traditional brokers. They make referrals, follow-up, and advocate for their clients. They have little clout and frequently rely on personal influence and persuasion to obtain services for their clients. Too often, case managers who rely on brokering can only get their clients put on waiting lists, with little indication of when services will be provided (Applebaum & Austin, 1990). Brokering reinforces rather than changes agency relationships. "Too often case' management is assumed to fail because of case manager failure, when it will fail without administrative and policy support" (Ooms, Hara, & Owens, 1992, p. ii).

What is the relationship between case management and delivery-system change? Coordinated and integrated delivery systems present different environments for case managers and case management. In an integrated system, case management is one of several tactics in an overall strategy to achieve system change. It is not the primary change strategy. More integration, however, is not a panacea. Baker and Vichi (1989) observed that "the conflict between continuity of care and cost control is likely to be greatest for those case managers who work in service organizations that are highly integrated, both administratively and financially" (p. 208). Policies designed to produce integrated systems are driven by restructured financial incentives.

Coordinated systems lack a substantial driving force toward system change. Case management is the primary change strategy in coordinated systems. By itself case management cannot produce structural changes. It provides a system-maintenance function designed to manage tension in the delivery system. In programs in which improving coordination is a primary goal, system change normally does not occur. Case management in coordinated systems is not designed to change system structure and funding incentives. Rather, it helps maintain the *status quo*.

All system change is not positive. Greater system integration will not produce improved service delivery if, in the process, financial support for the program is drastically cut. For example, although closing mental institutions and nursing-home-diversion programs may have merit as policy goals, inadequate and inferior community services will seriously compromise the quality of services clients receive. Rapp and Kisthardt (chapter 2) observe that "in many respects individuals experienced a diminished quality of life from what they had known in the hospitals."

Clearly, system change is not solely the product of the case manager's activities. A comparison of the programs included in this volume indicates that large-scale system change is accomplished only through significant reorganization of funding and system structure. As Rothman (1992) observes, "structural problems are not amenable to solution through actions of case managers" (p. 7). Structural problems require structural solutions. Yet, even when structural problems are appropriately addressed, case management is still necessary.

## ❏ Case Management as Part of a Large Change Strategy

Where structural and fiscal change has been initiated, case management is one part of a larger system-change strategy. For example, outpatient programs for the severely and persistently mentally ill are the result of policies that moved clients from institutions to community programs. Deinstitutionalization has been the dominant policy in mental health for more than 20 years. Implementation of these policies has significantly reduced the census in mental institutions. Institutional care was no longer attractive for ethical, clinical, and fiscal reasons. Total institutional care dehumanized patients who could live in the community with greater dignity and at considerably less cost. Thus, mental health programs have been transformed, emphasizing the development of independent living skills to prevent readmission. To this end, the structure of the delivery system and fiscal incentives have changed dramatically (Anthony & Blanch, 1989; Intagliata, 1982; Kanter, 1987).

Case management was not designed to produce desired fiscal and structural goals in the mental health delivery system. However, it remains a key component of the larger policy strategy. Case management services are part and parcel of community-based programs. These fiscal changes produced a modest reallocation of funding that has altered the shape of the mental health delivery system.

The primary function of case management in this setting is to direct and coordinate services to ensure continuity and quality of care for the client. Case managers aggressively support client independence with community care plans. The primary goal is to prevent readmission to costly institutional care. Community-based case managers work with clients to prevent readmission. As institutions were closed, patients were discharged to the community, in many instances without adequate discharge plans (Bachrach, 1983; Baker & Weiss, 1984; Harrod, 1986; Stein & Test, 1985). A coordinating and monitoring mechanism was necessary to guide these newly released clients. Enter case management.

Case managers deal with the anticipated and unanticipated consequences of large-scale change in service-delivery systems. Over time, optimistic expectations faded as the realities of homelessness, lack of access to health care, inadequate housing, unemployment, and family burdens became apparent. Case managers deal with these debilitating problems daily. They advocate for clients who are affected by the consequences of imperfect policies.

The development of community-based long-term-care services provides another example of the limits of what case management alone can produce. Although case management was an important component, community-based long-term-care programs required a funding source. Until the mid 1970s, Medicaid funds could be used only to pay for nursing-home care. Medicaid waivers made it possible to pay for community-based services to prevent or delay nursing-home admission. Subsequently, preadmission screening was introduced to ensure that only clients who met screening criteria would be admitted to a nursing home. Costs of care plans provided to clients through Medicaid waivers had to fit under a specified cost cap, usually a percentage of the cost of nursing-home care. In this program, case managers authorized the purchase of services on behalf of their clients. Modified Medicaid funding, preadmission screening, service authorization by case managers, and capped care plan costs were introduced into the system in time. In combination, they have contributed to modifications in this delivery system (Applebaum & Austin, 1990; Callahan, 1989; Kane & Kane, 1987; Quinn, 1993).

## ❏ Health Care and Managed Care

A major difference exists between health care and managed care and the other service sectors reviewed in this volume. In these two settings, case managers have been caught up in rapid and ambitious fiscal and structural changes. Policy goals in these settings concentrate on cost containment to a greater extent than in other program settings (Hurley & Freund, 1988). Over the past decade, fundamental change in the financing and organization of health care has been mandated by federal legislation, policy, and regulations. The prospective payment system (PPS) and the introduction of diagnostic related groups (DRGs) were designed to affect the delivery of hospital-based care by imposing admission-based payment, depending on the diagnosis. Financial risk introduced by PPS reflected a fundamental shift of incentives in acute care (Estes & Swan, 1993; Wood & Estes, 1990). This massive change effort to restructure delivery systems reflects a top-down phenomenon as opposed to the bottom-up product of case management. In a real sense, PPS created the demand for case management. In fact, some case managers in health care are responsible for implementing the new incentives and sanctions. Berger (see chapter 7) is tentative in her discussion of the role of case management in health care and its capacity to produce system change, noting that "if case management has as its goal cost containment, central authority to fund services will be a critical role."

Authorization is the power to allocate resources. In health care, the case manager's authority is controlled by the same incentives and sanctions that are in place throughout the delivery system. Provider risk means that if the system cannot operate within specific fiscal parameters, the provider must absorb any excess costs (Leutz, Greenberg, Abrahams, Prottes, Diamond, & Gruenberg, 1985). In health care, as in other program areas, case management is part of a larger intervention. The difference is that case management in health care is not the primary system-change strategy. The architects of change in the health delivery system did not rely on or expect case managers to restructure and refinance the system. In health care, more powerful interventions, like basic changes in fiscal incentives, have successfully produced system change. In health care, some case managers undoubtedly deal with the negative consequences of large-scale system change. For example, case managers are particularly challenged to advocate for clients in a system that imposes sanctions and incentives that are not always client centered. When fiscal management becomes the dominant focus, it is necessary to be even more vigilant about potential deterioration in the quality of services.

## ❏ Inequality among Target Populations and Delivery Systems

In many program settings, case management is seen as the primary vehicle for producing delivery-system change, if change at this level is a goal. Even in programs in which case managers control resources, the magnitude of system-level change pales when compared with system-level change in health care. In the majority of human service programs, case management is a weak intervention. By itself, it cannot produce desired system outcomes.

In health care, major system change has been the goal of powerful stakeholders. Fiscal incentives and sanctions have been used to motivate the cooperation of providers. The health care experience demonstrates what can be accomplished when the clear goal is large-scale system change. Case management alone compared with DRGs (as one part of a wider system-reform strategy) are not in the same league when it comes to promoting delivery-system change. Does this mean that system change is not feasible or expected in other programs or that only minimal change is expected? Does interest in producing fundamental system reform vary within the human services? Perhaps programs that benefit the general public receive higher priority than do programs designed to serve marginalized groups.

The social status of client populations varies. Stigma is not attached to individuals who use health care services. For the uninsured, negative stereotypes are associated with their lack of insurance, not their need for health care. Massive and growing expenditures, combined with a mainstream clientele, have allowed for considerable system change in health care. The recent growth of home health care is a case in point (Estes & Swan, 1993). As patients were being rapidly discharged from hospitals on the basis of DRG limits, it became apparent that the supply of home health care resources in the community was highly inadequate. For example, "Public policy concerning hospital care for the elderly . . . resulted in a significant increase in demand for and utilization of home health care services" (Estes & Swan, 1993, p. 108). The shape of health care has changed substantially, with home health service becoming more important in the delivery system and an increasingly attractive investment opportunity for nonprofit and proprietary providers. Expenditure patterns shifted; a market was created; a funding source was available. And because the client population carried no stigma, it was easier to justify the costs of home health care.

On the other hand, many of the other populations discussed in this volume are considered deviant and not in the mainstream of society. Examples of marginalized populations include the severely and persistently mentally ill, AIDS patients, individuals with substance-abuse problems, welfare mothers, high-need families, the frail elderly, and severely mentally disturbed children and adolescents. For many of these clients, participation in case-managed programs is not voluntary. Clients are mandated to receive program services. Programs directed toward these populations emphasize cost containment; budgets are cut, further limiting already insufficient program funding. Budgets for community-based programs are funded at a fraction of the cost of institutional care, making cost saving possible, at least in theory. Someone must be responsible for managing these inadequate resources, and case management has become a familiar response to lack of money, a fixed point of fiscal accountability. To a certain extent this is true even though some case managers can authorize the purchase of services and allocate resources. Some settings have initiated modest reallocation and restructuring of the delivery system. However, case management is no substitute for adequate funding.

Case managers working in programs that have been severely cut by recent governmental action face difficult dilemmas. In this context, involuntary case management clients become targets of increased social control and potentially punitive actions. This can be seen in changes in welfare programs. How will case management services change when recipients of Aid to Families with Dependent Children have two years to be trained and to locate a job? How effective can case management be when employment for their clients are few and far between? How will case managers advocate on behalf of their unpopular clients in such a negative environment? In these difficult circumstances, how will case managers avoid becoming agents of the program and reducing their client-advocacy efforts? Case managers' commitments and values will be tested as these policy changes are implemented.

## ❏ Alternatives

Case management is a public-policy master stroke. It seems to include something for almost everybody, and its popularity among policymakers continues. Its adaptability means that it can be provided by different agencies and professional groups in myriad ways. One size definitely does not fit all. Even in a highly integrated system, some form of case management will be required. Case managers deal with the negative residuals of poorly conceived and inadequately implemented policy.

Case managers determine eligibility, allocate resources, negotiate with caregivers, and monitor providers. Frequently, they are in the best position to understand the problems in the local delivery system. Case managers are the front line. However, they are not miracle workers and cannot cure the ills of dysfunctional delivery systems. Case management is a pragmatic service.

Pragmatism implies compromise. Compromise produces mixed expectations and results. Expectations for case management frequently are inflated, leaving those who fill this role frustrated. The strengths of case management have been exaggerated and its weaknesses underplayed. Although case management has its limitations, it is nevertheless a valuable buffer among the demands of clients, providers, and funders. Case management absorbs conflict, frustration, and confusion, all of which are rampant in a fragmented delivery system, while appearing to deal with these problems. Its services should be understood in this context.

Expectations regarding the effectiveness and efficiency of case management are a product of the policy and service-delivery contexts in which it is delivered. Clearly, case management is acceptable to enough policymakers and constituent groups that it will endure. Because case management plays such a central role in the human services, it requires ongoing examination and analysis to ensure that its popularity is supported by empirical evidence of its effectiveness. But the question remains, "Is this the best we can do?"

## References

Aiken, M., & Hage, G. (1975). *Coordinating human services: New strategies for building service delivery systems.* San Francisco: Jossey-Bass.

Aldrich, H. (1978). Centralization vs. decentralization in the design of human service delivery systems. In R. Sarri & Y. Hasenfeld (Eds.), *The management of human services* (pp. 51–79). New York: Columbia University Press.

Anthony, W., & Blanch, A. (1989). Research on community support services: What have we learned? *Psychosocial Rehabilitation Journal, 12*(3), 55–81.

Applebaum, R., & Austin, C. (1990). *Long term care case management: Design and evaluation.* New York: Springer.

Applebaum, R., & Wilson, N., (1988). Training needs for providing case management for the long term care client: Lessons from the National Channeling Demonstration. *Gerontologist, 28,* 172–176,

Austin, C. (1983). Case management in long term care: Options and opportunities. *Health and Social Work, 8*(1), 16–30.

Bachrach, L. (1983). An overview of deinstitutionalization. *New Directions for Mental Health Services, 17,* 387–392.

Baker, F., & Vichi, T. (1989). Continuity of care and the control of resources: Can case management assume both? *Journal of Public Health Policy, 10*(2), 204–213.

Baker, F., & Weiss, R. (1984). The nature of case management support. *Hospital and Community Psychiatry, 35,* 925–928.

Benson, K. (1975). The interorganizational network as a political economy. *Administrative Science Quarterly, 20*(1), 229–249.

Callahan, J. (1989). Case management for the elderly: A panacea? *Journal of Aging and Social Policy, 1*(1–2), 181–195.

Case Management Association of America. (1995). *Standards of practice for case management.* Little Rock, AR: Author.

Compton, B., & Galaway, B. (1994). *Social work processes* (5th ed.). Belmont, CA: Wadsworth.

Connecticut Community Care. (1994). *Guidelines for long-term care management practice. A report of the national committee on long term care case management.* Bristol, CT: Author.

Estes, C., & Swan, J. (1993). *The long-term care crisis: Elders trapped in the no-care zone.* Newbury Park, CA: Sage Publications.

Fleischman, J. (1990). Research issues in service integration and coordination. In *Community based care of persons with AIDS: Developing a research agenda* (pp. 157–167). Conference Proceedings, U.S. Department of Health and Human Services, Agency for Health Care Policy and Research. Washington, DC: Public Health Service.

Galaskiewicz, J. (1985). Interorganizational relations. *Annual Review of Sociology, 11,* 281–304.

Germain, C., & Gitterman, A. (1886). The life model of social work practice revisited. In F. Turner (Ed.), *Social work treatment interlocking theoretical approaches.* (3rd ed., pp. 618–643). New York: Free Press.

Gilbert, N., & Specht, H. (1974). *Dimensions of social welfare policy.* Englewood Cliffs, NJ: Prentice-Hall.

Grisham, M., White, M., & Miller, L. (1983). Case management as a problem solving strategy. *Pride Journal of Long Term Home Health Care, 2*(4), 21–28.

Harrod, J. (1986). Defining case management in community support systems. *Psychosocial Rehabilitation Journal, 9,* 56–61.

Haw, M. (1995). State of the art education for case management in long term care. *Journal of Case Management, 4*(3), 85–94.

Hepworth, D., & Larsen, J. (1993). *Direct social work practice: Theory and skills* (4th ed.). Belmont, CA: Wadsworth.

Hurley, R., & Freund, D. (1988). A typology of Medicaid managed care. *Medical Care 26,* 764–774.

Intagliata, J. (1982). Improving the quality of community care for the chronically mentally disabled: The role of case management. *Schizophrenia Bulletin, 8,* 655–674.

Kane, R., & Kane, R. (1987). *Long term care: Principles, programs and policies.* New York: Springer.

Kanter, J. (1987). Mental health case management: A professional domain? *Social Work, 32,* 461–462.

Kingsley, C. (1991). *Local inter-institutional systems are necessary to support effective case management.* Waltham, MA: Brandeis University.

Kirst-Ashman, K., & Hull, Jr., G. (1993). *Understanding generalist practice.* Chicago: Nelson-Hall.

Leutz, W., Greenberg, J., Abrahams, R., Prottes, J., Diamond, L., & Gruenberg, L. (1985). *Changing health care for an aging society: Planning for the social HMO.* Boston, MA: Lexington Press.

McDaniel, S. (1993). Caring and sharing: Demographic aging, family and the state. In J. Hendricks & C. Rosenthal (Eds.), *The remainder of their days: Domestic policy for older families in the United States and Canada* (pp. 121–144). New York: Garland.

Miley, K., O'Melia, M., & Dubois, B. L. (1995). *Generalist social work practice: An empowering approach.* Needham Heights, MA: Allyn & Bacon.

National Association of Social Workers. (1992). *NASW standards for social work case management.* Washington, DC: Author.

Ooms, T., Hara, S., & Owens, T. (1992). *Service integration and coordination at the family/client level.* Washington, DC: Family Impact Seminar.

Quinn, J. (1993). *Successful case management in long-term care.* New York: Springer.

Radol Raiff, N., & Shore, B. (1993). *Advanced case management.* Newbury Park, CA: Sage Publications.

Rogers, G. (1995). Educating case managers for culturally competent practice. *Journal of case management, 4*(2), 60–65.

Rose, S. (1992a). Empowering case management clients. *Ageing International, 19*(3), 1–4.

Rose, S. (1992b). *Case management and social work practice.* New York: Longman.

Rothman, J. (1992). *Guidelines for case management.* Itasca, IL: F. E. Peacock.

Scott, W., & Black, B. (1986). *The organization of mental health services.* Beverly Hills, CA: Sage Publications.

Sheafor, B. W., Horejsi, C. R., & Horejsi, G. A. (1994). *Techniques and guidelines for social work practice* (3rd ed.). Needham Heights, MA: Allyn & Bacon.

Shulman, L. (1992). *The skills of helping individuals, families and groups* (3rd ed.). Itasca, IL: F. E. Peacock.

Stein, L., & Test, M. (Eds.). (1985). The training in community living model: A decade of experience. *New Directions of Mental Health Services, 26,* 210–223.

Weil, M., & Karls, J. (Eds.). (1985). *Case management in human service practice.* San Francisco: Jossey-Bass.

Wood, J., & Estes, C. (1990). The impact of DRGs on community-based service providers: Implications for the elderly. *American Journal of Public Health, 80,* 840–843.

Wood, G. G., & Middleman, R. R. (1989). *The structural approach to direct practice in social work.* New York: Columbia University Press.

Zastrow, C. (1995). *The practice of social work* (5th ed.). Belmont, CA: Wadsworth.